King Hui

Jonathan Chamberlain was brought up in Ireland and Hong Kong. After graduating in Social Anthropology at Sussex University, he returned to Hong Kong where he lived for many years as a teacher and writer. His other works include *Chinese Gods* and *Wordjazz for Stevie*, also published by Blacksmith Books, and *Cancer: The Complete Recovery Guide* which is available from www.fightingcancer.com.

In addition to his writing work Jonathan has founded two charities: The Hong Kong Down Syndrome Association and Mental Handicap Network China Ltd.

King Hui

The Man Who Owned All the Opium in Hong Kong

Jonathan Chamberlain

BLACKSMITH BOOKS

King Hui: The Man Who Owned All the Opium in Hong Kong
ISBN 978-988-99799-8-0
© 2007, 2010 Jonathan Chamberlain

Published by Blacksmith Books
5th Floor, 24 Hollywood Road, Central, Hong Kong
www.blacksmithbooks.com

Typeset in Adobe Garamond by Alan Sargent

This book is for Patrick and Christie

Acknowledgements

My thanks to Louise Aylward, Arthur Hinton, Françoise La Toison, my brother Simon and my father, Terence Chamberlain for reading the manuscript and making comments. I would also like to acknowledge the help, interest and enthusiasm of my wife, Bernadette, and of Lyn Austen, Lau Yan Tsun and Robert O'Brien. I wish to thank Lincoln Potter for presenting me with a photograph of Peter Hui taken shortly before his death and for his letting me use it. I would also like to acknowledge the editorial advice of Colin Day at Hong Kong University Press who persuaded me of the merits of cutting the book by twenty-five percent!

I am of course responsible for any errors that remain.

Foreword

Gladstone called it a barren rock. For all intents and purposes, Hong Kong then was indeed just another pink dot on the map of the British Empire – indistinguishable from so many other islands, dwarfed by India and subsumed under China. Yet, in the end, this tiny barren rock proved to be the real jewel in the British crown – 150 years of flourishing trade and a decisive return to China without even half a drop of blood shed nor any of the usual simmering post-colonial quarrels saturated with resentment and bitterness.

But going almost unnoticed from the outside are the intrigues of trade, of nepotism and corruption, of loyalties and treacheries, of fortunes and misfortunes. In this, Hong Kong, a hybrid society with a Chinese population under British rule, is no different from any other great city. It too is replete with its full cast of heroes and heroines, refugees and despots, tycoons and beggars, saints and scum.

To what extent has Hong Kong, with over 150 years of British heritage, inspired English writers? I am afraid 'not much' is the answer. There has been Clavell's *Noble House* and John le Carré's *The Honourable Schoolboy*, and even Somerset Maugham's *The Painted Veil* – which has recently been made into a film, but, alas, irritatingly its original Hong Kong location was switched to Shanghai! So in print, there ain't much at all to record old Hong Kong. For nostalgia, we have to rely mostly on old photographs and a few films like *The World of Suzie Wong* or *Love is a Many-Splendored Thing* or *The Inn of the Sixth Happiness* or indeed my firm favourite *The Road to Hong Kong*, although none of its stars (Bing Crosby, Bob Hope, Dorothy Lamour, Joan Collins, Robert Morley, Frank Sinatra, Dean Martin, David Niven and the young Peter Sellers – what a cast!) came out to the colony, as it was then. By the time Inspector Clouseau, aka the mature Peter Sellers, came to film *The Revenge of the Pink Panther*, Hong Kong was already past the golden age of Chinese and British intrigue.

Mind you, W.H. Auden did pass through in 1938 and wrote a poem about our city:

> Its leading characters are wise and witty,
> Their suits well-tailored, and they wear them well,
> Have many a polished parable to tell
> About the *mores* of a trading city.

It is a pity indeed that there isn't much good English writing to speak of to tell us what this old Hong Kong was like. We seem to have missed out on a proper descriptive record of the first half of the twentieth century – most particularly, of the vernacular life of this city: the lives lived by millions of refugees who came from the mainland to live in the British colony. How desperate some of them were; how fortunate others became.

So I am thrilled that Jonathan Chamberlain has produced a book which paints a vivid picture of the minutiae of ordinary life in old Hong Kong, as seen through the eyes of one Peter Hui, who – part rogue, part hero – is a true son of Hong Kong.

Peter Hui, or 'King' Hui as he was nicknamed at Queen's College, emerges from these pages as a man of certain rare, and not always enviable, qualities – whose life twisted and turned through all levels of Hong Kong society from the top banking families to the lowest street porter. In these pages we meet gamblers and playboys, pirates and triads, bankers and con men – and, of course, the girls who entertained in the dance halls of Hong Kong, the pleasure houses of Macau and the flower boats of Canton.

The history of Hong Kong is so bound up with opium – that infamous tarry substance that stevedores smoke in dark corridors of staircases, sucking in the smoke from silver foil, or the more decadent from ivory pipes prepared for them while they lie propped up in divan beds – that it is perhaps fitting that Peter Hui's own life should, ironically, include the curious fact that he once owned all the opium in the territory. In many ways, this is the definitive story of Hong Kong.

What makes this book particularly inviting is the descriptive background of Hui's life. This is an intimate history of this city. We catch rare glimpses of ordinary lives in the streets of Hong Kong. We are soaked in the attitudes and behaviour of the local Chinese people whose lives would otherwise have remained hidden from our gaze.

Jonathan Chamberlain has therefore done Hong Kong social history a great favour. And this is not the first time that he has delved into the mysteries of Chineseness. He has already written a classic work on Chinese folk religion, with his book *Chinese Gods*.

This is a true story but it reads like a novel. It is a cracking read.

DAVID TANG

Above: Peter Hui at the age of ten, with his father.

Previous page: A very young Peter (centre) with his family.

Above: Peter at the age of eighteen.

Above: Peter with friends at an outdoor restaurant on Cheung Chau.

Below: Peter at a barbecue a few months before his death.

Photo credit: Lincoln Potter

Introduction

T HIS IS THE STORY of a man's life. He was not an important man, if importance is measured by social position, but he was a man who was at one time rich and socially well-connected, and he might have continued to be if only he had been just a little bit different – but then this book would not have been written. Instead, like Icarus, he revelled too much in the glorious sensation that all possibilities were open to him. Then, singed, he fell headlong, tumbling down through the layers of Hong Kong society – now and then his descent was interrupted, occasionally he wafted upwards briefly on a favourable thermal – but always, inevitably, the fall continued until he hit rock bottom.

He was a man of certain uncommon gifts whose destiny it was to be drawn irresistibly to folly. His story is the living story of Hong Kong. This book is, therefore, a subjective, intimate history of this curious territory: where Shanghainese money and industry, Cantonese grit and fiery doggedness, and British phlegmatism and sense of order created a place where East and West worked out a way of living together.

Histories of Hong Kong have unanimously ignored the man in the street, concerning themselves instead with the dry bureaucratic colonial facts and particularly with the prisoner-of-war experience. But what of the local experiences of World War II, and more importantly perhaps, of daily life during the peaceful years both before and after the war?

There is a smell that distils for me all the essential ingredients of Hong Kong. It is the smell of browned cubes of tofu being heated in a dry wok by a street hawker. Black heat waves vibrate upwards carrying the stench, worse than diesel fumes, of the marinade that this tofu has sat in, seemingly for days on end: vinegar, sesame oil, chilli and shrimp paste. Not for nothing is it called *chow tofu,* stinky beancurd. This is the authentic smell of Hong Kong. This book is a stinky beancurd history of this city.

The island of Cheung Chau lies about eight kilometres south south-west of Hong Kong's main harbour, less than an hour by ferry from the centre of the city. It is a small but densely populated island. In the spring of 1976 I came to live on Cheung Chau. I had come for the simple reason that it had everything an island should have. It was a fishing village with a waterfront and a pier where the ferry came, and when you got off the ferry, there you were, right in the middle of the village. There was no ugly hinterland of docks to walk past.

The island was still quiet then. It is amazing to remember a deserted waterfront on a midsummer Sunday. Now, of course, it has been discovered and the ferries are packed with day-trippers. But back then it was a place known only to those in need of cheap rents or a quiet, unruffled life.

Among the people I met very quickly was a slight, dapper Chinese gentleman who went by the name of Peter Hui. He had an easy, charming smile and a reputation for borrowing money and not repaying it. He would have been in his early sixties then. The flesh on his face was taut and he complained of ulcers or a mysterious heart complaint which seemed to prevent him from working full-time, as he insisted he had to in order to survive. Yet he did survive. No one was really sure how he managed it.

From time to time he would hint of a past that would be worth telling – but, naturally, he said, he couldn't tell the whole truth. In particular, he often talked about the years of the Japanese occupation. 'You wouldn't believe how rich I was in those days,' he would say to me over a bottle of Tsingtao beer. 'During those years I had the largest string of ponies at the Jockey Club. Believe me, Jonathan, I'm not lying to you. I gave them brandy while people were starving.' He shook his head at the perplexing iniquities of fate.

We would be sitting at a small round table under the open sky. Girls from the fishing boats would pass by, dressed in thin cotton pyjama suits and wearing conical rattan hats. The older women had deeply tanned and heavily creased faces and, as they laughed, flashed rows of gold teeth. Where have they all gone? It is an age that has slipped quietly away. Time slips past us so fleetingly. It is difficult to stop and capture the small human details.

There was a general consensus among the European community that Peter Hui was not to be entirely believed. He would say anything to get you to buy him a drink. But the stories he told over the years didn't change. If he was a liar he had an impossibly good memory. And the purple swollen knuckles on his hands were testimony enough to the *kung fu* prowess he claimed for himself.

The years passed. Cheung Chau ceased to be a haven from the city. Life became busier. The year 1997 loomed. It posed questions. One of the questions for me was what life in Hong Kong had been like for the local people in the years gone by. It seemed to me important to capture the past now that we were still there. For the present seemed already like part of the past – and no one knew what the future, after 1997, would bring. There wasn't a book that gave any real sense of the place in an informal way. I didn't know that this was exactly the kind of book that was to fall to me to write.

One day, Peter stopped me in the street.

'I need to talk to you, Jonathan. Are you in a hurry?'

I shook my head cautiously. We had known each other now for coming on thirteen years.

'I'm getting old. I should tell my story. If you have time, maybe you can write it.'

As we stood in the glare of the sun I looked at Peter and it seemed he had hardly aged at all. He was still the same: alert and impish. I nodded slowly. It was true I was busy but then again, Peter's life story might be worth listening to. I had always been curious to know more about the racehorses and the years of the Japanese occupation. It occurred to me that there would be no harm in spending a few evenings with Peter. I would get to hear a few stories. Maybe they would be interesting. Maybe not. It didn't matter. Or maybe they would be everything that Peter had always promised they would be. I had no idea what to expect. As it turned out, Peter's stories were everything he said they would be. Over the months and years that we talked there was never any sense of discrepancy or contradiction. As we talked I set him small subtle tests. He passed them all. I have no doubt at all this is a true story.

This then is the story of Hui Shen-kei, also known as Hui Tak-kwong, also known as Peter Hui, also known as Hui Lo-sze – Respected Teacher Hui. (Hui rhymes with 'boy'.) Known too, when still a schoolboy, as

'King' because of his *kung fu*. This is the story of a true son of Hong Kong, a hero in his own way, though most readers will probably see him as an anti-hero. This is the life story of a Hong Kong playboy, gambler, fighter, wartime collaborator with the Japanese, CIA agent, mastermind of armed robbers, associate of triads; a man who once, for a very short time, owned all the opium in Hong Kong.

I am in Peter's rooms overlooking the beachfront. Ostensibly it is the island's RSPCA clinic but Peter has taken it over – he is the RSPCA man on the island. Usually the room is bare and functional but today it is bright with flowers. It is Chinese New Year. His few photographs line the walls – 'I have lost so many things. I have been so careless!' This, as it turns out, is an understatement. Although Peter professes to be a Christian there is a porcelain Buddha and another set of figures showing the folk deities: Fu'k, Lu'k and Shao – the human embodiments of Happiness, High Rank and Long Life – the three great traditional desires of the Chinese.

Otherwise the room is spartan. There is an office desk with a telephone on it and a metal table for the veterinary inspections. Under it, in separate cages, are two mynah birds. Their sharp shrieks burst out from time to time: 'AAANGAANG! . . . Grrrek Grrrek! . . . Ngahwee . . . Ngahweeeee . . . Warrowarrowarrow . . . wooowwooo . . . ngeow . . . ngeow!' It is a wide repertoire of noises. Have they learnt them from the animals that file in every Wednesday when the RSPCA vet comes? Two dogs mill around. 'Shut up! Sit down!' Peter slaps them and they obey.

Occasionally there is a loud whirr as a helicopter approaches, red lights flashing. Behind Peter's house is the hospital – little more than an emergency out-patient clinic and a geriatric home. Two hundred yards along the beach is the helicopter landing pad. Someone has to be taken into town for serious medical treatment. There is no point talking now. The sound is deafening. Eventually the aircraft takes off and the sound drifts off into the distance and merges with the other sounds that come in from outside. There is a basketball court not far away and sounds of laughter and shouting interrupt the silence but we are at the back of the village and it is mainly quiet. Of course there are the yapping village dogs. But we can also hear the hush of waves gently slapping against the sand.

I fix the microphone to Peter's shirt, press the record button, check the batteries, check the tape is moving, nod to Peter that we're ready to start and then I lean back in my chair to wait.

'What shall we talk about today?' he asks.

'Tell me about your first memory,' I say.

In the beginning

MY FIRST MEMORY? I was four years old. It was the day of my eldest sister's wedding in our home village of Taam Shan in Punyu district of Guangdong Province. And do you know what I remember? I was really terrible. My very first memory is of biting my mother's arm very hard. I can remember every detail. I can even remember the taste of her skin. I was so furious. I was angry with her and I was angry with everyone else because they were allowing my sister to be carried away. My sister was crying and wailing and pleading to be rescued but the strange men were carrying her away and none of our relatives did anything to stop them. They just stood there and let my sister be kidnapped. I remember it was getting dark. Maybe it was already dark. Of course I must have been very excited. We had been entertaining people from the neighbourhood all day. I didn't understand what was going on. I knew my sister was being taken away from me and I didn't understand why. There would have been a lot of firecrackers. Strings of them suspended from the roof of the house exploding like a machine gun. Of course that's not the sort of thing I would remember. I am just imagining how it would have been. That's how I know it would have been dark, or nearly dark. It is our belief that the sun is the seat of male influence and the moon is the seat of female influence. So there is a superstition that if the bride leaves her home when the sun is still strong in the sky then she will be oppressed by her husband and perhaps badly treated. The easier a husband gets a wife the less respect he will have for her. So a wife should not be too cheap. And no one would think of giving a girl away. Our Chinese custom is that a girl must be taken away by force. She must be captured and kidnapped. She must be taken like a treasure from her home to her husband's home. But while the groom will want to take her away as soon as he can so that their marriage will be ruled by the sun, so the bride's relatives will seek to delay the 'kidnapping' for as long as possible. It is a natural compromise then that twilight is the time agreed upon by most couples for their departure from the girl's home. My brother-in-law's village was a few miles from ours. He had a sedan chair with four bearers to carry her back to his house. It is normal for the bride to cry out and wail. But of course she was happy. It is rare for a girl not to welcome marriage. But she has to pretend. I didn't understand. I was only four years old.

It was late afternoon and preparations were being made to take my sister away from me. I cried to everyone to stop them but of course they just laughed at me. The more they laughed the more furious I got. All I could think of was to stop them somehow. The servants couldn't control me at all. I loved my mother. She was the only one who could control me. I think she was scared I would run down the road after the sedan chair to fight them all by myself. And I would have done. I am like that. So, my mother put me on her back but I continued to struggle and fight and when I found I couldn't get free, I bit her hard in the arm. I can still remember the warmth and taste of her skin as I bit hard and she yelled and slapped me and I screamed for someone to help my sister.

I think this was the first time I could feel in myself a terrible temper. On that day, I discovered something very important: I had a fighting heart.

Now, I can tell you that my sister was nineteen years old when she got married. I can calculate it like this. I was four. My second sister was thirteen years older than me and my first sister was two years older than her. At that time, this was considered to be quite old. Most girls got married at the age of sixteen. I think the reason my sister didn't marry until she was nineteen was because my parents were very serious about who they wished to have for a son-in-law.

When the match-maker came to us with details of Ho Tim, my father accepted. Although we were quite rich then and Ho Tim's family was poor, it was obvious that Ho Tim would make a good son-in-law. He had started work at the age of ten. He now had a good job at the Hongkong Hotel, which at that time, this must have been in 1918 because I was born in 1914, was the best hotel in all Hong Kong. The Peninsula Hotel wasn't built yet. But when it was, in 1928, Ho Tim was the man in charge of all the staffing arrangements.

I don't remember anything more of the wedding. But I can tell you that the day after the wedding Ho Tim would have sent back a whole roast pig and some fish. This gift is like a final seal on the wedding. It means the husband has spent a night with the bride and found that she was indeed a virgin. Not to send this present would be a big insult. After three days they would have returned in person to pay their respects to my parents so that they could see that my sister was well.

So my sister was taken away from me. I missed her very much because she loved me with all her heart and took care of me. Now there was just my mother and my second sister to take care of me – and, of course, at home there was also an amah and a *mui-jai,* a slave girl.

Although the wedding took place in Punyu, we actually lived in Hong Kong. We were all born in Hong Kong, all three of us – but because both families came from the same area it was thought a good idea to have the wedding in our native district.

Let me tell you about this district. Hong Kong is on the south China coast on the eastern side of the mouth of the Pearl River. Actually there is no such thing as the Pearl River. 'Pearl River' is the name we give the joining of three rivers: the West River, the North River and the East River. Canton city is situated more or less at the junction of the West River and the North River on the northern bank. The estuary lands south of Canton are flat and rich in rice and river fish. We call this area Nam-Pun-Shun. This is really three districts joined together: Nam-hoi, Punyu and Shun-tak. Nam-hoi is the richest, Punyu is the second richest. But this didn't mean that the farmers were rich. It was the middlemen who grew rich: the rice merchants. The farmers, like farmers everywhere, worked hard and earned little money.

Perhaps the most important reason for having the wedding in Punyu was that my grandmother was still living there. She was old and paralysed. My grandfather had died. I never knew him but I remember my grandmother clearly. Not from this time but a few years later when I was sent to live with her during the great seamen's strike. She was in her nineties when she died. My grandmother was old and paralysed so she was always lying on a couch or bed. She could do nothing for herself. She always asked me to go to her and kiss her. I was the only son in our generation and so it was natural for her to love me. In fact, I can tell you, I was a little bit disgusted by her. She was old, ugly and wrinkled. I remember, she always drooled from the corner of her mouth. But I knew it was very important that I show her my respect so I always did go up to her and kiss her. I know many boys my age would have refused to kiss her but I knew it would make her happy. I was very naughty in other things but not in this.

As for my grandfather, all I know is that he was a wood merchant. Now, there are many different kinds of wood. There is wood for furniture and wood for building. Obviously wood for furniture is the best quality and wood for building is of a lower quality. Our family business was to sell wood of the poorest quality – wood for fuel. It was a hard job. He had to collect the wood and put it into bundles and then he had to carry it to the houses of all his customers. I suppose it wasn't a bad business. He could afford a house. But he only had one wife and one son: my father. I have no records of any sort of our family before my grandfather. Who or what my earlier ancestors were I really cannot say. They were country people. Perhaps they were farmers or perhaps they had always sold firewood.

When my father grew up, perhaps he was like me, perhaps he was a gambler. He knew he could never have a good life if he stayed in Punyu district. For a few years he helped his father by carrying wood to people's houses. Then, for some reason, he decided to try his luck in Hong Kong. I don't know why he didn't prefer to go to Canton city which was closer. He never felt that Hong Kong could be a proper home for a Chinese. Not while it was ruled by foreigners. Although he lived there all his adult life and made a lot of money, he never bought any land or property in Hong Kong. Every piece of property he owned was in China. I really regret that. I can say that things would have been very different if he had invested in Hong Kong. I would still be very rich. Perhaps it was God's will. My father was a man of contradictions. He was not a man who wanted to be like the foreigners, and yet he arranged for me to have a Western education. He never dressed or appeared to be rich but when I got married I had the biggest wedding Hong Kong had seen for over ten years.

Now, let us go right back to the very beginning. I was born a few months before the start of the first European war. My father had come to Hong Kong in his early twenties and he hadn't married young. So by the time I was born he was nearly fifty and my mother was about three years younger than him, so she was forty-six or -seven when she bore me. Of course such a thing is certain to make people talk. A lot of people from our home district believed that I had been adopted. Actually, this would have been a very common arrangement and would not have caused any surprise at all. Perhaps there was surprise that he hadn't already adopted a son. Only a son can carry on the family name. A man without a son has no respect.

Now, it seems that a man from the same village was heard to express his suspicions that I was really only an adopted son. My father was angry when he heard this. At last he had a real son of his own, after trying for many years and only having two daughters. A son of his own flesh and blood. And everyone was saying he had adopted a son into the family. The only way to settle a case of this sort was to take it to the council of Taam Shan village – what we call the council of the ancestral hall. So my father and the man who had expressed his reservations both went back to Punyu and put the case to the council. There was plenty of evidence that my mother had been pregnant and had been aided by midwives at the time I was born. Naturally, my father won his case. He wouldn't have won any money, just a few catties of roast pork. The purpose of the case was to ensure that people accepted that I was a real son of his flesh. In fact I have no doubt that I am his real son.

My father first came to Hong Kong when he was a young man in his twenties. Of course he didn't have any money but he was a clever and hard working man. I remember he used to tell us stories of his early life. At one time he operated a cinema. Not really a cinema. Everything was much simpler then. Maybe it was what they call a lantern show. It must have been something like that because he operated in the street. He charged just a few chien-jai to see a show. Nowadays ten cents is the smallest unit of currency but in those days ten cents was worth something. Even with one cent or less you could buy something. There were ten chien-jai to one cent. Then, after a while he gave that up and got into the clothes dyeing business and this is what he was doing when I was born.

In those days there was a lot of dyeing work. It was a good business to be in. People didn't buy new clothes like they do now. When their clothes started to look old they would get them dyed. They always dyed them a darker colour. If they were originally white they would be dyed light blue. If they were light blue they would be dyed dark blue. My father was already very well known by the time I was born. He would walk from Central to Causeway Bay. He carried everything he needed

with him. He had a big wooden box with his name on it: HUI KUM KEI –
DYEING MERCHANT. His name was Hui Kum. Kei means 'company'. This
box was about two-and-a-half feet high and about twenty inches square.
In this he kept all the dye stuffs and utensils he needed, a stove for heating
up the water and also there was space for all the clothes he collected that
didn't need to be dyed urgently. These he could take home and dye there.
However, some people insisted he did the dyeing on the spot, while they
waited, so he also carried a large tin tank in which he had some water.

He carried everything on a hawker's pole. At the front he tied his box
and at the back he tied the tank. But the tank was light compared to the
box with everything in it, so he put water in the tank. He was a very
strong man. I know he could carry up to a picul in weight: that's about
100 catties (130 pounds). He put his shoulder under the pole and lifted
it up. Then he would walk with quick short steps that made everything
sway and dance, like a spring. That makes it easier to carry a load like
that. He would walk down the streets calling out: 'Hui Kum is here.
Dye your clothes.' In those days it was easy to tell everyone you were
coming. None of the buildings was more than four or five floors high.
Everyone could hear what was going on in the street. If anyone wanted
him they would just shout down from the windows. In those days there
wasn't any mains water. All the water came from wells. He would go to
the nearest well and draw up the water he needed. Then he would heat
up the water, add the dye, stir it until it was just right and then he would
dye the clothes. Later, when he had made a name for himself, he always
refused to do the dyeing in the street. Instead he would collect the clothes
and take them home. By the time I was born he was doing good business.
He was quite well off. But he wasn't rich. Maybe I brought him luck.
Within a year of my birth he was to be a very rich man. How? It was
like this.

When war broke out in the summer of 1914, people became nervous
and this had an impact on the economy. Obviously at a time like this
no one buys new clothes and no one worries if their old clothes don't
look very smart. No one spends money on looking good. So naturally
the dyeing business was very bad. But later it turned out to be lucky
because soon there was more dyeing business than ever before because
people preferred to dye their old clothes rather than buy new clothes.

The very best clothes dye was made in Germany. Before the war broke out my father had bought twelve drums of this dye. Soon it became impossible to get this so there was a very big shortage and the price shot up. My father sold his stock of dye and for each tub he sold he was able to buy a large property in Canton. He bought warehouses and blocks of flats, three- or four-storey blocks. So we became very rich. But even though we were very rich we lived a very simple life. We had a two-storey building in Staunton Street, just above Hollywood Road – but we just rented it. We lived upstairs. Maybe it was about 700 square feet with a slanted, tiled roof which was very common then. My father did his dyeing in the kitchen. With the money he earned in rents from the properties in Canton he bought more property. We were rich but you could never tell that by looking at him. He dressed in very simple Chinese-style clothes.

Anything I wanted I just shouted for it

I WAS A VERY SPOILT CHILD. Anything I wanted I just shouted for it. I had a house full of women to do things for me. If they didn't do things quickly I would get angry and I might even hit someone. I wouldn't hit my mother or my sister but I once hit my *mui-jai* because she was slow to get me a bowl of congee.

Now I must explain something. After my elder sister had got married my parents talked to my second sister and suggested to her that she should stay single in order to take care of me. Of course I was the only son so such a thing couldn't be left to the amah or to the *mui-jai*. My mother had to go often up to Canton to look after the properties and collect the rents – and maybe she invested the rents in more property. I know we had over a hundred acres of riceland in our home village which she rented out to farmers. We never sold this land. I don't know what happened to the ownership papers. Maybe my elder sister got them. Maybe my nephew has the documents. But in fact they should belong to me. I am the only son. But it doesn't matter. The Communists own it all now.

Yes. My second sister agreed to sacrifice herself for me. This wasn't so strange in those days. I am certain my parents would not have forced her not to marry against her wishes. They were very kind. They would have asked her. But she was a very obedient and filial daughter and so she was happy to obey. She cooked my meals, did my washing, mended my clothes. She would stop me eating the wrong food and she made sure I was always very clean. She even bathed me. Later when I went to school, I had the reputation of being the cleanest student of the whole school. I remember all the European mistresses at Ellis Kadoorie School always praised me in front of the others. They would say: 'Shen-kei is clean and tidy. You should all follow his example.' But of course it wasn't my efforts but my second sister's. I can tell you that I enjoyed being neat and tidy and well dressed. I was born to be vain. I have always had the ability to dress well. It is an instinct. I like to look handsome.

My sister also taught me my table manners and how to use chopsticks, and more importantly how not to use them. It is very bad manners, she taught me, to pick through food on a dish before selecting the morsels you wish to eat. Also don't reach across the table to eat the food on the other side. You must eat what is closest to you. Once your chopstick has touched something you must pick it up and eat it. I remember my father hated me to leave even a grain of rice in the bowl. I remember once when I did this, my father quietly put his chopsticks down on the table and turned them round. Then he picked them up and rapped me hard over the knuckles with the top ends. After that, whenever I saw him doing this I would quickly pick up my bowl again to pick up every grain. The way my father explained it was like this: 'Every grain is the result of energy, sweat and even blood from the peasants. They work hard to grow the rice and you just waste it. You aren't giving respect to the peasants. And you don't care about the value of rice. That cannot be tolerated.' That's what he said to me and that's what I said to my children. I am sure every father tells his children the same thing in the same way. We have a saying that if a person doesn't eat up every grain of rice they will marry a spotty-faced husband or wife. This is just a joke of course, a way of scaring people into doing the right thing without wasting time on explanations.

I loved my second sister very much because she was so good to me. She would read me stories so I know she had received some education. Even now, much of what I know of Chinese literature I first heard from my sister when she read aloud to me and told me stories. She told me the stories of the Hung Lau Moon – the Dream of the Red Chamber – and of the Water Margin and the Story of the Three Kingdoms. I loved to listen to her tell these stories. Even after she was married my elder sister would come back to our house most days in the afternoons for a few hours. She loved me very much and she was always bringing me sweets or candy or toys. She and second sister would sit and embroider socks or stockings. These stockings were made of pure silk or wool. In the old style of things any money they made from selling these wasn't their own to keep. They had to present it to my parents to put towards the general living expenses of the household. In fact my parents never accepted this money so they did have a little extra. It wasn't necessary for her to do this as we had plenty of money but perhaps this was the only way she could get her own money to spend on things without asking for it.

As for me, I was always very fierce. I think it started at my elder sister's wedding when I lost my temper. Maybe it was my character from before but I was always damned fierce. Now I never did anything cruel to my servants. Of course, if they did anything wrong I would shout at them or even smack them. I remember once, when I was twelve or thirteen, I punched my *mui-jai* in the face. I had demanded a fish congee. This is very easy to make. There is always congee, just plain rice porridge, ready in the kitchen. It just needs to be heated up. Then you put some thin slices of raw fish on top so that they are lightly cooked in the congee. It's easy to make. On this day, I remember, I had come home and shouted for the *mui-jai* to bring me a bowl of fish congee. Then I waited and waited but she didn't come so I went to the kitchen to find her and saw that she had forgotten about it. So I hit her. I can say this was a very rare event. That's why I remember it so clearly. I was terrible. When I grew older I learnt respect for my parents and for my sister. I would never dare to show any anger to them, especially not to my father. Now, if my mother was angry with me she would never show it, but if my father was angry he would get a feather duster and holding it by the feathers he would whip my legs with the cane handle. If he was very angry he would bend me over and whip my buttocks. There is an old Chinese saying: 'Youngsters suffer in the flesh. The old suffer in their minds.'

Let me explain about the *mui-jai*. *Mui-jai* were slave girls. They had no rights at all. They were young girls who were sold off by their parents because their families couldn't afford or didn't want to bring up useless daughters. So they were sold to wealthier families who could do whatever they wanted with them. Some were treated very cruelly but I can honestly say we treated ours well. There was a strict prohibition against amahs or *mui-jai* eating at the family table. But in our family it was different. Most meals the *mui-jai* and my amah would eat with us. I didn't think anything of this until I was fifteen or sixteen and I saw the custom in other people's houses. Then I asked my mother why we allowed our *mui-jai* and amah to eat with us when this wasn't normal. My mother put on a very stern face: 'My dear son, don't ever talk about this again. Other people have their ways and we have ours. Even a *mui-jai* and amah are human and should be respected.' This impressed me very much.

Our *mui-jai* at this time was Wong Tsui. She was a few years older than me. We had a few others and I was given one when I got married and my first wife had one. When Wong Tsui was eighteen, I remember, my father took her to a restaurant where he often went. There was a waiter there that he knew. He introduced them. Maybe we went one or two times. I can't remember. Then, on one visit, father asked: 'Do you like this girl?'

The waiter nodded: 'She seems very nice.'

Father: 'Would you like to marry her?'

'Yes, I am sure she would be a good wife for me.'

'How could you support her?'

'Well, my salary is. . . .'

That's how I remember the conversation. It didn't take long. I don't know if the girl's wishes were taken into account. I think everyone assumed she would be happy to get her freedom and a husband. Naturally, my parents spent some money on the wedding. Not as much as on a real daughter but a bride has to provide furniture for the future home. In return the bride's family will get some lucky money from the husband. This is reasonable as they have brought the girl up and fed her and clothed her. Then she has to leave her family and join the family of her husband. It is right they should be compensated. If she marries into a rich family the compensation may be very large indeed. I am sure, if Wong Tsui is still alive, she will say that she was well treated by my family.

One day, I must have been seven or eight, I found myself surprised by my mother. She took me aside when my father was out and she said to me: 'Ah Kei, listen to me. I have something important to say to you. If your father asks you would you like another mother you must say "no".' I didn't understand anything about this but I was happy to agree. It turned out that a few days later my father did ask me. 'Ah Kei, how would you like it if you had another mother? Would you like that?' Naturally, I loved my mother very much and I wanted to make her happy so I immediately shook my head violently and said 'no'. My father didn't mention it again, but for a few months he went around with a very serious expression on his face. And naturally he didn't marry a second wife. But that didn't stop him having fun. My father was very clever. He never fooled around in the evening. He never went out at night. Every evening we all had dinner at home and then he would spend the evening chatting or listening to the radio or maybe go to bed early. But during the day was a different matter. Later, when I was much older I saw him several times walking in the street with a girl and then he would go into a lodging house with her. He didn't go into high-class hotels, just boarding houses. So whether or not he married a second wife made no difference to him. He was a romantic man who enjoyed the company of many young beautiful girls. Of course, I never let him see me nor did I ever mention it. It amused me to see him.

Now I'll tell you a story that happened a few years later. This was sometime before the war. I was working. At that time I liked to take my father out to lunch or dinner once a week. It gave me great pleasure to invite him to eat with me. One day, I said to him, 'Where shall we go for lunch?' He understood that I was going to pay. So he mentioned a well-known restaurant in Central which was quite expensive. I didn't know his reasons for wanting to go to this restaurant until we got there. When we entered, one of the hostesses bowed and greeted my father with a warm smile.

'Welcome sir, please follow me!'

Now this girl was a great beauty. I suppose she was about twenty years old. She was younger than me. I must tell you, when we entered this restaurant I was very well-dressed in a suit. I was a handsome young man. My father was in his sixties, and dressed very casually. But this girl didn't even look at me. Not for a second. She just looked at my father and greeted him. I was a little bit surprised. Naturally my father was very pleased to be greeted by such a young beautiful girl. During the meal she came over to our table several times and my father introduced me to her. But I could see that she didn't pay much attention to me. I understood my father was a regular customer. Her attention was all on my father. I was very surprised. I understood that she was the kind of girl who was interested in money. She wasn't interested in a handsome young man like me. She was interested in catching a rich man.

At the end of the meal the girl brought our bill and my father insisted on paying, even though it had been clearly understood between us that I was to pay. I remember every detail very clearly. We had chosen some quite expensive dishes and the bill was $3.70. Normally you could eat four dishes for just $1 so you can see how exceptionally expensive this lunch was. My father waved my wallet aside and paid with a five-dollar note. When the girl brought the change he just smiled and said: 'Please, it's for you!'

I was stunned, a $1.30 tip. That was enough for dinner by itself. It was a thirty per cent tip!

After we had left I asked him: 'Why did you tip so much?' he just waved me away: 'Never mind. It's a small thing!'

A few days later I decided to go back. I was curious. I took a half-bottle of brandy with me. I had a normal lunch. This girl was polite but she didn't pay much attention to me at first. Towards the end of the meal she came over to my table and started to talk. I remember thinking to myself: 'You should take the son not the father!'

She pointed to the brandy.

'I see you are a strong drinker like your father!'

I laughed and said: 'Yes. But I'm not such a strong tipper!'

Then I asked for my bill. She smiled at me.

'Please,' she said, 'this time let me have a chance to invite you.'

Whoever heard of a waitress buying a customer a meal? Why did she do this? Naturally she must be interested in getting to know me. She wanted to catch me. But I already understood that she was only interested in money. A rich old man is one thing but a girl who is after money should not marry him. Instead she should marry the son. Then she would have the best of both love and money! I was not pleased with this. I supposed that there was some relationship between her and my father. Perhaps I was a bit rude. Abruptly, I said to her: 'I know my father likes you very much but you must know that my mother will never allow him to take a second wife. But if anything happens outside marriage that is another matter. I respect my father. He is free to enjoy himself.'

Now, to go back to my second sister, I really have no idea if she regretted not being married. It's possible she was happy to remain single and live at home with us. It wasn't always good for a girl to marry. She would have to move in to her husband's family home and put up with bullying from her husband's mother. It was very common in those days for the wife to be under her mother-in-law's thumb. Often she wasn't entirely accepted until she had provided a son. So maybe second sister was sad sometimes that she never married but maybe she was also happy to be more independent. It is also true she wasn't strong. When I came to be aware of such things I saw that she was very thin. So she looked after me all her life. She cooked for me and washed me. I was fifteen years old when she stopped washing me. Maybe this shocks you but the fact is I was a late developer physically. I think males usually reach the age of having sexual power at the age of sixteen, but for me it was around seventeen. I finally asked her to stop washing me when a rather embarrassing incident occurred. It was like this. I enjoyed having my bath on the balcony of the flat, on the first storey, so that I could look down on what was happening in the street. My sister would rub me and scrub me all over. You must understand that I was always surrounded by women and had been since I was young. It was natural for me to be naked at home and to be spoilt in every way. So I was growing up physically but I never noticed this and no one told me anything. Maybe second sister had noticed. Maybe she was aware of the changes but, as with a nurse, even if she was embarrassed it was her job. Actually, I must confess that I had become aware that I enjoyed the feeling when my sister washed me between the legs. Perhaps I noticed that I was getting an erection. But I didn't really pay any attention to it. However, some other people did see it. Across the road from our house was a small jewellery melting workshop. I was very friendly with all the workers. I often went into the workshop and saw them melting the gold and making rings and chains. I was fascinated by their work. I loved to watch them blowing fire on the ornaments and making the settings: silver and gold. They all loved me and I loved them. We could talk about everything and they liked to tease me. Even now I can remember all their faces. Then one day I went in to the workshop after a bath and they all laughed at me. I asked them what they were laughing at. 'Wah! Your sister rubs you and your prick stands up!' someone said. They would say everything very straight to me. Of course my sister couldn't hear them but I was very embarrassed and so I told her the next day that she wasn't to wash me any more. Naturally, everyone knew the reason for this.

My poor, dear second sister. I loved her very much and she loved me very much. She was thirteen years older than me. She was my constant companion when I was very young. Sometimes fate can be very cruel.

I nearly drown

WHEN I WAS NINE YEARS OLD I nearly drowned. It happened like this. I was with my father and my mother's nephew, Kwok Lau, the son of my mother's brother. Of all my mother's relatives, he was the only one I could stand. Actually Kwok Lau and I got on very well, even though he was ten years older than me. He was a big, strong country boy and he could swim like a fish but I was a city boy. I couldn't swim at all. My father hadn't taught me to swim. Maybe he didn't think of it. Maybe there was some other reason because later he forbade me to go swimming. Maybe that was because he was shocked by what happened on this warm spring day in 1923.

I guess it was spring, probably about the time of the Ching Ming festival, because father, Kwok Lau and I were climbing the hillside above Pokfulam on the south side of Hong Kong Island. We were going to visit the ancestral grave of the people from the Punyu district. It's still there high above the road. It takes about an hour to climb up. Every year at Ching Ming and Chung Yeung festivals it is the custom to go to our ancestors' graves and sweep them clean and make offerings of food and paper money and so on. But for people living in Hong Kong it wasn't so easy to go back to China, and it was very expensive. Some people couldn't afford to go. So the people from the different districts built communal shrines in Hong Kong where they could go to pray to their ancestors. These graves were built on remote sites because the government didn't want any land that might be used for development to be occupied by graves.

On this day, we were on our way to the grave to pay our respects. I don't remember that there were many other people on the hillside so most probably it wasn't exactly on Ching Ming. Maybe we were going up the hillside before or after the festival when there were fewer people about. It was a hot day and on the way to the grave we came to a large rock pool. Kwok Lau decided to go for a swim to cool down. Father couldn't swim, I suppose, at least I never saw him swim. He sat down at the side of the pool. For a while I just played by the side of the pool watching Kwok Lau. It struck me that there wasn't anything very difficult about swimming. Kwok Lau was a good swimmer and he swam easily across the pool. I got undressed and got into the water. I suppose my father thought the pool was shallow and that with Kwok Lau there it wouldn't be dangerous. Actually, the pool was about eight or nine feet deep. At first I held on to the side but the more I watched Kwok Lau splashing away, the more I realised that swimming was a simple matter of moving your arms and legs. Obviously it was very easy. I was always bold. I decided to try it out for myself. I pushed myself away from the side and started to move my arms and legs but it didn't work as I thought. I started to sink. This didn't worry me at first. I wasn't scared. I thought it would be no problem to get up again. I sank all the way to the bottom. I still wasn't afraid. I was very clear-minded. I can still remember every detail as if it happened just yesterday. Even when I got to the bottom I still didn't think I was in any difficulty. My father was watching me all the time and it didn't occur to him either that I was in difficulty.

He could see me, I suppose but all I could see was the light at the surface of the water. I remember that light above me very clearly. After two or three minutes I began to feel a great pressure in my chest. It was very painful. I just wanted to get rid of that pain but I couldn't get to the surface. I started to struggle. I don't know why I couldn't put my feet on the bottom and jump up. But then a strange thing happened. I have no feeling that I myself did anything. I was just struggling. Suddenly my body jumped up out of the water. I can't explain this. Suddenly I was above the surface. I tried to snatch something and hold on but I missed so I went down again. Again, a second time, I popped up and I tried to grab hold of a rock but again I missed. So I sank under the water again. The third time I jerked up out of the water I managed to grab hold of a rock and clutched it as tight as I could as I now realised this was life or death. I hugged the rock and pulled myself to the side. Then I called for help and father quickly got up and pulled me out. My cousin was still swimming around unaware that anything was the matter. My father called Kwok Lau to give a hand as I was shivering violently. I wasn't cold. It must have been the shock. I couldn't say anything. Kwok Lau rubbed me down and they dressed me and after a while the crisis was over.

I don't know if it's true but there is a Chinese saying that a drowning man has three chances. He will jump up to the surface three times. No matter how deep under the surface, he will jump up. Even if he's ten feet down his body will jerk him to the surface. My own experience seems to confirm it. Certainly, I believe that I would have drowned if I hadn't caught the rock with my third attempt. To this day I can't explain it. I don't know of any scientific explanation. I can still remember the pain of suffocating. It was torture. I can imagine the cruelty of dying in the gas ovens or from lack of oxygen. I know that drowning is not an easy death. It is better to be shot dead.

I think my father was surprised how easily I might have drowned. It only takes a few minutes. We all gave thanks to the ancestors afterwards when we got to the grave.

You would think that an incident like this would put me off swimming. For some people, maybe, but not for me. I was born not to be scared of anything. Really, I don't know why but I have no fear.

A year in China

NINETEEN TWENTY-FIVE WAS THE YEAR of the great labour strike. I was eleven years old. This was a turbulent time for everyone. Many people went back to China. My father sent me back to Taam Shan Village in Punyu district with my mother and second sister while he stayed behind in Hong Kong.

The only way to get to the village in those days was to take a steamer up to Canton and then take another smaller boat back down the river to Punyu district. Then it was still a good distance to Taam Shan village itself. There were no buses in those days. People didn't have bicycles. If we had to move a lot of heavy goods we would hire a cart that would be pulled by a man. Otherwise we would just have to walk. It was cheap to hire porters to carry your baggage. Some people would get to Punyu directly by walking all the way from Canton. That would take two or three days. Now you can take a jet catamaran and it only takes a few hours.

We went to stay with my grandmother. Now, I am going to tell you a very strange story about my grandmother. At this time she was over ninety but ten or so years earlier she had died. That's right. She died and then came back to life. She told us about it later. She said it was like a dream. She told us she remembered going down and down into the world of the dead under the earth. She found herself face to face with the King of the Underworld. He was a big man with a long black beard and a ferocious brown face. He looked at her and then apologised: 'I'm sorry,' he told her, 'you have been brought here by mistake. You're not going to die until you are ninety-two.' So she woke up again. And it was a fact that she was ninety-two years old when she died. But the incident had left her paralysed so she couldn't move. She could only lie and watch us play. She was just like a corpse, old and wrinkled and ugly. But she loved me very much and always asked me to kiss her and I always did.

My grandmother's home was a typical village house. When you went in the front entrance, there was a yard with a well. Straight ahead was

the visiting room and on either side of this sitting room were the two
bedrooms. There was a shelf at the back wall of the visiting room for the
household shrine. There was a cockloft at the back of the main room
where we stored rice, clothing and the bed quilts. The floor was
earthenware tiles. The whole area of the building was maybe 1,000
square feet. The kitchen was in a separate building at the back. The
toilets were in a communal building somewhere in the village. No one
in the village had a private toilet. The sewage was used in the fields so
it was easy to arrange for it to be collected from one place. There was
however a room for washing in. For me, I would be washed in the front
yard by my sister. She would draw up water from the well and pour it
over me. If the weather was cool she would mix the well water with some
boiling water that she had got ready before pouring it over me. I was
always naughty and laughing and playing tricks on her so she would hit
me with her hand. My grandmother would be lying on a step watching
me. If she saw my sister slapping me she would call out very weakly. Her
voice was so weak we would have to go up close to her to hear what she
said. Then my sister would hear: 'Don't hit him.' But of course she wasn't
hitting me hard. It was just a game.

I have very good memories of this time in Punyu, in particular the
food. There are two main snails that we eat in China. One is what we
call the thick-shelled snail. The other one has a thin shell and we call it
the horned snail. It grows in ponds and of course in my home district
there are lots of ponds. I can tell you they are delicious. When they are
cooked you take them out of the shell and eat them with a little oil and
soy sauce. You can't get them in Hong Kong. Of course they have to be
fresh. And there is a kind of asparagus with black spots on the stem.
When you take it fresh from the fields and just cook it, it tastes
wonderful. I went into the countryside a few years ago to see if I could
get some but I was disappointed. I couldn't find any asparagus anywhere.
Maybe it was the wrong season. Ah! Country food! There is nothing
better.

I remember there were some fruit trees in the village. The fruit was a
sort of Chinese orange but much sweeter. Originally, it is supposed to
come from the Laozhou area. We call it *lao chan*. We were always trying
to steal some of this fruit. There is only one thing sweeter than fruit
straight from the tree and that is when it's stolen! Also in those days

every village had a hunter who would go off and shoot birds. There were quail, wild duck, rice sparrow. I haven't had rice sparrow for many years. If you ever get the chance you should try it – either roast, fried or steamed. Now there aren't any birds because of that damned Mao Tse Tung, but at that time, really, I'm not joking, the countryside was full of birds. Not many people had guns so they were safe. Each village would have only one hunter at most. Many villages didn't have any. They used very old fashioned guns – long-barrelled muzzle-loaders. They would come past our house to sell their birds to my mother. When she got a bird she would pluck it and clean it and then put it in a special jar with some herbs and just a little water. Then she would put this jar in a larger pot with more water which was heated up until it just simmered. A rice sparrow steamed in this way was wonderful. It was also very nourishing. My mother made sure there weren't any lead pellets left in the flesh as they could make the meat go bad. Sometimes the hunters brought us a stork or a crane. My mother would cut these birds into several pieces and salt them to preserve the meat.

I had cousins in another village that we sometimes went to visit. These were cousins on my mother's side. I was playing with one of them, a boy five or six years older than me.

'Let's catch some birds,' I said to him.

'How?'

Here was my older cousin asking me how to do something. He was a country boy who should know all the tricks and I was just a town boy. But I had an idea how we could catch a lot of birds. We had been with my cousin's family a few days and I had noticed that they stored their rice in a barn behind their house. I had seen how it was common for the birds to fly in and steal grain whenever the door was open. My plan was very simple. There was only one door in the barn and no windows. Once we had lured in the birds by leaving the door open we would close it suddenly and then between us we would catch birds in a fishing net. That's exactly what we did. The birds flew wildly around and we caught them in our net. We caught maybe thirty or forty in half an hour. We put them in a cage. We did this for three or four days running.

There was something else that we ate that was delicious! Rats. Europeans and city people think rats are disgusting but actually rice rats are very clean. They are also very big and fat. Very tasty. I often had rice rat steamed with congee. You can get preserved rats and they are considered a delicacy but they are not as good as fresh rats. I tell you, fresh rice rat is even better than pigeon.

We stayed in the village a year. There wasn't a real school in our village but a teacher had been employed by the village council to teach in the village temple. I continued my studies here and soon I was respected as the leader of all the students because I was the cleverest and also the naughtiest. I suppose there were about thirty or forty children in the school and students were from about ten to fifteen years old. In the Chinese calendar I was twelve at this time.

I really was naughty. One morning I was so damn naughty that the teacher – I remember his name was Yeung – ran after me and chased me all around the hall. Chinese teachers have the right to beat their students and I knew he intended to do that so I ran off. Actually, it wasn't just fear of the punishment. I knew that if he didn't beat me he would tell my mother and that she would beat me. I could never escape a punishment. I knew that. It was the devil in me. I don't know why but I did anything I wanted without thinking about it. So, it happened one morning that he was chasing me around the hall and all the other students were watching and laughing. I knew that he would be able to catch me eventually as he was a man and I was only a boy so I got to one of the pillars of the temple, which are quite thick – at least a foot in diameter. It was quite smooth and plain but I climbed up the pillar like a monkey and was quickly able to get out of his reach. I climbed right up to the roof, which was about fifteen or sixteen feet above the ground. Now, naturally, the teacher was terrified I would fall so he begged me to come down and promised he wouldn't beat me. Actually, I didn't believe him. I thought it was just a trick to get me down. But it wasn't easy for me to hold on to the pillar. I was just holding on by clasping it tightly. It was tiring. I knew I couldn't stay up there long. I realised I would have to come down. When I did come down, I was quite surprised that he didn't beat me. But, of course, he did tell my mother and she scolded me like hell.

At this time, I was very thin. I had no muscle at all. All the village boys were very strong. One of them was a bit jealous of all the respect I received from our classmates. We used to play jacks in the dust in the squares where the rice was threshed or pickled vegetables were laid out to dry. The way we play this game the loser has to pay a penalty. He has to hold out his knuckles to the winner who gives them a rap. Now, this boy wanted to fight with me and prove he was better than me. He wanted me to respect him as the leader but I wouldn't do this. He wanted to pick a fight and this was his way of doing so. When I beat him at jacks he wouldn't hold out his hand for punishment. Naturally, I shouted at him.

'Hey, come on. Play the game. You have to hold out your hand.'

'Try and make me!'

That's all he said. Well, I let it go a couple of times.

'Ah forget it,' I said. It was a small thing. This happened a couple of times over a couple of days. Whenever I won he would not hold out his hand. However, when I got home, I would think back on it and I knew that I couldn't avoid fighting him sooner or later. If I didn't I would lose the respect of my classmates. It didn't matter if I won or lost, I had to show I wasn't scared. Actually, since he was such a big fellow and I was so thin I didn't expect to win.

'The next time this happens,' I said to myself, 'I'm going to fight him.'

So it happened that I won again and he refused to hold out his knuckles.

'Okay,' I yelled at him. 'If you don't hold out your knuckles I'm going to fight you.'

He just laughed.

'Okay. Come on!'

He was much stronger than me but he had no brains. I attacked him and knocked him down. I don't know how. I think my fierceness scared him. He was surprised that I could knock him down. He wasn't a natural fighter. That's my opinion. He was just big and strong. After that, of course, I had no more problems with him and my reputation got even bigger.

I think it was after this that people came to see that I had a special spirit. One day a relative of mine stopped to talk to me. He must have been in his seventies. His hair was white.

'Well, Shen-kei,' he said, 'you're a bright lad. You study hard. You are a keen fighter. Do you think you're brave?'

I shrugged.

'Do you think you are scared of the dark?'

'Well, not much,' I said. 'Maybe if it's pitch black and wet.'

'I could teach you not to be scared of the dark,' he said. 'Would you like that? In fact I could teach you not to be scared of anything at all. What do you say to that?'

I told him I was interested to learn. Of course. Why not?

'It's not easy to learn. You have to be prepared to face hardship.'

'I can face hardship. What do I have to do?'

'Would you be scared to go to the graveyard at night?'

'I might be scared,' I admitted.

'Don't worry. We can do it one step at a time. Are you interested?'

'Yes,' I told him, 'I want to learn that. I want to learn how to be brave.'

'Well come to my house after dinner before it gets dark.'

So that evening after dinner – we normally ate at about five – I went to visit the man.

'Come. I'll take you to the graveyard.'

Dark was just falling as we walked up to the cemetery. When we got there we sat down and waited. Night fell around us. It became pitch black. Remember, in the country, the only light at night is from the moon. There was no moon that night. When it was completely black the old man stood up.

'Now, I trust you to do what I tell you to do,' he said.

'Yes,' I said.

'I'm going to go now but I want you to stay for twenty minutes and then come down to my house.'

I can tell you that I was really scared. To be in a cemetery alone at night! Of course I couldn't stop thinking of ghosts and dead people. It's natural. But I sat there for what I thought was about twenty minutes and then I scrambled down the path back to the village.

The next day, I went back to the old man's house after dinner and we talked about what had happened. That was when the old man told me I had made a mistake. The stone I had been sitting on was a *to dei* stone. *To dei* are earth spirits. When people die their spirits return to the underworld but part of the spirit is an earth spirit. So it is common for a grave to have a small stone on top as a home for this earth spirit. That's what I had sat on. He hadn't said anything the night before as he hadn't wanted to scare me. He warned me to be careful and that if I did do anything improper to a *to dei* stone that I should apologise out loud to the stone. Otherwise the spirit might do something bad.

Now, the problem was that my mother didn't allow me to stay out after dark. This meant I didn't have much time to sit in the cemetery and learn how to be brave. I discussed this with the old man. Finally he made a suggestion: 'Let's do it like this: for the time being this is a secret between you and me. If anything happens I shall reveal what we're doing and why but until then let's not tell anybody. They wouldn't understand. Now, instead of coming to see me after dinner you should wait until your family are asleep and then creep out quietly, maybe at ten or eleven o'clock at night.' So that's what we did.

The worst time was when it was dark and moonless and there was a slight drizzle. I would slip out of the house and make my way to the old man's house which was about fifteen minutes walk away. He had prepared something for me. He had collected a lot of small, smooth pebbles which he had painted red and then put into a cloth bag. What I had to do was to drop one of these pebbles every ten paces as I walked up the path to the cemetery. There were three or four ways up there. Each time I would take a different route. On the way up I had to drop the pebbles and on the way down I had to pick them all up again. It took me about forty minutes to walk up to the graveyard stopping every ten paces to place a pebble on the ground. I was really scared I can tell you. But I learned something. If it is dark and you can see something white or light it must be a stone. If it is black it is mud and if it is shiny it must be water. I did this fourteen times a month and kept it up for about ten months. That's how I trained myself not to be afraid to be all alone in the dark. After that, any kind of hardship appears to be very common. Of course it isn't just the fear of darkness that you overcome. It is all fear.

My grandmother died while we were staying with her. She died one morning at about nine or ten o'clock. She was just lying in the courtyard on a bed as she had done since she had nearly died at the age of eighty. I seem to remember it was a cool day. Maybe no one noticed she had died for perhaps an hour because she always lay very quietly. Of course, it wasn't unexpected. She was an old woman. She couldn't live forever. She would already have had her funeral clothes ready. That is the normal custom. In our village there was no undertaker so we had to do everything ourselves. Obviously we had to get her a coffin. Now with coffins it's like this. Most people don't buy a coffin until someone has died. But some people like to be completely prepared so they buy a coffin and keep it at home. They will prop it up against the back wall and cover it with a red cloth. Then the whole family will pray to it saying: 'Now the person who will be buried in you is still alive and well. You, coffin, must always be prepared to receive him. You must be joyful and not make any trouble for your future master.'

We bought my grandmother a coffin. I can't say if it was Liuzhou wood which is reputed to be the best. We have a saying that if you want beautiful girls you must go to Suzhou and if you want the best coffin wood you must go to Liuzhou in Kwangsi Province.

When she died her eyes closed but her mouth was still open. In our superstition that means that something is still unsatisfactory. I think in her case the reason was she loved me so much. I was the only grandson. For five generations there had only been one male born in each generation. I think she wanted to live longer because she wanted to see me. Now, if the eyes and the mouth remain open what we do is put a silver coin in the mouth. I don't think this is just superstition. I think there must be a chemical reaction with the silver that causes the mouth and eyes to close. We Chinese are very superstitious. For example we avoid anything to do with the number four because the sound is similar to the word for death. My mother got a silver coin ready but she was afraid to put it in grandmother's mouth. Maybe it has to be done by a male. I can't remember. I do know that we asked some relatives and they refused. When I saw that it was so difficult to get someone to do it I volunteered. No one thought of me as I was still a young boy. I took the coin and put it in grandmother's mouth. Soon the mouth closed. I had no fear.

Soon after grandmother's death we returned to Hong Kong. The strike was over and things were returning to normal. I never saw the old man again either. I was young and soon forgot him as I got on with life in Hong Kong.

Kung fu

WHEN I RETURNED TO HONG KONG I was sent to a new school. Instead of going to the Chinese school at the Man Mo temple, my father decided to send me to Ellis Kadoorie School. I don't know why he decided to send me to an English school. At that time there was still some friction between the Chinese and the British because of the general strike. Actually, very few if any pure-blood British students went to Ellis Kadoorie. It was for Chinese, Indians and Eurasians. The school provided a British education for all those who couldn't get into the schools reserved for the British. The Kadoorie family are Syrian Jews. They also own the Hongkong Hotel and the Peninsula Hotel. Maybe that was the connection. Maybe my brother-in-law Ho Tim suggested it because he had a good job at the Hongkong Hotel. Maybe he advised my father that an English education would be a big advantage for me. Or maybe he understood that the sons of most rich Chinese families went to one of the leading English schools.

At Ellis Kadoorie, we could wear either European- or Chinese-style clothes. I insisted on wearing Chinese-style clothes. In fact, at that time I hated everything to do with Europeans. I was very patriotic. My mind wasn't open. I was very proud of everything Chinese. I think I was affected by the mood of the times. There was still a lot of bad feeling because of the General Strike. Our school uniform was a Chinese jacket over loose black trousers. But the jacket wasn't a man's jacket with buttons down the centre of the front but a woman's jacket with the buttons going across to the right and then down the side. Sometimes people in the streets made jokes that we looked like girls but everyone knew this was the uniform at Ellis Kadoorie and also at Queen's College so we weren't ashamed to wear it. Actually I was always very proud. I knew I looked smart.

At this time, I remember, I only thought about fighting. I used to lose my temper very often. I had no patience for arguing. If I didn't like something or someone I just hit out straight away. I would hit other students just for wearing European-style uniform. Now, maybe it surprises you to know that everyone was scared of me and everyone respected me. I am a very slight man and I was very slight as a boy. But I never lost a fight. Why? I can't say. It surprises me too. Nearly everyone was bigger than me but I lived for fighting. Always, my whole life, I have been fierce and I have always been very concentrated on myself. What do I mean by this? I'll give you an example. Most people when they walk down the street they look here and there, they are undecided, they see something attractive and their eyes turn. We can say that their identity is scattered. But me, when I walk in the street I just look straight ahead. I am very proud of myself. I only know what I want to do. Everything else can go to hell! So when I say to myself: Damn you! I'm going to fight with you. I am going to hit you. Well, then, I just go straight ahead and hit you. You may be stronger but I will never give up. You will have to beat me badly if you want to win. That scares people. That's why I can say I have never been beaten in a fight. If you want to win against me, you have to kill me first.

Why did I suddenly become such a fighter? I think the reason is that I am small and slight. When I first went to Ellis Kadoorie all the big boys, the bullies, wanted to pick on the smaller boys. They made the mistake of picking on me. I looked so easy to beat up. That was their mistake. I quickly got a reputation. The bigger boys soon learnt to leave me alone.

The teaching at Ellis Kadoorie was very bad. The teacher would just talk about the subject in English, reading from a text book. We had to work out what they were talking about. We had the books and we had to try and follow the words as the teacher spoke. We had to struggle hard to make sense of it. Actually, I don't think this is so bad. It forces students to learn and use their brains. All the teaching was like that. Our English teacher, Mr Crozier, was an intelligent man and he knew his subject but when he came into the classroom he just read the book in a low monotonous voice. From time to time, he might explain things as he went along. I always sat in the front row but those in the back couldn't hear him at all. He didn't know how to teach or to make things interesting. Later he became the Director of Education!

As a student I always concentrated hard on what the teachers said. I never tried to memorise anything. I tried to understand and make sense of it. That is the old way of studying. Students are supposed to study the whole book on their own at home and to think about it and come to understand it in their own way. If you still didn't understand it the teacher might give a rough explanation. Actually, the classical Chinese is very difficult to understand because there isn't any punctuation and a word can be a noun or verb or adjective. So it is very possible that even the teacher didn't understand it clearly. I was one of the best students at the school. I was naturally good at mathematics and I had a good grounding in Chinese from the Man Mo School – most of the other students hadn't studied Chinese as hard as I had so I was top of the class in two of the top three subjects. My English wasn't so good at that time but I struggled to learn it. I can concentrate very hard. That's how I was always able to do well in exams without having to study very hard. Some of my schoolmates would spend hours every evening doing homework. I never did any studying in the evening.

Now, I want to explain something. When we went back to China to our home village of Taam Shan, everyone understood that my father was well off and that I was his only son. In the country areas, all the old people are very superstitious. They always look for signs. They think that a big forehead that bulges out slightly is very fortunate. That's supposed to mean long life. Now, my forehead doesn't bulge out but I have a long forehead and long ears, like a Buddha. These are very good signs. One old lady examined me and said I was so handsome and had such favourable signs that I should be the Emperor of China. Now some of these old people still thought it was possible there would be a new dynasty with a new emperor. Why not? That's how it has always been – and the new emperor was often just a simple peasant, like the founder of the glorious Han dynasty or later the founder of the Ming dynasty. One old lady told my mother that I had the signs of an emperor. I was handsome, intelligent, and I had a strong spirit. But when I heard this I said to myself: 'Rubbish! The empire is dead. China is now a Republic!' I knew that much at the age of eleven. But later, when I was middle-aged and I thought back to that I realised she wasn't mistaken. I really was once a king. At Ellis Kadoorie and later on at Queen's College I was called 'King' or 'Tai Wong'. They respected me so much that even older boys would call me 'King'. Everyone understood I was the famous fighter who never lost a fight. They respected me even more than the headmaster. I have never had such respect since then. It gave me a special spiritual pleasure. The days glowed like they never have since. Everyone, even the teachers understood me and respected me truly with all their heart.

It was at this time that I started to get interested in *kung fu*. I was such a fierce fighter and I always won so students would ask me: 'Do you know *kung fu?*' Or maybe they would say: 'Hui Shen-kei must know *kung fu*. That's why he can win all the time.' But actually I didn't know anything about *kung fu*. So I started to think about it and it seemed to me that one day I would meet a fighter who knew *kung fu* and he would surely beat me up. So that made me want to find out more about it.

Now, when I was thirteen or fourteen, I could think of nothing more important than to be a hero. And I was a hero later as I shall tell you. I was a hero many times. So I decided that I had to learn *kung fu*. I discovered that the best teacher in Hong Kong was Lam Sai-wing. He was one of the leading students of Wong Fei-hung. If you mention these two names to anyone who knows anything about *kung fu* they will immediately recognise them. Wong Fei-hung was the hero of over a hundred films. He wasn't in the films. The films were about him and his exploits. Naturally they were all just stories but it shows how famous he was. I discovered that Lam Sai-wing had a school at the top of Pottinger Street, just below Central Police Station.

But before I could start learning I had to get my parents' approval. I talked to my father first.

'Father,' I said, 'I think it would be good for me to learn *kung fu*. I am so small and skinny. I need to build myself up.' He accepted this reason and didn't make any objection. But I also had to get my mother's permission. I knew that would be more difficult.

'What's the point of learning *kung fu?*' she asked, 'I don't want you to be a fighter. I want you to be a scholar and a learned person.' I explained that I needed to do exercise to be healthy. I wanted to learn *kung fu* so much that in the end she also agreed. So I started at Lam's school when I was fourteen. For the next two years I really trained hard. I learned all the movements. I trained with all the eighteen weapons. I did weight lifting to improve my strength. I smashed my knuckles into wood and metal over and over again until they were sore and bruised. Eventually they became so hard and big they were like knuckle dusters. Also I told my fellow students to hit me hard. At first they pushed me and didn't hit with their full strength. But later they beat my stomach and my chest with their full strength and I could resist it. By the time I went to Queen's College when I was sixteen, I can tell you: I was damn strong and tough.

I never recognise the word failure. My only fears at school were not getting high enough scores. I was usually in the top three or five in the class, so I knew I didn't have to study hard in the evenings to keep up with the lessons. That meant I had plenty of time to learn *kung fu*. After class I went swimming with my friends. Then I went home for dinner. After dinner, say about half-past seven or eight o'clock, I went to Lam Sai-wing's studio, which was only five or ten minutes walk away from home, and trained for about three hours. Then I would go home to bed.

Lam Sai-wing was a butcher by trade before he became a famous *kung fu* teacher. He was a short, stocky man. You could almost say he was fat. But he was very strong and very brave. When I started at his school he was about fifty. Sometimes he would teach me himself and sometimes he would leave it to his assistants. One of the other students in the class was his nephew, Lam Chu, who I became very friendly with. He eventually took over the school and kept it going when Lam Sai-wing died.

Of course, Lam couldn't teach. No one could teach. They didn't know anything about teaching. One of the classic starting movements was what we call 'the horse'. In this movement you put your feet together and bend your knees. You make fists with your hands and bring them down to your waist with the finger tips facing up. Then you push your arms forward and open your palms as if you are pushing something away. Now, in the old days, some *kung fu* teachers made their students do this simple movement for up to six months or even longer. Of course it isn't easy to stand like this. At first, maybe you can stand it for only a few minutes. Later you can build up to half an hour or longer. But, nowadays who has the time to spend six months on one movement? Even in those days we didn't have the patience for that and Lam never tried to make us just study this one movement. Now, no one explained the purpose of this movement. No one said: 'This movement will help you to protect yourself from a strike coming from above.' It was expected that students would think about it and come to understand it in their own way. No one explained these things to me but I immediately understood the value of everything I was taught. Just as the son of a fisherman understands water because he is in it all the time so I understood fighting. If you aren't a fighter how can you understand fighting? If you go to the park in the morning you will see many old men and women doing exercises. They move slowly as they do *tai chi*. But *tai chi* isn't just a system of exercises. It is a martial art. The movements have value for fighters. But unless you are a fighter you can't understand this.

In the class there would be anything from two to ten boys. The teacher would teach a set of six movements and we would all follow that until we had learnt it perfectly. I learnt these movements very quickly while the other boys always had to struggle and kept making mistakes. So while the other boys were still working on the first six movements, I was learning the next six, or the six after that. So I learnt two or three times faster than the others. Naturally, I quickly became a favourite of Lam's and I was always included in his demonstrations when we did a public performance. I was his star pupil. Because I was so young and small and so good I always did a solo demonstration. I remember Lam often boasted during these performances: 'If any of you think you are good at *kung fu* or any other kind of fighting come and prove it. You don't have to fight me. You just have to fight the smallest and youngest student in my academy.' Then he would point at me.

Opium and acrobats

THE FIRST TIME I WENT to an opium den I was maybe thirteen or fourteen. My father took me. I don't think he wanted to take me but probably it was too inconvenient to take me home first. And then after that first time it became normal for me to go with him.

My father didn't go to the den very often. He never went by himself. Long ago he had been an addict. But he wasn't an addict at that time. In fact it was because of me that he gave up. As I've told you, he was in his mid or late forties when I was born. I think a few years before I was born my mother had miscarried a boy child. So, when I was born he was very, very happy and he determined to quit his opium addiction. He did it himself without any help from anyone. He just stopped smoking. To help him get rid of his addiction he made up a special drink. He would dissolve some opium in double-distilled Chinese wine. Maybe an ounce in two catties of wine. Then he would shake it up and pour himself a small glass. I remember him pressing his thumb against the cork in the top of the bottle as he shook it up. At first maybe he drank it quite often. Naturally, I have no idea about that. But when I became aware of it he drank it only once every ten days or two weeks. Sometimes he might go a month or more without having any, and then he would remember and say: 'Ayah! I haven't had any opium wine for a long time!' and he would shake up the bottle and pour himself a small glass. So that is how he stopped his addiction.

But some of his friends liked to smoke opium, especially the seamen. People either smoked or drank alcohol. It wasn't common to do both. If you were a heavy drinker, normally you wouldn't be an opium smoker. If you smoked opium you would have just a little brandy or double-distilled wine or maybe just tea. If you had tea it would be the very best quality. But you wouldn't drink a lot. Maybe just one or two glasses. So when my father met some of his friends they might suggest going to a den and so we would all go.

The dens we went to were of a good class. Not the highest class, maybe, but a good class. Usually the den was just one large room with two or three opium couches. Each couch was for two people. They would lie down side by side with a small lamp between them. Maybe there would be some chairs as well. All the furniture was of black wood. If all the couches were occupied when we arrived we would just sit and wait and soon the smokers on one of the couches would get up. People in those days were very polite. They didn't like to lie on a couch just talking if they saw someone was waiting. But if no one was waiting they would lie on the couch with their head on a small porcelain pillow. In the old days Chinese liked to sleep with a rectangular porcelain pillow. But the pillows used in the opium dens were different. They had one slanting side for the head to rest against. Normal pillows were just square edged.

People would normally bring their own opium pipes but my father didn't have one, so he either borrowed one from his friend or he hired one at the den. An opium pipe was usually a long bamboo tube. If you were rich and you wanted to show off your wealth maybe you would have an ivory pipe – but experts generally preferred bamboo. About six inches from the bottom end there was a hole and into this hole was fitted a metal bowl. It had to be metal to withstand the heat. The opium itself was provided in a small earthenware pot. Usually smokers would ask for half an ounce. It was in the form of a wet paste. To get it out of the pot you used a metal pin. It was about the size of a toothpick but thicker and flat. You put this in the opium and twisted it so that the opium would stick to the pin then you would transfer the opium and let it drip into the bowl. There were usually some attendants to help you do this if you weren't used to it. Even if you were, they might help you just to give you some service. Some of these attendants were women. They were all experts in making opium pipes. When you had enough opium paste in the bowl you would turn the pipe and place the hole of the bowl against the top of the glass cover of a small oil lamp.

The smoker lies on his side on the couch with the hole of the bowl receiving the heat from the flame rising up through the glass funnel. The smoker must inhale with a long slow deep breath. This is the real trick of smoking opium. You have to breathe in for at least one-and-a-half minutes. Some people can do it for three or four. You breathe in through your mouth but some have mastered the art of breathing out through their nose at the same time. When you inhale, the pipe makes a soft buzzing sound like a bee and you can hear how long the smoker is inhaling for. Expert smokers always like to show off their skill. Smokers would inhale and then lie with their eyes closed and chat. Usually they didn't sleep but they would lie with their eyes closed, very relaxed. It always amused me to see them talking with their eyes closed. Then after a while if they wanted to they would smoke some more. Half an ounce of opium would be enough for three or four pipes.

There were three grades of opium. The cheapest grade cost a few dollars at that time. The middle grade would cost double that and the top grade double again. My father said the difference between the grades was very clear. Even I could tell the difference just from smelling the smoke. The top grade had a much richer smell. I watched them filling their bowls and I practised this myself until I became very good at it. I remember the seamen friends of my father most. They would tell me stories to entertain me. I enjoyed listening to them. Sometimes my father – or one of his friends – would invite me to try opium. I found I could inhale for over a minute. All my uncles at the den were very impressed: 'Wah! Very good!' they would say. Then they would ask me: 'How do you feel? Do you feel faint? Do you feel sick?' But I never felt sick or faint or anything like that. This surprised everybody. I think they thought I hadn't inhaled it properly but I had. I have always been very little affected by drugs or alcohol. When I was young I could drink a whole bottle of brandy without getting drunk.

Opium wasn't all bad like they say now. It wasn't so harmful. Some people even said it was good for you. They said it could cure some stomach pains and other aches. In those days it was legal. There were many opium dens – both low and high class. Also, if you wanted to smoke opium at home then you could go to the government outlet and buy what you wanted.

In those days, many people smoked opium with their friends when they wanted to have some amusement, or just to relax after a day's work. The British brought opium to China but they didn't make the Chinese smoke. The Chinese didn't need to be taught about opium. They adopted the custom very quickly and happily. They didn't have cinemas or bars or theatres. The only other cheap amusement places were the open markets. There was one at the end of Hollywood Road at a place called Tai Dat Dei. It's gone now but it was an open area where there were acrobats and story tellers, fortune tellers and fried food hawkers. I loved to go there. I often went with my father. Every time we went he would have his fortune told. There were many different ways of having your fortune told. Some people would read the soles of your feet. Others would shake coins in a tortoise shell. Others would throw sticks on the ground. There was another way which was very special using birds. These birds – usually there would be three in a small cage. If you wanted your fortune told, it cost just a few cents. The man would let one of the birds out of the cage and it would select a card from a spread-out line of cards. The fortune teller would then interpret the marks on the cards. When the bird had selected the card the owner would reward him by letting it peck out one grain of rice that was kept in a matchbox. He would half open the box by pushing his thumb in the other end then when the bird had pecked out a grain he would quickly close it again. The birds never flew away, just hopped back into the cage. My father loved to have his fortune told. He went to hundreds of fortune tellers and they all told him exactly the same thing. They all said: 'No matter what, you will only have one son. But this son will have many children.' And that's what happened. Very strange. I remember that was what my father said even before I was married.

I loved the acrobats best. They were *kung fu* men who had developed some special skills. I remember there was one who hit his chest with a long flat-sided rod of iron. He hit it hard with his right hand against his chest. He didn't do this just to prove how strong he was – but actually he was very strong. After this demonstration he would say: 'Even if I hurt myself I don't mind because I have this very powerful medicine here.' And he would point to a pile of cloth or paper squares. Each of these had a smear of some kind of ointment in the middle. He would pick up one of these squares and press it over his heart. He had hit himself in the same place so often it was like a black bruise. Most of these *kung fu* men made their money selling some kind of medicine. Sometimes there might be a man with a few snakes, maybe a cobra. He would have a large glass container like they have in chemist shops and inside there would be a dead snake. He would sell little jars of this snake lotion.

Another demonstration I liked to watch was done with small brown earthenware teapots. These are very fragile. The acrobat would put six or seven of these teapots one on top of the other. Then he would stand on top of the pile. This requires tremendous skill in balancing. You also need to have some of what we call 'light' energy: the ability to be light. With *kung fu* we have two different powers: external and internal. At first you study external power. Only when you have mastered external power can you start to develop internal power. If you try to master internal power first you will destroy your mind. I never studied internal power but even so I developed some just through learning external power. For example, once I was able to lift an eighty-pound boy with one arm right up over my head. I just lifted and up he went. I asked myself: 'Can I really do that? Is it really so easy?' So I asked another boy to curl into a ball and I tried to lift him but I couldn't. How can we explain that? Later I tried again and I had no trouble doing it. Even if you have internal power you can't always control it and use it in the way you want. Sometimes you just know you can do something and other times you doubt it. I remember once I was with some friends in the coffee lounge of the Hongkong Hotel. This was when I was in my twenties. We were talking about *kung fu* and they asked me to show them something of my powers. I picked up a Ronson cigarette lighter. Then I checked that the table was strong enough for the trick. It was marble so I knew it could stand the force of the blow. I put the lighter on its side on the table and then I hit it hard with my middle knuckle. Just one hard blow. I flattened it. It was made of some kind of hard metal. At home, alone, frankly, I would not do this trick. I would have been scared of hurting or breaking my knuckles. But at that moment I had no doubts about it and I had no problem performing the trick. That is what I mean by internal power. And I never once saw an acrobat break any teapots. When he had done his trick he would ask the people watching to put some money in a box. His son or his wife would go round asking for money. It was up to you if you gave any money. I always liked to give a few cents to everyone I watched.

These street markets were good fun and there was always some stall you could get a bowl of congee or a length of fried dough or a deep-fried fish-paste ball or something like that. I really miss those days. They will never come back.

The richest man in Macau

I WAS THIRTEEN OR FOURTEEN when my cousin Kwok Lau took me to meet the richest man in Macau. He was a relative of ours. His name was Ko Hor-ling. He owned the gambling monopoly. I remember he was an old man then. He lived in a large Chinese-style mansion. I remember very little of this visit except that Kwok Lau said: 'Mr Ko still has his begging basket.' Mr Ko laughed and nodded his head. He pointed it out. It was hanging on display in his visiting room. He wasn't ashamed of his past. 'That's what I collected money in when I was a beggar!'

Kwok Lau later told me the whole story. Ko's father had died when he was still a young boy – maybe seven years old. They were a poor family and his mother couldn't afford to bring them up herself. Ko had an elder sister. She was married off to my mother's elder brother. That's how we became related. My mother's family were very poor too. Ko, himself, was sold to a man who adopted him as his son. Now shortly after buying him, maybe a year or two later, the adopted father also died. Ko took back his own surname and went back to live with his mother. She couldn't keep him but she taught him how to earn a living as a beggar. So from the age of about ten to thirteen he went around from village to village begging. Then, when he was thirteen, he was taught how to be an entertainer. He was given a bamboo pole at the end of which there was a wooden model of a dragon boat. He was also given a drum and taught some folk songs.

So Ko now spent the summer months going from village to village entertaining the people with his songs. At night he would stay in the ancestral hall that each village had. Anyone was free to sleep there but of course you had to bring your own bedding.

In those days there was little official control over the country areas. In fact the situation was quite chaotic. Villages often attacked each other – especially just after the harvest. It is a countryside with many streams and rivers. The water people could often turn into pirates. There were gangs that would take charge of an area and tax people and impose charges on any boats passing through their districts.

If you go to this area now you will see that all the villages have watch-towers, all built recently. You can see this from the styles. One village might have four or five towers. Often the doors of the houses open onto narrow alleys to stop attackers from being able to break open the doors easily. Naturally there was a great deal of opium smuggling. Ko knew all these people and they knew Ko. He was a familiar face. One of the problems for the smugglers was how to distribute the opium to the villages without raising any suspicions. One day, a smuggler saw Ko passing by with his drum and his bamboo pole and had an idea. He waved Ko over. Ko was fifteen or sixteen by this time.

'Hey, Ko. How much do you earn?' He told them.

'How would you like to earn a month's pay in just one day?'

Naturally Ko agreed. Why not? He was game for anything. The smugglers hollowed out Ko's pole and filled it with opium. They told him that he was to give five taels to this man in this village and another five taels to that man in another village and so on. The smugglers told Ko that each time he made a delivery he would be paid and when he returned to them he would be paid some more. Ko didn't ask what it was all about. He was a simple uneducated lad and he just knew that it was good to earn more money. So life carried on for a year or so. Then Ko gradually became curious as to what it was he was carrying around. So he asked them and they told him it was opium. He had saved up a bit of money by this time so he asked if he could invest in the enterprise and share in the profits. The smugglers agreed and so Ko became one of the gang – a partner.

Year followed year. Ko grew older, and wiser in the ways of the world, and richer. One by one the other partners changed, or died, or had accidents. Time sieves out people. When he was in his twenties Ko gained control of the gang. He controlled a network, a district, and became very rich. He invested in other businesses. He got involved in gold smuggling as well. This too was a very profitable business. Then Macau made a move to control the gambling syndicates that had established themselves in the territory. They decided it would be more profitable for the government to have a monopoly on gambling which could be tendered for. One way or another Ko teamed up with a man called Fu Lo-yung who was a rich businessman in Hong Kong. The Fu family still owns a lot of property in Hong Kong, including the Furama Hotel. I knew his son when I was at school. Fu Yum-chiu. I haven't seen him for over twenty-five years. In fact, I introduced him to his wife!

So Fu and Ko were partners in the gambling syndicate. They controlled it for many years until Stanley Ho stole it from them in the 1960s. Even though they are my distant relatives I have no sympathy for them. They were too complacent. Too arrogant. They didn't believe Stanley Ho was a threat. But that's another story.

But although Ko Hor-ling became very rich he never forgot his origins and he never became ashamed that he was once poor. Actually he was proud he had made such a success of his life. But although he was a rich and powerful man, he didn't control Macau. In fact, one time, he had problems with the authorities and he and his family had to leave hurriedly. It was a tax matter. Naturally Ko and Fu didn't declare their true earnings at their gambling establishments. Maybe they declared ten per cent. How can anyone know how much a casino earns – so much money is going in all directions? But there was an investigation and somehow they discovered his smuggling activities. Naturally, being a rich man, he heard what was happening before the police could arrest him. He fled to Hong Kong.

It took Ko Hor-ling about one-and-a-half years to settle everything so that he could return. Naturally a boy of thirteen or fourteen won't be told all the details but from what I remember then and what I learned later, I believe this trouble was connected to the events that led up to the murder of a very famous man in Hong Kong, Lee Hysan.

Anybody who knows Hong Kong knows the Lee Gardens area, and the main road there is called Hysan Avenue after him. The story behind this is interesting. Lee Hysan was a superstitious man and he believed a lot in *feng shui,* the art of wind and water. This is a way of measuring and controlling the natural forces that affect a particular place. Now the *feng shui* experts pictured a large goose across much of Wanchai and Causeway Bay. The goose's neck went up Canal Road and the head of the goose was the area of land that Lee bought and developed and called Lee Gardens. He thought this was the most auspicious spot: the goose's head! It wasn't so auspicious for him. One day in 1928, when I was fourteen, he was murdered. No one knows who killed him. No one was ever arrested. But I know who ordered the killing and why. I have read many reports of the case but Ko Hor-ling's name never appeared in any of them. But he was the man behind the killing. This is a fact.

Lee Hysan was the man who owned the government opium monopoly in Hong Kong. He had also owned the monopoly in Macau but for some reason he had lost it. I am sure this was all connected. His secret partner in the opium business in Macau and China was Ko Hor-ling. They also cooperated in smuggling large amounts of opium to America. Together they were a very good team. The educated Lee who spoke English and the uneducated, illiterate Ko.

Although they were close partners, whenever they had important business with each other they would draw up a contract between them. When they got into the opium smuggling business the contract between them said that Lee would handle the sales of the drugs and would pass on to Ko a fair share to be decided by Lee. Since they were old friends Ko trusted Lee and signed his name to the contract. Ko in fact was completely illiterate and the only thing he could write was his signature. I think it must have been his wife or maybe a son who convinced him that at least he should be able to sign his own name. It was a matter of face. Actually, many people didn't know how to sign their own names and instead they used a chop on any documents. This was very common and even if you are well educated you might still prefer to use a chop.

Lee, it must be said, was a very stupid and greedy man. How could he expect to get away with cheating Ko? Around Lee and Ko there were many associates who were friendly with each other because they cooperated in so many illegal businesses. Naturally they could add up one and one and make two.

The main way of smuggling the opium was with the help of seamen on ocean liners. On a large passenger ship there are a million and one places to hide small parcels. Seamen were very glad of the chance to earn more money. One or two of the crew would be associates of Ko and Lee. So every liner that went from Hong Kong to America was carrying opium. How they got the opium off the ship on to shore I have no idea. Perhaps they bribed the customs men. Maybe they lowered it off the side into small boats. It didn't take much intelligence for the associates to calculate exactly how much money Lee was making. They knew how much it cost to buy the raw materials and how much it cost to transport and how much money changed hands at every step. They knew every-thing to the last cent.

I heard the whole story from my father. He knew all the details. He was a very well-connected man. He thought it was funny. No one was sorry for Lee when he got killed. Every time he told me the story he said: 'Lee was making seventy-nine times his investment. Every month. On millions of dollars of investment. And how much did he give to Ko? They were supposed to be equal partners. How much did Ko get? Only five times! Only five!'

Of course this was very good money. If every month you invest one million and get back five million you would be content. Of course Ko was happy and didn't question anything. But the young associates quickly understood that Lee was making phenomenal profits. One day, one of Lee's associates mentioned this in front of Ko. Perhaps Ko made a face. It was clear to everybody that he was displeased.

At first Ko did nothing. He wanted to be sure that what he suspected was true. As he gathered more and more evidence it became clear, without any possibility of doubt, that Lee was cheating him. There was only one solution. Ko hired a gunman to kill Lee. Naturally, because Lee and Ko were such good friends they knew all about each other's habits. Ko knew that Lee liked to go to a certain opium den in Second Wife Lane which, in fact, was just behind our house in the neighbour-hood known as Kao U Fong. I don't know why it was called Second Wife Lane – maybe because it was a narrow, unimportant lane. Second wives never had any power or authority in the traditional households of China. Everything was under the thumb of the first wife. The assassin had no problem killing Lee as he was leaving the den. He just stepped up to Lee and shot him dead. How could he miss? The police inves-tigated the matter but no one was ever caught and no one knew who might have been responsible. But some people like my father knew. He told me the story often enough before the war. Lee was killed when I was fourteen or fifteen.

AUTHOR'S NOTE: *Hong Kong Inc.* magazine (January 1990) carried this description of the killing:

As the *China Mail,* the *South China Morning Post* and several
Chinese newspapers reported on April 30 and May 1 1928: 'At
noon on April 30, Lee Hysan was heading to the Yue Kee Club at
Wellington Street as usual. Outside the club, he was shot three
times at point blank range and died on the spot. The murderer,
under the shelter of a succession of firecrackers, managed to
escape, leaving behind the murder weapon, a 38-calibre Smith &
Wesson.' The killer had planned Lee Hysan's murder carefully. He
had a clear idea of the club's surroundings and Lee's everyday
habits. He obviously followed Lee for a while, picked the quietest
spot for his task and knew his way out. The Yue Kee club, on the
second floor at 196–198 Wellington Street was popular with many
well-known Chinese businessmen. Despite its Wellington Street
address, the entrance was by way of a flight of underground steps
or from a maze of alleys off Kau U Fong, on the other side of
which is the Chinese Theatre. The killer followed Lee through the
door and along a passageway. About eight paces in, he drew his
pistol and fired three shots. The first two hit Lee in the left
shoulder and the stomach. The third grazed his chest as he turned
around. Two waiters rushed out of the club and found Lee
covered in blood, supporting himself against the wall with one
hand. There was no sign of the killer.

The lottery

HOW WAS IT THAT MY FATHER knew all these secrets about Ko and Lee? Well, my father was a very sociable man. He had time to go to the teahouses and drink tea and chat with his friends. That's how he got the chance to be the controller of the lottery in Central district. Someone offered him the opportunity. People knew he could be trusted. It wasn't very big money but it was good enough.

I need to tell you something first about the lottery – the *po biu* as it was called: That just means 'ticket shop' but that's what we called the lottery. It is still operating in Macau. Nowadays Hong Kong people aren't interested in it. It's too small. It's not interesting. But in those days it cost very little to buy a ticket and there wasn't any alternative form of gambling in Hong Kong except the horse races. The horse races were very popular but not so regular as they are now. Maybe they would be held only once or twice a month, not twice a week like now. The *po biu* was held every five days. I remember my father saying: 'At least we can eat dinner six times a month!' and in fact we did all go out for dinner every fifth day when the *po biu* was drawn – just the men: my father, my cousin Kwok Lau and myself. Kwok Lau was my father's assistant. Although he was my mother's relative in fact he was very similar to my father. They both liked to enjoy themselves.

It worked like this: everyone got a ticket with 120 characters on it. This was an extract from the four-characters classic that every student used when they started to learn their characters. The first 120 characters from the book were printed out on a sheet. Then the banker in Macau pre-selected twelve characters. If you wanted to make a bet, you would mark ten of the characters. The ticket-shop manager then noted down exactly how much the bet was and kept a record. Every fifth day the selection was declared. If the gambler got four of the characters right they would win back something. If you had seven correct characters you won the jackpot.

The *po biu* was operated from Macau. There were plenty of shops in Macau you could buy a ticket from. But of course there weren't any *po biu* shops in Hong Kong because it was illegal. Instead there were agents. Each agent controlled a territory. When the results were announced in Macau, people in Hong Kong would hear the results over the radio. But they didn't just rely on that. The syndicate also sent messengers to their agents carrying certified announcements of the result. Then these would be posted up or even printed in the newspaper. The agents would get three to five per cent of all bets, and they would also get tea money from winners. It was an easy income. I am sure my father did well out of it. But my father was not a gambling man himself. He didn't care about making millions of dollars. My father was very relaxed. He only cared about three things: children, food and women.

The lottery was run from an office, not from home. Later he handed it all over to Kwok Lau, who did very well out of it. Kwok managed to keep going through the years of the Japanese occupation. Even then there were enough people with money enough to bet. That's how he survived those years. I don't suppose he was a millionaire but he wasn't short of money.

Now why did father give up the lottery syndicate? The reason was this: Ho Tim, my brother-in-law, had just been promoted to superintendent of the Hongkong Hotel. This was the most senior position that a Chinese could rise to. The managers of the hotel were all Europeans but the Chinese staff did all the real work. Ho Tim was a very capable man in his twenties or early thirties. One of his responsibilities was to arrange all the food for the staff canteen. There were hundreds of staff members. This was a job that Ho Tim knew nothing about. He had to put it in the hands of someone he trusted. That is our way. If we can, we put relatives into key positions because we feel we can trust them better. Ho Tim asked my father to take over this job for him. My father wasn't happy to do this. The lottery business was earning him good money and he didn't have to do much work. If he took on this responsibility he would have to get up early in the morning and organise many assistants. It would only take an hour or so but it would be hard work bargaining and arranging the delivery. However, my mother was on Ho Tim's side. She didn't want anything to stand in the way of his success. She pressed my father until he had to agree. That's why he handed the lottery business over to Kwok Lau and took up the job of buying the staff provisions.

Early every morning he went down to the market to buy hundreds of catties of meat and vegetables. He had porters to carry it to the hotel for him. Actually, it was very easy. All he did was bargain and say: 'I'll take that and that and that.' And then he was finished for the rest of the day. Maybe he worked two hours a day. And obviously he earned good money from this. As I remember it he was given an allowance of two dollars per man per month. With hundreds of staff members, even if the profit margin was low he could earn quite a lot. Day in, day out. There was no competition. There would be tea money from suppliers. It suited my father very well.

Naturally he spent most of the rest of the day sitting around the staff quarters of the hotel. There was always a lot of activity there because the staff worked on shift duty. He would sit and chat or play Chinese chess. Sometimes he would do some small business with the staff. He was a very jovial man. Everyone trusted and respected him. Sometimes I went with him to the hotel or I would go there to find him. They all called me 'Ah Kei!' That's how I came to meet one of the most famous pirates at that time, or perhaps you would call him a bandit, or is brigand a better word? His name was 'Teacher' Tuen.

In those days, southern Guangdong Province wasn't safe. There was no law and order in the countryside. In the cities everything was corrupt. The area between Canton and Hong Kong was under the control of four gangs of bandits. They controlled all the waterways. Boatmen had to pay them a small sum every time they passed by. I came to know many of them later. I don't really remember how it was that I did know them. I think it was because many of them at one time or another came down to Hong Kong to hide out. Now, first of all I need to explain something. When the Peninsula Hotel was built obviously it was necessary to get staff. My brother-in-law was responsible for this and once again he asked my father to help him. First we look to family, then to neighbours, then to people from nearby districts. Very rarely do we trust people from other areas. This is typically Cantonese. Shanghainese are different. They are more extravagant and generous. Even though I am Cantonese I have to say that I admire the Shanghainese character. The Cantonese are hard working but miserly and distrustful. They are very careful. They don't like to take big risks. It is harder for a Cantonese to borrow money from friends than a Shanghainese. So, naturally, when my father and Ho Tim needed to find staff for the Peninsula Hotel, they went back to our home districts and recruited there, or if they recruited people in Hong Kong, they gave preference to people from Punyu district or the Namhoi area. In this way my father had a very strong influence with the staff of the hotel and much later when I was down on my luck this influence was still helpful to me.

In those days the only way to cross the harbour was by ferry so, especially in the heat of summer, my father would take the food over to the Peninsula – he now had to organise the staff provisions for two hotels – and then stay there until evening before returning home. The staff quarters of the Peninsula were on the roof of the hotel. That's where I found him one day chatting to a man I didn't know. I assumed he was just another worker.

'Ah Kei,' my father called me over to where he was sitting, 'come and meet Mr Tuen.' I nodded to him. That was all that was said. He wasn't a very impressive figure. I didn't realise until later who he was. Naturally, my father didn't say: 'This is Teacher Tuen, the well-known bandit who is hiding out here for a while.'

At that time, the Chinese authorities had launched an anti-bandit drive. It was dangerous for them to remain in China. Tuen had a relative working at the Hongkong Hotel and this relative had asked my father to help. My father arranged for him to stay at the Peninsula Hotel staff sleeping quarters.

Tuen's story was rather amusing. He actually was a poor village teacher. One day he was kidnapped by a gang of bandits and held for ransom. The problem was he was poor, like all teachers, and his family was poor also. So they couldn't pay the gang any money. However, the gang wouldn't let him go. Most people at that time were illiterate so the gang leader made use of Tuen's ability to write by making him write ransom and demand notes. He became the secretary of the gang. A few years later the chief bandit died. The other bandits had to choose another leader and they chose Tuen. I suppose they respected him for his education. So Tuen became the gang leader. These gangs had a great deal of influence, not just over the waterways but also over the farmers of those districts.

'King' of Queen's College

I WAS ABOUT SIXTEEN when I went to Queen's College. This would have been in 1930. At that time Queen's College was the top school in Hong Kong. All the sons of the richest Chinese families sent their sons there. Dr Sun Yat Sen, the founder of modern China, was also educated there.

When I arrived for my first day at Queen's College I was already famous among all the students. They were waiting for me to come. 'King is here!' they said when I arrived. They still knew me as 'King' because many of them had also been to Ellis Kadoorie. Now why were they so happy to see me? Well, the situation was like this. There were about 1,000 students altogether. Of these about 700 were Chinese and 300 were Indians or Portuguese or mixed. Now, perhaps you would think that the Chinese students would be dominant but that wasn't the case. In fact, the non-Chinese students bullied the Chinese students. There were three play areas in the school but the Chinese students were forced to use only one. If they tried to use the others they would be beaten up. The reason for this is quite simple. The 300 non-Chinese knew they were in a minority so they ganged together very tightly: they were better organised and they were physically bigger and stronger: some of the Indians were six foot tall. They matured much earlier than the Chinese students. Also, it is true, most Chinese students were discouraged by their parents from physical activities or from doing anything that might hurt them. I was different. That's why I was so popular when I arrived at Queen's College. They wanted me to be their hero.

I enjoyed being called 'King' but actually I wasn't looking to be a hero, a fighter. In fact, the other students respected me so much they didn't just call me 'King'. Wherever I walked they would make way for me. Naturally, I enjoyed this respect very much.

Before entering Queen's College, I had just had six months of intensive *kung fu* training because I had left Ellis Kadoorie in February or March and didn't go to Queen's College till after the summer. All those months I trained at *kung fu*. I was fitter and stronger than I have ever been in my life. Even though I am such a short, slight man I could then knock down a six-foot-tall man weighing 200 pounds. But after six months of training I had had enough of it. In fact I stopped training after that. I decided there were better things to do. I had achieved all I wanted to achieve in *kung fu*. I was now ready to get down to school-work. Also I started to take up other courses at this time. I took up Chinese music, photography, Chinese painting, typing; many different subjects. Most of them I didn't study for long, but I studied painting for several years. I wasn't interested in being just a fighter.

The top fighter in the school when I arrived was a Macau Portuguese by the name of Abbas. He was the big bully. When I arrived I was very much welcomed. 'King has arrived! Now we've got someone to fight against Abbas!' they said. But I had no desire to get involved in a fight. So when people came to me and asked me to fight Abbas, I always said to them: 'Why don't you fight him? Why should I do it? There are hundreds of you. You outnumber them. What's the problem?' But they never did. They were too scared.

Abbas was a big, strong boy who would hit any Chinese student who got in his way. One day during recess I came out of the toilets and I saw him in the playground hitting out. He must have hit six or seven students. To do this in front of me! This showed no respect! I couldn't stand that. I suddenly lost my temper.

'Get out of my way!' I shouted and all the Chinese students cheered as I rushed out to fight him and they cleared a path. But it was a funny thing that I immediately lost sight of him. I think what happened was that all the other students started to crowd round because they wanted to see the fight. I remember thinking at that moment that I could not avoid fighting: it was my fate to be a fighter. And since I was a fighter I might as well hit out at anybody who got in my way. So I looked round for any non-Chinese students. I caught sight of a tall Indian. He was also known as a bully. Of course he didn't know I intended hitting him so he was taken completely by surprise. I hit him hard and he fell down crashing against a pillar. He was saved from being seriously injured because he was wearing a turban on his head. I turned to look for someone else and saw another Macau Portuguese boy. I punched him and he too just flew away. Finally a space cleared and I could see my enemy and so I went up to him and punched. He was quite good. He stepped back and I missed. He was a boxer. He tried to hit me but he missed too. He held his hands out like a boxer but for me this was no problem. I hit him over the arms and before he could react I punched him on the chin, knocking him to the ground. That was all I did. Just then the bell rang. We dispersed to our different classes. This was on a Saturday morning. There was just one more class before the end of the day. Throughout the lesson my thoughts were on Abbas and his friends. What would they do? I knew they would be scared of me after what I had done. I expected that they would try to leave together for protection. For my part, I didn't feel yet that I had won conclusively. I wanted to destroy his reputation completely.

Ten minutes before the lesson ended I told the teacher I was feeling a bit ill and left the classroom. I went to the main gate and waited. As I expected they tried to leave early. There were twelve of them and Abbas was in the middle. For a moment I was a bit concerned that they would all attack me. One Chinese against twelve. The odds weren't good. But they were scared of me.

'Abbas,' I challenged him, 'let's you and me fight, one to one.'

He hesitated because he knew he couldn't beat me – but he couldn't say that in front of everyone. So we started to fight there next to the front gate of the school. He was a boxer and I was a *kung fu* man so our styles were different. By this time my blood was up. I already expected to be expelled so there was nothing to restrain me. I quickly knocked him down.

'Get up!'

'No!' he shook his head. 'You win!'

Then I challenged all the others: 'Anyone else want a fight?'

Naturally, no one said anything. But I wasn't satisfied. It was all too easy. I wanted to hit someone. Abbas picked himself off the ground and collected his rattan school-bag.

'Come on. Why are you such a coward?' I yelled at him. 'Why don't we fight some more?'

He just shook his head. His face must have been hurting badly. 'No,' he said, 'I don't want to fight.'

But, how can I explain this, when you are prepared for a fight and you are all worked up you must have something to release that tension.

I was just blind with anger. I was not rational. So I just stepped up to him and punched him hard again. He fell to the ground. I would have hit him more but there was a policeman there.

'Stop that!' he shouted and grabbed my arm.

'Let go,' I told him, 'or I'll hit you too.' I gave him such a furious look that he immediately let go.

'You're coming with me to the police station,' he said.

'I'll come but you must take him too!' I pointed to Abbas. So both of us went to the police station and a report was made. There they took down details of the incident and warned us not to fight again. They told us they were going to report the incident to the headmaster. And they did. He gave us a big scolding!

That was the only time I ever did fight at Queen's College. I didn't have to. I was 'King'. No doubt about that. From that time on everything changed. Everyone came to respect me. I remember, a long time after leaving school, I would bump into Abbas in the street and he would always come up to me and shake my hand.

Those years that followed were the happiest days of my life. Really, when I look back at them I feel a kind of golden glow over all my memories. It was complete. I had everything I wanted. I was 'King'. Everyone loved me. Everyone respected me. Even the teachers. I was a bright student and I enjoyed my studies. I was young and handsome. I could have been anything I wanted. I think something happens to a person when other people show they respect him. I know that I radiated a kind of golden aura. Everything revolved around me. I know that other people have to work hard to keep up, but I never had to work hard. Everything always came easily. I made sure I understood what the teachers said so I never did any homework. I didn't have to. The concentration that I learned from *kung fu* I also applied to my class studies.

I sometimes wonder how it could be that such a wonderful, glorious, young man could fail. How could I fail? But I can tell you, fate has been against me. If not for fate, how could I possibly fail? It wasn't possible.

Getting married

IN 1935 MY DEAR, DEAR SECOND SISTER DIED. She was only thirty-two years old. How short and sad her life was.

Not long after, my parents had a talk with me.

'Ah Kei, now that your sister is dead you must think about marriage.'

This was not the first time the subject had been mentioned. I think I was sixteen when they first started to talk about it seriously. I always refused.

'How can I get married?' I always argued, 'I'm still a student. Anyway, what do I need a wife for?' I was not at all interested in girls. This time my mother was not to be put off. Obviously, an important factor was that she was getting old, she had already had a slight stroke a year or two before and she wanted to be alive to see her grandchildren. There was another problem which she explained.

'Ah Kei. Who is going to look after the house? Now there is just the amah and the *mui-jai* and you. I am going up to Canton regularly to see to our property up there and collect the rents.' It was true. As we grew richer, she was having to spend more and more time managing our property. By this time we owned a lot of rice fields in our native village which were leased out to farmers. We would split the income from the crop fifty-fifty. In addition to the fields, we owned large godowns, warehouses, in the centre of Canton. One was the size of four football fields and occupied the site between the railway station and the river.

'So,' my mother concluded, 'this means that either you get married or you will have to stop your studies and supervise the home.'

Now, I enjoyed my studies. I was very happy at school. I had no wish to leave. Indeed I was beginning to have thoughts of going to university, perhaps to Harvard to study medicine. Anything was possible. To stop now was out of the question.

'Are there any girls you are attracted to?' my father asked. 'We have no objections. Perhaps, one of your schoolmates has a sister you would like to marry?' It was true there were a few mothers who tried to get me interested in their daughters. Fellow students at Queen's College would talk about me at home. I was a hero. Naturally the mothers would take note of this. They would ask around and discover my parents were quite rich. This was the most important thing. Then they would send a go-between to our house with photographs of their daughters. But I never paid any attention to them. The subject of who I married was of absolutely no interest to me.

'I have nobody in mind,' I said.

Then my father ended the conversation: 'I am ordering you to get married. Your mother and I will select some suitable girls, but I won't force you to marry anyone you don't like. When I have selected a girl you will be able to see her and judge her for yourself.'

'Anybody you choose will be fine with me,' I said.

'Ah Kei, don't worry about your wife. If you don't love her and later you find someone you do love, don't worry. Just marry a second wife.' Even my mother said this to me, though she wouldn't let my father have a second wife! So that's how I thought about it. Either I would like my wife or I wouldn't. In any case, it wouldn't affect the way I led my life.

My parents' first thought on the matter was that Hong Kong girls were not so suitable. They were too 'modern' for my parents. They wanted someone more old-fashioned, more conservative. I remember at this time that my father stressed several times that China was the land of our origin. Hong Kong was just a colony. We would eventually return to China. That was why he invested all his money in property in Canton and that was another reason why we should go back to Canton to find me a wife.

This didn't make much sense to me. 'Just because our estates are in China doesn't mean that I have to marry a girl from Canton. I don't see anything wrong with Hong Kong girls.' Finally they agreed to consult a match-maker in Hong Kong. The go-between came back with the photos of two girls, cousins who had been brought up together. One was fat and the other was slim. In fact I knew the slim one vaguely because she, like me, was a keen swimmer. She was the women's freestyle and backstroke champion of Hong Kong. The girl's father owned a shop that sold roast pork and duck. They came from the same district in China. Naturally I said the slim one was preferable. My parents were pleased that I was taking sufficient interest to make a choice. So the match-maker was sent to discuss the matter with the girl's family. They knew that father was well off so they were very pleased to agree. Now, when a boy and a girl get engaged the boy's side has to give the girl's side a lot of presents. The most important present is the *lai beng,* the courtesy cakes. At this stage we had a tentative agreement but for some reason we didn't move quickly to the formal stage, probably because we still had to have our horoscopes matched to make sure our stars were compatible. In fact we never did send the courtesy cakes because shortly afterwards the two girls went back to China to visit their native village. While they were there they went swimming. Now, even in Hong Kong it was considered very modern for a girl to go swimming. In China it was unheard of. It was considered a matter of gross indecency for a girl to expose her body to public view. Actually, not much would have been exposed to view because they wore long skirts in those days. Still, it was considered outrageously immodest, especially as they all knew she was about to be engaged. Word quickly reached my parents. I remember my mother being furious that the girl should 'show off her thighs in public'. They immediately called the engagement off. They were now more than ever insistent that my wife should be a girl from China. So we took the train to Canton.

In Canton, another match-maker was contacted and she suggested the daughter of a private tutor. He wouldn't have been wealthy but that wasn't a concern of my parents. It was far more important that the girl be respectable and well brought up. Arrangements were made to meet in a teahouse. The father refused to come but he sent the girl with the go-between. We went to the teahouse early. Just before the appointed time my father suggested that I go with him outside to the street and pretend to buy fruit. In this way we would be able to catch a glimpse of the girl as she passed by with the go-between on her way to the teahouse. That's what we did and shortly later we saw them approaching. I remember the girl was nice looking and very gentle. Very thin and delicate.

'What do you think?' my father asked me.

'She seems fine,' I said.

'You don't think she's too thin?' he asked.

I shrugged my shoulders. Thin? Fat? What difference did it make? We went back to the teahouse to wait but the girl never came. Maybe she was too shy. Maybe if her father had been there she would have come. Anyway, everyone seemed happy that I had no objections. The next stage was to do a thorough investigation of her family's background. My parents' main concern was that the girl might have TB. They insisted that a check should be done. A doctor's certificate was sent to us to show that she had no health problems. But it was not unknown for medical records to be falsified. Finally, my parents could not shake off the feeling that there was something unhealthy about the girl's thinness. Remember, my second sister had also been very thin. So they decided to pull out. The go-between insisted the girl was healthy and that, in addition, she was polite, obedient and – being the daughter of a teacher – very learned. But go-betweens can never be trusted. They have sweet tongues and it is in their interests to promote marriages. Naturally they will say anything. My only concern was that the girl should not be ugly. What did it matter if I didn't love her?

A second go-between came to us with photos of another girl. Her father owned a big farm not far from our native village. The first contacts were made through the go-between but as soon as we knew where the family lived my mother hired a car and we drove there to look them over. We did this without informing the go-between. We didn't want to warn the family so that they could get prepared. In fact, when we arrived, we found the girl washing a pig in front of the house. She was a large, healthy farm girl with a full round face, red and tanned by the wind and sun. Her long thick black hair was tied in plaits on each side. She was more attractive even than the first girl.

'Well?' my mother demanded.

I shrugged. 'She looks all right.'

My mother laughed.

'All girls look all right to you!'

Negotiations began but again nothing came of it because her father stipulated that after the marriage she would stay with us for three days but then return to the farm for three years. This was quite a common arrangement in those days. The way of thinking was this: the girl's family had spent a lot of time and energy bringing the girl up. Then suddenly the girl is married and taken away to join another family. This was felt to be cruel. To the parents, not the girl. They would get no benefit from her labour. For these three years the husband would not be allowed to visit his wife. It was felt that the husband and wife would naturally want to be together and there would be consequences which would interfere with the girl's ability to work. This arrangement did not suit my parents at all. My mother wanted me to get married and to have a wife to look after the house. She was getting old and wanted to see her grandsons before she died. Again my parents pulled out.

The next girl was from Foshan, a town very famous for its milk and desserts. It lies half an hour by train to the west of Canton. We went there by train and were invited to lunch at a teahouse by the girl's father. The go-between was with us in the restaurant. When we were ready she was sent off to fetch the girl. Then, a little while later, my father turned to me and winked.

'Come on Ah Kei! Let's go to the toilet.'

In fact everyone understood we were going out to the street to look at the girl before she arrived. This time the girl was very modern and fashionable. We knew that she often came down to Hong Kong and she copied the Hong Kong styles. Now, the new modern styles were nothing out of the ordinary in Hong Kong but here in this provincial market town they were stunning, perhaps even shocking. She was wearing a long gown with a slit up the side, what we call the *cheong-sam*. But while conservative girls had the slit up to the knee, the modern style was to have the slit much higher. In addition, the dress she wore was vividly coloured. She carried an umbrella to protect her self from the sun. She was quite a sight. Very beautiful and elegant. Her hair was cut short in the modern style and waved.

'What do you think?' my father asked.

'She's all right,' I said. Actually, I thought she was quite attractive.

'Don't you think she's too fashionable?' he asked.

'She's just like any girl in Hong Kong.'

'Yes,' he said doubtfully. 'But this is Foshan.'

Now, it's a funny thing but this girl also didn't come up to the teahouse. I think what happened was that the go-between knew we had seen the girl so didn't feel there was any need for the girl to come to the teahouse. Of course we didn't say we had seen her so her parents invited us to their home after lunch. Even when we got there she wouldn't appear.

'She could come out and let us look at her,' my mother said. An amah was sent to get her. This time she was dressed in a cotton trouser suit with wooden peg buttons – simple home wear. She seemed very gentle and polite but she had made a bad impression on my father with her stylish clothes so nothing came of her either.

The next girl was the daughter of a factory owner. He was very rich. He had the biggest canned food factory in all of south China. He met us in a teahouse and we chatted together. Then the go-between was sent off to fetch the girl. This time I made an excuse and went out with the go-between. I wanted to ask her about the girl. We walked a little way down the street. 'What's she like?' I asked. 'And tell me the truth. I don't want any lies.'

'She's a very clever girl,' said the go-between. 'She can write long and learned compositions. She enjoys writing poetry. And as for her physical attractions, she is known as an attractive girl by every shop-owner on Tung Wan Street.'

Tung Wan Street was famous for its shoe shops where all the girls went to buy pretty slippers. I can tell you now this was all lies. She could hardly write anything at all and she could only read a little. She had some education but not much. In those days it wasn't considered that a girl needed much literary education. She should be able to read and write common things but that was all. And as for being beautiful? I would say she was plain with a touch of beauty. I waited in the street while the go-between fetched the girl. I saw them coming but I found I was on the wrong side of the street. The go-between was between me and the girl. Did she do this deliberately so that I wouldn't get a clear view? I can't say. Anyway, it was of no real concern to me. Even if she was ugly what did it matter as long as my parents were happy? I went back into the teahouse. Again she didn't come in but went straight home. Her father made a great show of impatience and then suggested we should all go to his home nearby and see the girl there.

'Don't worry, Mr Leung,' I said, 'I will tell you honestly. Just now when I was outside I saw your daughter. She seems to me to be very nice and I have no objections.' My parents were very pleased and immediately agreed to send the marriage offer.

'As for you, young man,' Mr Leung said, 'I think you and I should have a private chat. Just the two of us.' Everybody agreed that this was a good thing and I arranged to have lunch with him the next day.

The following day we met as arranged at the same teahouse. I wasn't at all nervous. Why should I be? I was a handsome, intelligent young man. I expected he would want to find out about me: my abilities, my ambitions. That sort of thing. When the tea and some of the dumplings arrived, Mr Leung leant forwards.

'Well, Ah Kei. Tell me about your parents' property. Do you know what your parents own?'

'Only a little. I don't take much interest in these things and they have never told me exactly what they own.'

'Do you own property here in Canton?'

'Yes. From what I know we own a few blocks,' I replied cautiously.

'Can you tell me some details? Where is this property, for example?' he asked. I told him a few names. They didn't mean much to me as I didn't know Canton very well but he was a Canton man so he knew everywhere I mentioned. Naturally he was very impressed because some of these blocks occupied prime sites in good districts. It was like saying we owned a block on Mayfair and another in Oxford Street in London. I had only mentioned two or three blocks when he held up his hand. 'That's enough! Enough! You don't have to tell me anything more. That's fine!' And then he just sat there quietly, smiling at me and offering me things to eat. Actually I was a bit annoyed. All he was interested in was what we owned, how much money we had. When I got back to the hotel I told my parents all about it. I was disgusted.

'That bloody man! He's only interested in your money!'

'That's only natural,' my father said, 'you are going to marry his daughter. He just wants to make sure your financial standing is good.'

In fact later I discovered he was a very nice and kind man. I liked him very much but he just had one failing. He was very mean with money.

When the engagement formalities had been completed my future father-in-law said to my parents: 'Have you any objection to coming up to Canton for the wedding? We can have it here.' Now, our custom is like this. The man's family is considered the 'top' family and the girl's family is considered the 'lower' family. The boy's family meet all the expenses of the wedding and in return all the wedding presents, except of course presents of gold that go to the girl from her side, go to the boy's parents. In those days it was rare to give cash, not like now. It was customary to give gift certificates, or blankets, or gold. Now since my father was going to pay all the expenses he felt he had the right of choice about where the wedding was to be held. He was an important person in Hong Kong. He had many friends here. I was his only son. He wanted the wedding to take place in Hong Kong. He explained this to Mr Leung.

'That will be rather expensive for us!' Mr Leung said. Of course he could easily afford it but as I have said he didn't like to give away money. If my mother hadn't been there I don't know what would have happened. My father was also not an extremely generous man. My mother was different. She would lend money to anyone she thought had an honest need. She was a little annoyed at this situation. Such a disagreement could easily end up with the engagement being broken. I can't say if that was likely or not because my mother stepped in.

'Please don't worry about it. We will take care of all the expenses of you and your family and any servants you need to bring with you.' Mr Leung could say nothing against that so it was agreed that they would come down to Hong Kong. We paid all their fares and we put them up at one of the more prestigious Chinese family hotels. They took three or four rooms for about ten days altogether. Not including rooms for the servants. It wasn't cheap.

For the wedding dinner, we booked the entire Tai Tung Restaurant, which was five storeys high. On each floor there would be twenty to thirty tables. Each table would seat ten people and I seem to remember the cost then for the banquet was $100 a table. But even this was not enough. We had several sittings. One at eight-thirty. One after ten. And finally there was one after midnight for all our hotel friends who had to work late and then go and get changed before coming to the restaurant. Some didn't arrive until one-thirty or even a quarter to two.

I think my father spent maybe $40,000 on the wedding. How much would that be worth today? Millions. The presents that came back would not have covered more than twenty per cent of this. My father-in-law presented my parents with a fine suite of black wooden furniture and we had these in our sitting room. It was only then that we all really understood how wealthy my father was. We didn't live in the grand style.

We lived very simply, like any other family. But actually we had a lot of money. I don't think there had been such a lavish wedding party for many years before. All the newspapers covered the event.

It's a funny thing but, until the morning of the wedding day, my wife had never seen me and I had only seen her fleetingly that morning outside the teahouse. I went to the hotel with a group of relatives and friends. These were my 'brothers' for the day. Some were kinsmen from my native village, some were friends from school, some from the *kung fu* academy. We all went to the hotel and knocked on the door of the room where my wife was staying. Inside she was all dressed up and waiting for us with some 'sisters'.

'Open up!' my brothers said. 'We've come for the bride.'

'Go away!' the sisters shouted back.

'Come on,' my brothers called out again, 'open up!'

'How much will you pay us to open the door?'

'Nine cents.' One of my brothers shouted out. 'Come on. I'll give you nine cents.'

'Nine cents? What can we do with nine cents? We want nine hundred and ninety-nine thousand, nine hundred and ninety-nine dollars and ninety-nine cents.'

It was all a big joke for them. All the numbers have to be in nines as this is the luckiest of all the numbers. The next luckiest is three. You must avoid 'four' because that sounds like 'death' in Cantonese dialect. I was dressed in a scholar's gown with a small black cap on my head. You know the kind of hat with a small red bobble on the top like a cherry. I couldn't join in the fun and games. Neither could my wife. We had to stay quiet and be modest and dignified. Eventually we were let into the room. I think we paid ninety-nine dollars. That was a lot of money then but the girls knew I was rich and that money was no object. That was like one month's salary for a senior manager. To give you some idea of what that money meant: a bottle of Chinese wine in those days cost thirty-two cents. My father would send me out to get the wine and give me thirty-five cents. With the three cents change I could buy a bowl of fried pork and noodles which now would cost you about six or seven dollars.

Naturally, my wife was very shy with me. Of course we evaluated each other. I could see she wasn't very beautiful but nor was she ugly. As I have said she was quietly attractive. But more important for me was her manner. You can tell a girl who has been brought up well in a rich family. Her manner, her way of doing things will show her class. A girl from a rich family will hold her chopsticks in a different way than a girl from a poor family. She will pick up a bun in her fingers in a different way. My first impressions of these things were very good. I was very satisfied with her manner. This was for me much more important than her looks. As for her, I asked her later what she had thought about me, never having seen me until this moment. Of course she had seen my photograph. She told me she had asked her relatives and friends and other people who had seen me what I looked like. Everyone said I was very handsome and intelligent and she knew everyone was very satisfied with me, so she was happy to hear that. But there was one thing that they had doubts about. They noticed in my photograph that my hair was slightly curly. This is a natural curl. They wondered, since I came from Hong Kong, whether perhaps I was not full-blooded Chinese. Maybe I was Eurasian. They were a little concerned about that I remember. They didn't want to marry a foreigner.

My wife's name was Yau-hang, which means 'perpetual patience'. My marriage name was Hui Tak-kwong. It is our custom to get a marriage name from our first primary school teacher so I went back to the Man Mo School on Hollywood Road. My first teacher was Mr Ip. But he wasn't teaching there any more. He was at another school. I traced him and asked him to give me a marriage name. *Tak* means 'obtain' and *kwong* means 'light'. At first sight it is a very auspicious name. But *kwong* has a secondary meaning of 'clearance'. Many years later, a friend pointed out that one way of interpreting my name was that you obtain a lot of things but then it is cleared. It goes away. I am not a very superstitious man but the more I thought about it, the more I realised that it was true. I had obtained many things but everything had just cleared again. So I changed my name back to my birth name. After that, it seemed to me the hard times were never so serious. So I am happier with my birth name.

After the bargaining, my wife and her 'sisters' entertained us. Then we took the girls back to our house and entertained them in return. There we paid our respects to our ancestral shrine by pouring out wine from three cups and bowing three times with joss-sticks in our hands, always three joss-sticks. Then we presented tea to my parents. They sat in straight-backed chairs and we bent down on our knees and offered them tea. Then we had to go to the restaurant. Even long before the dinner is served we had to be there. Many of the guests would come early to play mahjong in the afternoon. We all had to be there to greet them. From three or four in the afternoon until way after midnight we smiled and smiled and smiled until towards the end my cheek muscles were painful. During the dinner, it is the custom when the soup course appears – shark's fin soup – for the bride and groom to go round the tables toasting all the guests. Naturally, everyone is drinking brandy. There must be a bottle of brandy for every table. Now, imagine. There were 120 tables. There were two or three sittings. If you drink brandy every time you toast a table then you will have to drink about 250 sips of brandy. At some tables there are some young friends who want to have fun so they challenge you to finish off the glass.

'*Yam sing!*' they say and empty their glass. You have no choice but to do the same. That is one of the rules of the wedding day. You cannot refuse anybody. It is very easy for someone to get drunk but it is considered a very bad thing to get drunk. People remember it. It leaves a very bad impression. A new husband and wife must at all times be modest. My father warned me several times that I must stay sober, and so did my cousins. So what can we do? Actually, the waiters at the wedding are professionals. They know all the tricks. They follow you around with a tray carrying the brandy and when you finish one glass they hand you another. But the glasses don't contain brandy. They contain cold tea the same colour as brandy. So you go around all the tables drinking tea while everybody else is drinking brandy. Actually, I will tell you. I didn't just drink cold tea. I also drank a lot of brandy. I was used to drinking even at the age of nineteen. My parents always had a catty of Chinese wine with dinner and they would finish it between them. I often had a glass or two to try it out. We had to stay until the very last guests left. It would be very rude to show we were tired but I can say we were both exhausted. Finally we were able to shake hands with our last guests. That's one good thing about our Chinese custom: when we have finished eating we don't sit around talking. We get up immediately and go home.

But the day was still not finished. My 'brothers and sisters' escorted us back to our house in taxis. There, in the bedroom, it is time to break the ice between the new husband and wife. This can be an amusing time. It is a time for silly games – games that may be a little embarrassing for a girl with no experience of life. One game for example is to ask the wife to peel an orange and then to break it into segments. Then she must lick each one before handing it to her husband to eat. Another game is to get the man and woman to nibble each end of an olive. Of course, their lips must press together as if they are kissing. These are simple amusements and they serve a useful purpose. But sometimes they can go too far. The guests may be drunk. Husband and wife cannot refuse them. I have heard of cases where a girl has refused to take part in some trick that is too immodest and has been punished by having the ends of joss-sticks burn her cheek. This is very cruel. But our Chinese custom says that it is permissible if a wife refuses the requests of a guest. But this is rare. Normally it is a time of good spirits. We were fortunate. Our friends did not stay long. Now was the time for us to make love. This is important because if the girl is discovered to be not a virgin it is still possible to repudiate the marriage. We got into bed together and I started to make the first moves. She didn't resist but whispered to me: 'My dear husband. I am very tired. If it is not a problem for you, can we leave this till tomorrow night?' I too was exhausted and had no great desire to continue. And so we both fell asleep. It was on the second night that we both discovered the joys of love.

So young and handsome!

I LIKE TO LOOK AT A PHOTOGRAPH that I had taken before my marriage. I was so young and handsome. And my smile! People say to me that I have a very handsome smile. I remember years later, during the Japanese occupation, I was at the hotel dining room in Canton. One of the waitresses was chatting to me. I think she wanted to catch my eye. She said to me: 'Your smile is wonderful. When you smile we all fall down!' I have dimples. Even now. All my life people have said that I have a nice smile so I must accept it.

I remember after I was married, but when I was still at school, I bumped into Kwok Lau in the street not far from where we lived.

'Ah Kei,' he greeted me, 'Come. Let me show you something you need to learn. Come and visit some "chickens".'

Queen's College was at the site on Aberdeen Street now occupied by the police married quarters. The area next to Queen's College was well-known for prostitution – we call prostitutes 'chickens'. During the day everything appeared normal. But when night fell it was different. Then the girls were very visible. Everyone on the street then was looking for fun. People would be mad for fun.

'Come along, Ah Kei!' he said and took my arm. I still had very little interest in girls or sex then. I enjoyed my wife. That was all. However, I was happy to go with Kwok Lau and have a look. We went up a narrow flight of stairs to a flat where there were several girls. They laughed and greeted us. I just smiled at them all in a friendly way.

'How old are you?'

'So young and handsome!'

'Is this your first time?'

I just smiled at them. I didn't want them to think I was just a young schoolboy.

'So,' Kwok Lau said, 'just choose any girl you want. I'm paying.'

All the girls were very nice but the idea of buying sex disgusted me. I didn't mind Kwok Lau doing it but it wasn't for me. I was very pure then, I suppose. But the fact is, I have never been interested in buying sex. It's not my way.

'Go on! You do what you came up here to do,' I said. 'I'll just chat with the girls.'

And that's what happened. Kwok Lau went off into one of the bedrooms and I sat and chatted with the other girls. They all loved me. I was always clever with my tongue and I know how to talk smoothly to girls. Even though I was so young and inexperienced I had a way with women. I think it's because I don't try to charm them or cheat them or pretend anything. If I want to say something I say it straight out. Girls are always surprised by this. When we talk it is always natural. I think the main thing is I like women. Many men don't. They use women. For me I have very pure feelings about women – and I am never impressed by beauty. All my life I have known many very beautiful women. What's another beautiful woman to me?

After this incident, it happened several times that Kwok Lau would bump into me in the street and invite me to go to a bawdy house with him. I don't know if he ever told my father about these visits. Maybe he did. Maybe they both had a good laugh about it. He must have found it strange that I never went with any of the girls.

These bawdy houses were in Gough Street, which was famous for its nightlife – like Wanchai is today. There would be old women sitting on the pavement offering you girls but these were the lowest class of prostitutes. The others, the better class ones, were not visible from the street. Even lower down the scale were the whores in Temple Street in Kowloon who would accost you themselves. Sometimes, during the day when I was walking home from school I might pass by a girl who I'd met during one of these visits and she would smile and greet me. We called girls like these 'glamour girls'. I never dared to greet them back. Actually it was embarrassing. You have to keep face and your self-respect. You don't want the whole world to know that you associate with prostitutes. Maybe they did it because they liked to see me blush!

Now when I think back on this time I realise how innocent and simple I was. My parents told me I could marry another wife if I fell in love and I accepted that as I accepted everything else. Why not? But I can say this poisoned my mind. My attitude was wrong. It was an old-fashioned way of thinking. The times were changing. People of my generation followed more the Western ways. Now, most people had temporary concubines rather than taking a second wife. This way you didn't have to get your first wife's permission, or that of your father or elder brother. It was simpler. At that time I assumed I would have a second wife, and maybe a third if I wanted.

In those first few months of our marriage I discovered and explored the joys of the bedroom with my wife. She was, I found, a quiet, bashful, conservative, respectful, good-natured girl. Like all young wives her main concern was to get along with my mother, her mother-in-law. And in fact she and my mother did get on well. My wife was the sort of girl who would make sure they got on and my mother was easy to get on with. In some families there can be big problems in this area but I can say that peace reigned in our family. I continued to go to school. I continued to lead my life as I always had. Then she got pregnant.

Our flat was small and with my wife's arrival it seemed even smaller. In part because she brought her own *mui-jai* as well. Chinese-style buildings at that time didn't have any brick interior walls. It was up to the people living there to put up wooden partitions where they wanted them. For this reason it is easy to hear things from one side of the flat to another. Maybe Westerners think this lack of privacy is strange but it was normal to us. What happens when a couple make love, like my wife and I did every night? Obviously, you have to make a noise. It isn't something you can do silently. I can say that we Chinese don't worry too much about things like that. I don't know what my parents thought. Maybe they expected us to be noisy. If we were too quiet that might mean nothing was happening. If you're not noisy how can they get grandchildren? And they wanted grandchildren very much. I don't know if my wife was concerned. As for me, I only knew what it was I wanted to do. Noise? I didn't care at all.

For some complicated reasons, it was thought best that I should change schools and become a boarder at another school: Diocesan Boy's School. That's where I spent my last two years and that's where I met Chiu Kei-fan, who was to be my best friend throughout my life. He had the seat in front of mine in the class. He was a short, slight boy, you might say a weakling, but in fact that impression would be wrong. I remember, he was very impressed with my physique. Almost the first thing he said to me was: 'Shen-kei, you are so strong. How did you become so strong? What do you do? I want to be strong like you. Tell me. What can I do?'

I told him about my swimming but I didn't tell him about the *kung fu*. I didn't need to tell him. He already knew. He always stuck to me when he was at school but he was a day boy, not a boarder, and he only came to school two maybe three days a week. The rest of the time he fooled around. Perhaps you are wondering why the school allowed this. He had the charm of the rich. This is something that no one can resist. He was extremely wealthy. He used to come to school in a bright red, open-top MG. He was the only student who had his own car and drove himself to school. It was quite a sight to see him arrive in the morning. Naturally everybody was very impressed with him. Now, at that time I was never impressed with anyone just because they were rich. If someone said: 'So and so is very rich,' I just thought to myself: 'So what? I'm also very rich.' Wealth was not important to me. I had no particular desire to be friendly with KF but he stuck to me and he was amusing so we became friends.

His family background was very interesting. His grandfather was Chiu Yiu-teen, a very famous philanthropist. I remember my father often commented to me that I should model my behaviour on him. He was a wonderful, kind, old gentleman and highly respected, not just in Hong Kong but throughout China. Now I'll tell you a story about him. The family lived in an old three- or four-storey house in Kowloon, quite near Kowloon Park. One day part of the building collapsed, suddenly, without any warning. Several servants and relatives were killed. Old Chiu Yiu-teen was sitting in a large wooden armchair on one of the upper floors. When the building collapsed he was sent hurtling down to the ground floor, still seated in his chair. The chair hit the ground first and he was thrown out. When people rushed to help him they found he was completely uninjured. Everyone said the gods had saved him because of all his benevolent acts. In fact, one of the grandest of the families in Beijing, one descended from a very high-ranking official of the Qing dynasty, sent their daughter to marry his grandson because they were so impressed with his character. This grandson was KF's elder brother, brother Number Six. KF told me that they had an enormous garden, maybe you could call it an estate, which would take two or three days to walk around to see everything. It was second only to the imperial gardens which would require at least a week to walk completely round. Later, this daughter asked me to be tutor to their children. This was before the war.

KF was the thirteenth son. His mother was the third concubine of her husband. In fact she had been a servant in the house before becoming third wife. She was also the mother of his ninth, tenth and eleventh sisters and his twelfth brother. He always called his mother 'Third Auntie'. That's the custom. 'Mother' is reserved for the first wife. KF's father died when he was three years old and his portion of the inheritance was held in trust by his mother. But she was a simple uneducated woman and KF convinced her to hand it over to him when he was fifteen years old. That's how he could throw money around without a care in the world. In fact KF had immediately gone on a tour of Asia by himself when he was fifteen. He went to Japan, Malaya, Thailand and Singapore. He claimed to have lost his virginity at that time. He must have developed earlier than me. When we met he said he often fooled around with girls. He was about seventeen then and I was twenty. He hero-worshipped me. At that time, his English was the best of all the Chinese students because he had to learn it when he went travelling. He was more sophisticated than any of us. I remember he brought a phonograph and some records and we played them in the dormitory and learnt how to dance. Sometimes during holidays or days off we would go together with some of our classmates to a cabaret or ballroom. These places were considered very naughty then. And for us they were very expensive. Of course we only went to top-class ballrooms. We would have been too scared to go to one of the lower-class ones. Although I never studied dancing I found I was naturally good at it. I had good rhythm and balance. And I enjoyed it. Dancing with a girl, that was something!

At that time, I had little experience of social life and did not concern myself with fooling around with girls or anything like that. In fact I concentrated hard on my books. I gave up *kung fu* altogether. I had learnt as much as I wanted. I was beginning to see its limitations. I took up horse riding. It was KF who introduced me to this sport. He was very keen on it and in fact he was very good. Later he became a jockey. He rode under the name Henry Chiu.

He wasn't the only person to seek my friendship. I was very popular, especially with the younger boys. It was at this time that I met Siu. Siu later became one of the wildest of all of us playboys. He had no sense at all.

Then there was Cheng Chung-bong. He was another crazy, spoilt rich boy. He was pointed out to me soon after I arrived as the cousin of Cheng Kwok-yau, who was very famous at that time because of a murder trial. What happened was this. Cheng Kwok-yau was a rich and handsome man so naturally he had no trouble establishing a relationship with a famous actress. He set her up as his concubine. Not an official concubine, you understand, just a mistress.

Now I can't say I blame the actress. A girl may love a man for money but she has a heart too. Cheng had a right-hand man whose name I forget. It often happened that Cheng was fooling around with his friends or with other girls. Often when he did this he would send one of his associates to entertain his mistress. Take her out to dinner and to nightclubs. Otherwise she might get bored. Now if you put a man and a woman together often enough, friendship or love will blossom easily. It's natural. Cheng knew this so he tended to choose for this job one of his closest associates. Someone he thought he could trust. Inevitably Cheng Kwok-yau discovered the love affair between his chief associate and his favourite mistress. He was furious. A man like that is used to getting his own way. If he wants something he just reaches out and takes it. If something gets in his way, he just brushes it aside. That's how Cheng was and I can say also that's how I am. Cheng hired a gunman to kill his associate. Everything went according to plan and the associate was shot dead. No one knew who did it and the case was closed. Gradually Cheng dropped the girl. He didn't do it suddenly, openly. That would have been too obvious. Maybe the girl knew who had arranged the killing. Who can say?

Everything would have been fine except that there was the problem of the killer. A man who hires a gunman to do a job like this is always in the gunman's power. If he needs money he will come to you. There is no end to it. He went back to Cheng two, three, four times. Eventually Cheng refused to meet the gunman's demands. So the gunman decided to see if the police would pay him for the information. Cheng was arrested, tried, found guilty and sent to jail for fifteen years. When he came out he wasn't the same rich proud man he had been. He became very solitary. He brooded a lot about his fate. My friend Cheng Chung-bong told me the family found him very strange.

Cheng Chung-bong was also rich and wild. His mother tried to control him and when she failed she had him sent to Diocesan Boys' School in the hope that he would be under control there. But the warden in charge of the dormitory was a Chinese teacher called Chan. He was too respectful of the rich young boys. He was in their pockets. They spent the whole night fooling around and he didn't say anything. It was at this time that Cheng became an opium addict. All through his school years he smoked opium. Later he turned to heroin. He never married. He stayed at home. He was a sickly man. I think he had a girl who came to his house once or twice a week but she didn't live with him. He had a nurse who gave him his injections. I stayed in touch with him over the years. He was a rich man but, like many rich men, all his money was tied up in companies and trusts and so on. It's very difficult for one man to take control. All his adult life he spent trying to get control of his family's finances – or at least his portion. But although he was very rich and I became poor I never asked him for money, not even when things were bad. Later, when I was completely broke, my wife kept pressing me: 'He's rich! Ask him for some money! It's nothing to him to give you several thousand!' But it's the fate of all rich people to be sucked on by everyone they know. Cheng was the same and he despised them all for it. Cheng always told all his associates and servants: 'There's only one man who has never asked me for a cent. That's Hui. He's a true friend!' So when my wife pressed me to borrow from him I said to her that I couldn't. I didn't want to destroy his image of me. Also, if I borrowed money from him people would hear of it and they would laugh at him and say: 'Look! Even Hui is just after your money!' I didn't want him to lose face in this way. So I never did ask him. But he understood I was in a poor way. When I visited him, maybe four or five times a year, I would take my children with me and he would give them red envelopes. They contained two or three or even five hundred dollars each. That was his way of helping me.

One day he said to me: 'Now I am a millionaire but soon I will be a multi-millionaire. I have a plan. I want to set up a company. I want you to be one of the two top managers. I know a girl who will be the other manager. She is a very sharp and intelligent girl. Between you two, you will be my arms and legs. You will run the business for me.' I was very pleased. I knew this was his way of helping me. But we had to wait for a few months until the paperwork was sorted out. Then a few weeks later I bumped into one of his servants. He told me that Cheng was ill and in hospital, the Sanatorium in Happy Valley. I wasn't disturbed by this. It was quite common for him to have to go to hospital. I delayed visiting him a few days. By the time I got there he was already dead. The doctors had killed him. Yes, I blame the doctors. He was a heroin addict. He had been an addict for over thirty years. But the doctors said: 'This heroin is bad for you. We will cut it out. While you are here in hospital you won't be able to get heroin.' He pleaded with them but they refused. Ten days later he died of shock. So that was the end of that plan. It has happened many times. People who are kind to me and try to help me die before they can do so. This is my terrible fate.

So these were some of the people I knew at Diocesan Boys School.

The day after I matriculated I started work

WHEN I WAS STILL AT SCHOOL I remember I wanted to be a pilot. Sometimes we would see a plane flying over the city. I thought it must be marvellous to be way up there in the sky and to look down on the city. I wanted to be in a plane and turn somersaults and dive and roll over. I dreamt of all the flying stunts it was possible to do. In those days there were lots of photographs of pilots with leather caps over their heads standing beside their planes. It seemed such a heroic thing to be a pilot.

I asked my mother and she said I could do anything I wanted but my father was obstinate. He absolutely refused his permission. It was too dangerous, he said. It is true there were many crashes in those days. Maybe, it's true, if I had become a pilot I would have been killed. I put the idea out of my mind. I am not the kind of person to have regrets. Without his permission I couldn't do anything. He controlled all the family money.

The day after I matriculated I started work. I didn't have even one holiday. That wasn't my idea. I had intended to fool around for a while before getting a job somewhere. If it had been up to me I wouldn't have got a job under my brother-in-law. It was my mother's idea. She told Ho Tim to fix me up with a job at the Hongkong Hotel. I was given the job of cashier clerk in the cocktail lounge, or in the tea lounge as some people called it. This was the busiest place in the whole hotel. Everyone came to have tea in the morning or afternoon; all the European ladies and rich young Chinese, and after work businessmen and senior government officials came to have a gin and tonic or to meet their wives.

It was not an easy job. There were three of us and we worked non-stop all day. We didn't even have a minute to ourselves. We had to write out all the orders in different columns: soft drinks, snacks, alcoholic drinks and so on. Then we had to issue the bills. When the payment came we had to give the right change. There was no time even to go to the toilet. We had the hardest job in the whole hotel. Mistakes were common and we might often be ten or twenty dollars out at the end of the day. I was earning forty dollars a month.

I also led a very active social life. How I managed everything I can't remember. I was always going out with my male friends, drinking or going to the dance halls.

I knew almost everyone in society at that time – Chinese society. I paid no attention to the British or the Americans. I could speak English of course but we didn't mix at all in those days.

I already knew so many people but then they would introduce me to their friends and relatives and so on until I knew more people than anyone else. Although I was working hard at the hotel, the money I earned there was not enough to support my habits. I was earning forty dollars, but I needed four hundred a month! In order to make this extra money I had to develop some sidelines. It wasn't difficult. I was naturally sociable and friendly and the more people I knew, the more business I got involved in. Whenever anyone wanted anything they would come to me and say: 'Hui, I want to sell my car. Do you know anyone who would want to buy it?' Or: 'Hui, do you see that girl over there? Who is she? Is she just a glamour girl or is she respectable? Do you think you could introduce me?' and so on. If I made a deal for them I would make a commission from both parties. But don't misunderstand me, I never made any money from introducing men to girls. That's not my way.

Also I had a sideline in ties. I knew the owner of the wholesale company that imported Manhattan and Arrow shirts and ties. I persuaded the wholesaler to sell these ties to me at a wholesale price and when the spring and autumn fashions arrived by steamer from America I was always the first to see them. I had first choice. I knew what people liked so I spread the word that I had the latest ties. I would have them available a week or two before they appeared in the stores and also I was able to sell them for a slightly cheaper price.

I had to make a lot of money because my running expenses were so large. I liked to drink and eat and go to the best ballrooms and have fun. Obviously I couldn't survive on my salary of only forty dollars with, maybe, an extra ten dollars in tips. My friends didn't take me to be a professional broker. To them I was just a friend who did them favours. Naturally they knew I made a commission. Why not?

One time, my old schoolfriend Siu Yu-fong bought a car. It was a Buick. The very latest model. I think I remember that he bought it for HK$6,000. It was the only one of its kind in Hong Kong. Siu was a crazy playboy. He was very rich but he was always having money problems. So, a few weeks after buying the car, he phoned me and asked me if I knew anyone who wanted to buy it off him. He wanted the same money as he had paid for it. I told him I would ask around. Actually I knew already who would be interested, Lee Kim-bun. He was another crazy playboy who liked to throw his money around. I rang Lee and told him that the car was for sale at $6,500. 'I'll need a quick answer as there are other people interested,' I said. He didn't hesitate. Then I rang Siu back.

'I've got a buyer who's offering $5,700. Are you interested?'

'Okay. I need the money quick.'

So in half an hour I made $800. I remember that especially because it was the largest single commission I ever made.

Now I drove that Buick and I drove every kind of car around.

'Hey,' I would say to my friends, 'Let me drive your car.' And they would be happy to let me drive their car. The only kind of car I didn't drive was a Rolls-Royce. Why not? I'll tell you a story. My friend Lee Sai-wah – Lee Kim-bun's brother – bought himself a Rolls-Royce. He was just a young man but his father had died and he had got his inheritance. Everyone knew the Rolls-Royce was the king of all cars. So he got his Rolls-Royce and drove around in it. But after only a day or two he was contacted by the governor of Hong Kong himself.

'Mr Lee,' the governor said to him, 'I see you have bought a Rolls-Royce. I am sure you understand that this isn't just another car. It is the car of royalty. It is the car of the aristocracy. It is the car of high officials and of course it is the car of the very rich. Now a car like that has its own rules. You should know that one of those rules is that you don't drive a Rolls yourself. You must have a chauffeur. And the chauffeur must, of course, wear a uniform. In this way the status of the Rolls is maintained. I am sure you understand.' So Lee Sai-wah had to get himself a chauffeur.

Let me tell you about Siu Yu-fong. He was the seventeenth son of his father, that is counting sons and daughters he was number seventeen. In fact I still call him 'Number Seventeen' when I see him. His family owned a very famous porcelain shop in Central district. It was on

Queen's Road just next to the Queen's Theatre. But although they made very good porcelain that wasn't where their fortune was made. Someone suggested to them that one good way of making a lot of money was to use the pots to smuggle opium into America. They did it once and they were very successful. Then they did it again and succeeded once more. So they did it a third time. Again they were successful. But for some reason they decided that was enough. Probably they were afraid of being caught. So after three times, they stopped.

Now Siu was a wild and extravagant man. No one could control him. He was a sucker and he enjoyed being a sucker. I'll give you an example to show what he was like. Let's say you have a pen in your pocket. Let's say it cost two dollars. If he wanted the pen he would say: 'Here, Hui. I like your pen. Here is twenty dollars. Give it to me.' He was that kind of man. He liked to show off the power of his money. We were all playboys and we all liked to spend money but not so foolishly. People don't like it. I remember I was in Macau with him once. We went to the cabaret. Every night he would choose a girl and take her out for the night. He wouldn't just pay her the regular amount. He would insist on paying two or three times more. We tried to make him see sense. I remember I said to him: 'You're a sucker. You throw your money away for no purpose. If you want to be generous, fine! Pay a bit more. But not like that!' But he never changed his behaviour one bit. He wasn't the only one in his family to be wild like that. His younger uncle . . . in a big Chinese family it is quite common for uncles to be younger than their nephews. This uncle got to know a dance girl. He set her up in a flat and after only six weeks he gave her a present of a large American car. This was before the war. Cars in those days cost a lot. How can you get to know a girl so well in such a short time? He was a fool. He got the girl to go to bed with him but he paid too high a price for it. His family got to hear of it and his brothers and sisters and wife got together and forced him to cut all his dealings with the girl. They were frightened his infatuation would drain all their wealth. We were all brought up to be spoilt young men but still it is necessary to have some limits.

My classmate was Siu's elder brother Siu Hok-fong. Sometimes I spent the night at his house. This was a large, forty-room, two-storey house on top of Homantin Hill in the centre of Kowloon. There were no other buildings close to it. It was surrounded by trees and garden and rocks. You could look down on the city of Kowloon. That's how I came to know all his family. Siu Yu-fong was younger than me but he felt we were friends. But one day he did something very bad to me.

I was working at the hotel when Siu Yu-fong came to see me. 'Hui, you must help me. I've lost all my money in Macau. Can you arrange some hot cash for me?'

'How much do you want?' I asked.

'Oh, one or two thousand will do,' he said. I looked at him in amazement.

'Siu,' I said, 'do you know how much I earn here? Only forty bucks a month. Now I have some money and I can maybe raise some more but what you are asking for is impossible!'

'Oh come on, Hui!' he begged. 'At least lend me one thousand.'

'Okay, I'll see what I can do. Come back tomorrow.'

'Tomorrow? I need the money now. Immediately. I'm afraid to go home. I've only got a few bucks with me. I'll pay you back within two weeks.'

As soon as I could manage it, I took a break and ran across the road to Shell House. I went to the offices of one of Hong Kong's leading lawyers. I knew all the clerks there. I explained the problem and asked them to help. I promised to pay them back within a month. They all knew me and trusted me. They pooled their funds and collected $700 altogether. I took that back to the hotel and gave it to Siu. He went off with the money and he never mentioned it again. He never paid me back. Now, for the money, I didn't mind at all. For me money is nothing. But my reputation! That is something important. Naturally, I couldn't afford to pay the clerks back within a month. I think it took me about two months to pay it back. For me this was a very bad trick. If I have lots of money, all right! Why not? I can afford it. I can tell you, I lost some face over this business. That hurt me. That made me angry. In fact I met him the other day in the street and I got very angry with him. I shouted at him. He was in his wheelchair. I think he was frightened I would hit him. People watching us must have thought this was very funny: an old man shouting at a cripple about something that happened nearly sixty years ago! I had suddenly remembered how he had hurt my reputation. It made me so mad.

Later, Siu married a very nice, sweet young girl. She couldn't stand him. They had a daughter and then she left him. Before he got married he went out for a short time with Winnie Ho, one of the sisters of Macau gambling boss Stanley Ho. Now, let me tell you, I have a lot of respect for Stanley Ho. His father was a bankrupt but he is now one of the richest men in Hong Kong. In those days before the war they were dirt poor. I can tell you how poor they were. One day Winnie asked Catherine Ma if she could borrow a pair of silk stockings. This was when she was going out with Siu. A pair of stockings cost about $20 in those days. She couldn't afford even a pair of expensive stockings. How do I know this petty female gossip? It was Catherine herself who told me the story. But even though Winnie was so poor and Siu was so rich, she couldn't stand him and they broke up after about ten months.

Let me tell you I could have been Stanley Ho's brother-in-law. Then I wouldn't have any money problems now! Catherine Ma tried to get Winnie and me together. They were school-friends. But although I was contented with my wife, Winnie was very attractive and very smart. I liked her very much. I said this to Catherine. She passed this on to Winnie, who said: 'Well, Mr Hui is a handsome man.' We met several times and got on very well. Once I said to her: 'Winnie, you are really beautiful. If I weren't a married man I would chase you.'

'Well, love is one thing,' she said. 'But we can always be friends.'

But actually we didn't become close friends. I laugh when I think I could have married her as my second wife. My life would have been very different. I don't regret this. It's just funny how life turns out. Who could have predicted then that poor Stanley Ho would become rich and rich Peter Hui would become so poor.

When Stanley took over the gambling monopoly in Macau, Winnie went with him to take charge of the accounts, I think, or personal matters. Something like that. About ten years ago I was in Macau with my youngest son. We went to an expensive restaurant for lunch and I saw Winnie sitting at a table. I recognised her straight away. Her features hadn't changed at all. As I passed the table I greeted her.

'Hello Winnie.'

She looked up but didn't recognise me.

'We met a long time ago. I am a friend of Catherine Ma and Chiu Kei-fan.'

'Yes, I knew him well.'

I could see she still couldn't recognise me. I just smiled.

'You don't recognise me. It doesn't matter.'

I nodded and we continued on our way. There were two men with her, one on each side. Bodyguards. She has to be protected. Stanley is so rich it would be dangerous for her to be alone.

Family problems

WHY DID I WORK SO HARD at the hotel when I was making so much as a broker? At first I did it because it was new. It gave me a chance to meet people. But mainly it was because my mother insisted. Also I expected to be moved round the hotel so that I could learn the whole trade. Brokering isn't always regular and when I did make some money I always spent it immediately on clothes or fooling around.

In the past, when I had needed money, I always went to see my sister and borrow from her but our relationship became very bad soon after she gave birth to her son. My sister gave Ho Tim two children. My niece, Hau-ying, was eight years younger than me and then there was a gap of twelve years before a son was born. Throughout the years that I was growing up my sister lavished her love on me. I could do no wrong. But when she had a son of her own she suddenly withdrew all her love from me and gave it to her own son. This was something I couldn't understand. I still can't. One day she loved me, the next day her love for me vanished. Of course she should love her son more than anyone else but she cut everyone else off too. Even Ho Tim.

How these facts were connected I don't know but it was at this time that Ho Tim took another wife. He didn't tell my sister and he certainly didn't ask for her permission. He knew she wouldn't agree. But a second wife is not something that can be kept a secret for long. She wasn't hidden away. Ho Tim spent time away from her. Of course my sister soon found out but what could she do? In those days it was perfectly legal for a man to have two wives. She just had to accept it. Because of all this, my sister suddenly became very mean. She started to disapprove of me. She turned my mother against me. My mother's attitude affected my father's attitude. Life at home became unpleasant and I thought many times of moving my wife and children to another flat. But my income wasn't regular enough to do this.

Before these events my mother gave me anything I asked for. Afterwards, no matter how reasonable my request, she would say: 'Let me think about it.' I knew she would talk about it with my sister and then say nothing more about it. I became very angry towards my sister. I couldn't trust her anymore. In fact, later she cheated me out of my property. She borrowed money herself from my parents to buy property. She should have repaid this loan to me but she never mentioned it – not even when I was so broke after the war and I needed money to support myself and my wife and children. My heart is very heavy when I think of this, and when I think of her love which was taken away from me and never again given to me.

Although my relations with my sister changed so badly at this time, and my relations with Ho Tim were also not going very well, my niece and I were very good friends. She loved me and respected me as her dear beloved uncle. And I loved her too. She was a pure and innocent girl. Whenever I needed some money I would contact her secretly and she would always lend me some. She always had plenty of money because Ho Tim loved her very much. My poor, dear beloved niece. Fate is very cruel.

Ho Tim and I didn't get on so well either. He had put me to work in the busiest place in the hotel and he had given me the hardest job to do. The cashier was responsible for any mistakes. If I made a mistake and at the end of the day I was out one or two dollars I would have to pay the difference out of my salary. Naturally I understood that everyone has to have some experience of the difficult jobs but then I saw people being transferred to other restaurants – the grill room, the bar or the roof garden. But I stayed where I was. I began to get very angry. One day I had had enough.

'Brother-in-law,' I said to him, 'I must talk to you about my job. You have not been fair to me.'

He started to apologise.

'I'm very sorry Ah Kei. I had to show everybody that I wasn't treating you differently. I didn't want people to say: 'Of course Hui is having an easy time. He's Ho Tim's brother-in-law. I will find you another job.' But I was too angry by this time and I had no patience.

'You can keep your job. I'm quitting right now!' And I walked out. I was so mad. I didn't realise it then but this year at the Hongkong Hotel was going to prove to be very useful to me.

After I left the hotel I was free to fool around full time. From time to time I went over to Macau. I didn't go to the public casino. We went to a private club called the Nam Lau, The Southern Mansion. This was a club for the friends and associates of the gambling bosses. There they played *pai kau*. This is a complicated game using dominoes. I once bet five hundred dollars on one hand. That was a very big bet for me, a whole month's spending money. But for them it was small stuff. I suppose that there would be as much as twenty thousand dollars on the table at any one time. It was always crowded. There were always so many people gambling that often I couldn't even see the dominoes. We had to trust the croupier. He called out all the plays and we had to bet blind. I remember the croupier calling out 'Hui-jai, you win.' They called me 'Young Hui'. Now the front manager who stood at the door and decided who could come in and who couldn't later became the most powerful man in Macau. His name was Ho Yin. At that time he was one of Ko Hor-ling's trusted aides. He was put in charge of the gold smuggling. Macau was a big centre for gold smuggling before the war. Ho Yin was a very smooth and very clever man. Naturally he smuggled for his own account as well as for Ko's and he became very rich and powerful. For years he was the man who was the intermediary between the Macau government and China.

Ho Yin knew I was a relative of Ko's so when I went to the club he was always very welcoming.

'Mr Hui, you don't come often enough.'

And that was true because although I'm a gambler, and usually I am lucky at gambling, I prefer to fool around with girls. That's another story.

My first love affair

IN HONG KONG AT THIS TIME girls were lucky. It was rare for them to have their marriages arranged as in the old days. But girls still had to get married early. She would not get married until she left school but if a girl wasn't married by the age of twenty-one she would be very worried. So for girls, the need to find a good husband was very strong. They arranged lots of parties so that they could meet boys. That's how I fell in love. And KF too. He met Catherine Ma and soon they were together all the time.

I don't know where he and Catherine met but soon she was often to be seen seated next to him in his car. Actually, the three of us were always in his car driving around together. It was at this time that we really became close friends. He often suggested I go out with them for a drive. I had left the Hongkong Hotel and made some money from broking. I had no interest in getting another job. I wanted to enjoy myself. KF made it easy for me. He was always suggesting that I accompany Catherine and him. Why? I think there were two motives. One was that he wanted to impress Cat through his friendship with me. The other was that I would be useful if any fight broke out. Social life wasn't always polite and smooth. Sometimes there might be some aggression. That's why KF liked me to be with him. He had a sharp tongue. He often caused trouble. As for me, I was happy because KF had his money and could pay for everything. I never forgot that I depended financially on him a great deal at this time, in those years before the war when I had no money at all because my father was still alive.

KF would drive his MG around the New Territories where we went just for the drive or to go horse riding. This was KF's great passion. Often we would drive over to the beaches on the south side of Hong Kong Island: Repulse Bay, South Bay, Shek O, Big Wave Bay. We all sat in the front of the car. MGs were small but Cat, KF and I were all very short. Cat sat in the middle between us. Those months were the timeless days of youth and freedom. I spent very little time at home. My wife had a toddler to keep her occupied. Soon she was pregnant again. By the time of the Japanese occupation in December 1941, we had three children. She accepted the fact that I was a playboy. In those days a man's life and a woman's life were very different. It wasn't expected that a man spend all his time at home or help with bringing up the children. That was the job of the women: my wife and her *mui-jai* and my amah. We married off my own *mui-jai* when my wife came with hers. We didn't need two *mui-jai*s.

KF had been going out with Cat for about a year when old Mr Ma summoned him: 'You have been going round with my daughter for over a year now. It's time for you to make a decision. Either you marry her or you stop seeing her.'

KF had never given the idea of marriage any consideration. He was only interested in having fun and fooling around.

'I must think about it,' KF said.

Later, with me, he exploded.

'That bloody man! He's pushing me to marry his daughter now! I'm too young for marriage.'

'Mr Ma is right,' I said. 'Think about it. Cat is nineteen years old. If you go around with her for another year and then don't marry her, she will have to find someone else.' In those days a girl of twenty was considered quite old and if she wasn't married by the age of twenty-one, it would become very difficult to find a suitable husband.

'If she then goes out with another man and he also doesn't want to marry her then she will have a lot of trouble.'

I finally made him see sense and a week later he went back to Mr Ma to say he wished to marry Cat. They were married less than three months later.

At that time we were all not much more than boys and girls. Most of the girls we knew were still at school. If not they would be married off very soon after. It was a time of love and romance. We would get together and have parties. After school the girls would often come and have a drink in the tea lounge. I am sure that because of me many girls and boys came together and later got married.

I also fell in love at this time. I didn't mean to. I was happy with my wife. I respected her. But love is not something you can control so easily. I had been introduced to the two daughters of the Lee family. These were the daughters of Lee Hysan who was murdered outside the opium den. The two girls were Lee Shuen-kum and Lee Shuen-ho. They were very socially active and had many schoolgirl friends. On my side, I knew many men friends. As a result I suggested that we should get together and have a few small parties. In those days, parties were just gatherings where we drank tea or soft drinks and played cards or just talked. Not like nowadays with their discos and music. There were maybe only a dozen of us at these parties. Of the girls, the most beautiful one was Leung Chui-yee. Now all the others were single and mad for love but I was already married so I did not push myself forward. But Leung Chui-yee was attracted to me and I was attracted to her. The Lee girls warned Leung Chui-yee not to get involved with me as I was married and I also made it very clear to her that I was married and had no intention of leaving my wife. If she and I were ever to marry she would be my second wife.

Once it became obvious to us that we were falling in love with each other, we started to date. Sometimes we would go to the cinema, just the two of us. She was my first lover. In the evening we would walk together, hand in hand, on secluded paths. All that sort of thing. We loved each other very much. Until then I didn't know how love felt. But it's not so easy to talk of those times with the words we use now. What does 'lover' mean now? It means someone you go to bed with. Leung Chui-yee was my lover but our relationship was pure and correct and innocent. We didn't jump into bed with each other like boys and girls do nowadays. Now, girls are more straight-forward and maybe this is better. But although we were deeply in love, and I can say we were truly lovers, we acted differently. I have had maybe five or six true lovers and I never went to bed with any of them. That's not my way.

Leung Chui-yee and I were lovers for about a year. The Lee sisters were very unhappy about this. They already had plans to marry her to their fifth brother. They had already suggested to him that he marry Chui-yee and in fact, I know, he was already in love with her himself. He asked his sisters to do what they could to persuade her to marry him. But at that time, Chui-yee only had eyes for me. So instead of talking to Chui-yee they turned their attention to me. I remember, one day, Lee Shuen-ho drew me aside.

'Shen-kei, you are a married man. Why are you and Chui-yee getting involved? It's not good.'

'Why are you concerned?' I asked.

'Leung Chui-yee is my friend. I don't want her to be ruined.' That's what she said at first. She did not reveal to me straight away that she was really interested in getting Chui-yee for her brother.

'I am Chinese,' I said. 'My parents have always told me I can have as many wives or girls as I like if I love them. I love Leung Chui-yee. She loves me. When she graduates I will take her as my second wife.'

'That's an old custom,' Lee Shuen-ho said. 'In this modern world, there is no place for second or third wives.'

Of course, they were educated at the Italian Convent so it was normal for them to think this way. Also, women were becoming freer then compared with even ten years before. Even I had secret doubts. I had talked to Leung Chui-yee about her being my second wife but as a warning. Actually I had not yet asked her to marry me. But I knew that if I did ask she would agree. She loved me very much. I can say she loved me more than I loved her.

'Shen-kei, let me be straight with you,' Lee Shuen-ho said. 'My fifth brother wants to marry Chui-yee. He knows that she is in love with you but still he wants her. Now, you must admit, it will be better for Chui-yee if she married my fifth brother as his first wife than you as your second wife. Please think about this. If you truly love her then you will step aside.'

This made me think. I had been seeing Leung Chui-yee for almost a year. I had to make a decision. For her sake, I examined my heart. I asked myself what it was that I wanted for myself and what would be good for Chui-yee. It seemed to me that Lee Shuen-ho was right. I was still young. Did I want to tie myself down with a second wife? Even though I was a rich man's son and I knew my parents would be happy to agree, still there was a problem. I did not earn sufficient money to support myself. It was a matter of pride. Why should I be so eager for Leung Chui-yee? There were other girls. As for her, it was undoubtedly true that it would be better for her to marry into the very rich Lee family.

I told Lee Shuen-ho: 'I can give her up. If you can persuade her to give me up I will not stand in the way.'

Later Lee Shuen-ho came back to me.

'She absolutely refuses to give you up. She is too much in love with you.'

'So,' I said, 'there's nothing we can do about it. It is her choice.'

'That is very selfish of you,' Lee Shuen-ho attacked me. 'She won't do anything, so you must.'

I can tell you that if you start an argument with a Chinese woman you cannot win it. So I said to her: 'Lee Shuen-ho, I will do this as a very great favour to you. Tell your brother to do what he can to try and see more of Leung Chui-yee. From this moment on I promise you I have renounced my love for Leung Chui-yee. I will cease our relationship. I will be cold to her. This is no joke. It is for our friendship and because what you say is right. Your fifth brother is a quiet man. I have not met him but I believe he is a good man. But understand, this will be very painful for Leung Chui-yee. Girls are very emotional. She will be very hurt. This will be very cruel to her. This is your responsibility.' That is what I said to her. And from that day on I put all thought of Leung Chui-yee aside. At first I tried simply to avoid her, to have no further contact but she phoned me and finally I agreed to meet her. We met in a small coffee shop in Happy Valley. I explained the situation to her as clearly as I could. Tears trickled down her face as she pleaded with me but even though I could see how hurt and miserable she felt I made myself cold towards her. I said: 'I love you but I am a married man. I have children. Although I have the right to marry a second wife, and even my parents will agree to it, but still for me I am not sure I want to have two wives. The world has progressed a lot. It isn't such a good thing for a man to have two wives. From this very minute, no matter how much it hurts you, you must cut me out of your life. I have heard that Mr Lee is very much in love with you and that he is a kind man so you should consider being his friend or you may even decide to marry him. It is not so easy to find a good man. A rich good man is even rarer. Mr Lee has already inherited all his properties while I still have to wait for mine. This is the right decision.'

Then we parted. She cried when I left. I too cried but I didn't show her my tears. So Lee got his chance and eventually they got married. I myself was sad for maybe one or two years after this and didn't have another lover during this time. The group of friends around the Lee sisters still had parties but I stopped going and soon I had very little contact with that crowd. We all moved on.

Years later, after we had separated, it was during the years of the Japanese occupation, I met her once or twice in Happy Valley. I could see that she still loved me. But what could we have done?

I was walking one way and she was coming the other way. How awkward we were! She was accompanied by an amah. Maybe one of my amahs was present. Perhaps they noticed our awkwardness. We could not speak freely.

'It is not convenient for me to talk to you in the street,' I said and walked on. If we had talked our love would have flowed again. If she had left her husband it would have been a terrible scandal. Such a sacrifice was unthinkable. Maybe I am inventing it. Maybe she just wished to be on friendly terms. But this was also impossible. Love cannot become friendship. A man cannot let his wife become close friends with a former lover. You see what I mean? The circumstances were against it. The best thing to do was simply to accept the facts. That is what I did. We met two or three times like this. Society was small in those days and all the maids and amahs exchanged gossip between families. That's how her husband came to hear that we had bumped into each other. That's how I came to hear that he had forbidden her ever to speak to me again. I have not seen her since.

Love is something that can be wild or it can be tamed. There is a love of the heart and a love of the mind. This love of the mind is a practical love.

In love I have always been honourable. If I want to sleep with a girl I make sure she knows I'm married. Obviously I don't say this in a clumsy or serious fashion but maybe I will say something about one of my kids at home or I might look at her ear-rings and say: 'These are very nice. Where did you buy them? Maybe I will get a pair like these for my wife.' I do this because I want them to understand my position. If they don't want to continue that's fine. But also you can see this as a kind of test. Did they really love me?

When I was rich I knew all the rich beautiful girls of Hong Kong. I knew all the high-class people. Money is important. Rich girls should marry rich men. Girls from good families also should try to marry someone with money. It was because I did not wish to stand in the way of her happiness that I let the fifth son of the Lee family marry Leung Chui-yee.

I have a great deal of experience in love. I am now seventy-nine years old but that doesn't mean that I have forgotten about love. So what is my philosophy of love? Maybe this will surprise you but I say love is nothing! Obviously, love is sweet and we all like to taste its fruit. Love is a kind of pleasure, an enjoyment. For boys and girls who feel love for the first time, love must seem like it is forever and that if it goes, if it dies or is destroyed, then this is a tragedy, that love will never return. But this is not true. We may suffer for a year or two but then, when we have stopped looking for it, love will come again. Then you may say: 'Ah! That first love was not everything. Here is love again. This love is just as good as the first love.' So if anyone dies for love I have no sympathy for them. I think they are silly. You should never sacrifice yourself for love. So if love is not important, what is? I'll tell you. Money is important! We are all creatures of circumstance. We cannot avoid being affected by our circumstances. The circumstances we find ourselves in dictate what we can and cannot do. Bad circumstances will have a bad effect on love. First make sure the circumstances are good then think about love. If the circumstances are bad, you'd better forget about love. If a girl marries a poor boy then their life will be a struggle and sooner or later their love will be destroyed. This is a natural law. It is inevitable. Take the story of Romeo and Juliet. In this case finances weren't the problem but if I had been Romeo I would have recognised that the circumstances were bad and a life of true love with Juliet would have been impossible. I would have told Juliet to find someone else.

That is what I did with Leung Chui-yee.

The game of Ba Wong

W E HAVE A SAYING: If you go to a house of pleasure and spend the night we say you are 'playing the game of Ba Wong Yeh Yeen'.

Ba Wong was a mighty warrior who had a very beautiful wife. She is renowned even today as one of the great beauties in all of China's history. Her name was Yu Kei. In the end, having lost a battle, they committed suicide side by side because neither could bear to see the other dead.

Now these houses of pleasure were in the Street of Happiness in Macau. It wasn't cheap to take over a house for the evening but it wasn't much more expensive than taking out a cabaret girl from a dance hall. For a cabaret girl you would have to buy her out for the evening, then entertain her and then later, you would still have to bargain with her. Frankly, I can tell you, I don't like bargaining. Also you had to look around for a restaurant and a hotel, which might not be so comfortable.

Most of my friends were used to giving presents to girls but I never did. Not even to my lovers. I didn't mind spending a hundred dollars on entertainment but I refused to pay even ten dollars on a present. The way I see it: if you don't like to go out with me that's okay but if you like me and I like you, why should I give you a present? Sometimes a girl might explain that she needed some money, for example, her parent needed medical attention. I would check it out and if I saw it was true then I would lend the money. I would even offer before they asked. Asking a girl how much she wanted to go to bed was something I couldn't tolerate. But a house of pleasure was completely different. They have all gone now. They weren't like modern brothels where you just go to sleep with a girl. In fact, an evening in a house of pleasure was a marvellous thing.

These pleasure houses in Macau were different from the ones in Hong Kong's Shek Tong Tsui district. In Hong Kong they had flowery names like Peony Pavilion or Long River Chamber or something like that but in Macau they just had numbers. This number was written on a large plaque and placed over the door. Whenever I went to Macau I would go straight away to the Street of Happiness and I would walk along thinking to myself: Which one shall I choose today for my pleasure? At every doorway there would be beautiful girls trying to attract my attention. Now the way things worked was like this. If you booked a house you were in total control of the place for twenty-four hours and if you wanted to stay longer you were welcome. Naturally, if I already knew which house I wanted to patronise I would go straight there and book it. But even then, out of curiosity, I might spend a little time being entertained in one or two houses along the way. If I did that I would leave a hundred dollars. At that time this was a lot of money but obviously I must show my generosity or, at least, show that I wasn't a mean fellow. On leaving I would tell them whether or not I intended to return. My plan was usually to book a house and then go off for gambling or fooling around. Then I would return, either just myself or with some friends and we would have dinner at the house and play games with the girls.

The girls were always skilled at singing and playing drinking games. Some might even be able to play the couplet game. This is a kind of abstruse literary game. I was good at this because I had had some classical education. Most of my friends couldn't because they were educated in the modern way. To play this game you need to have a good knowledge of Chinese poetry. You take two or three lines of a poem and then you invent more lines. The girls were usually very good at this. So we would laugh and drink and play games all night and if I felt like it I would sleep with the diamond queen. That's what we called the chief beauty.

I didn't just fool around in Macau. In Hong Kong I enjoyed going to the ballrooms. When you went into a ballroom you would be greeted by managers. If you knew one of them you would greet him and he would take you to a table.

'Can I get you a girl?' he would ask. 'I have a specially nice girl for you this evening,' he would say. But this was just sweet talk. The 'especially nice girl' would just be the next girl in line. Each manager was in charge of a number of girls and his job was to get customers for them. The manager would sell you some tickets, say fifteen tickets for five dollars. If a girl sat down at your table it would cost three tickets for seven or eight minutes of her company. At the end of that period the manager would call her away. Maybe he would say: 'Miss Anna, another guest would like to see you,' and she would get up and go away. Sometimes you might sit and talk to a number of girls in this way. If you found one that you liked then you would tell the manager and give him enough tickets for the time you wanted to have her company. Then you would drink and talk and dance with her. Maybe you didn't want a girl to sit at your table but just wanted to dance. In that case you would go up to any of the girls sitting around the side of the dance floor and ask her for a dance. Each dance cost one ticket. Actually it would be very shameful to be so mean to give her just one ticket. I always gave two, sometimes three.

Now, if I found a girl that I liked and wanted to have her company for the whole evening then I would ask her if she wished to come out with me. If she agreed then we would have to bargain. It would depend entirely on the girl. Naturally, a young, handsome, rich and joyous man like me would not have to pay as much as an older, less handsome man. The minimum fee was fifty or sixty tickets because that went to the ballroom – anything over that was for the girl herself. Of course the girl got a percentage of the ballroom's takings too. If you wished her to spend the night with you that was another matter again. A night out with a ballroom girl would cost several hundred dollars – and remember, this was a time when the average monthly wage was only forty or fifty dollars.

I was well-known in the ballrooms and the girls knew I liked to be generous and have a good time and that I wasn't just interested in sex so I usually paid just the minimum. And most times I didn't sleep with the girl. We usually just went to other ballrooms or to a restaurant or a nightclub. We just fooled around until five or six in the morning and then we would part. And if I did sleep with a girl I never paid for it. If they liked me then maybe we would go to a hotel room. It was up to her.

Now, in this matter of sleeping with girls I must tell you I was always very careful. Even if I knew the girl was a family girl who didn't play around too much. But who knows. Maybe she has made love to another man and got some sexual disease. It only takes one man. I was always very frightened of getting some sexual disease. Why was I frightened? I remember when I was fourteen. In the street markets there were herbalists. They always had pictures of medical problems. These pictures were really disgusting. Bodies with ugly skin diseases. Boils. Scabs.

Swellings. Infections. Especially around the anus and the sexual parts. I remember the ones that showed people's faces and their sexual parts eaten up because of sexual diseases. Men and women. I remember being so scared that my own handsome face would be eaten up in that way. I wanted to remain handsome and mentally alert all my life. That was why I was so concerned about catching sexual diseases. That's why I didn't make love so much. Except when I was drunk and the girl encouraged me. But, for me it is like this. First I must like the girl very much and I must know that she likes me too. Then the situation must be comfortable. Then after making love I must do two things. I shower and wash myself all over and then I go straight away to a doctor to have a penicillin injection. That's how it was with me.

The girls liked me. I have always been a gentleman. But not everyone was so well-mannered. One man who had bad manners was Lee Kim-bun. He was the spoilt man who bought Siu's Buick. He liked to use his money like a weapon. He was very proud of his wealth. The managers of all the ballrooms all knew him and hated him. Naturally they didn't show this directly but they knew I was a friend of his brother's so they talked to me about him. When he went into a ballroom he would say to a manager. 'That girl over there,' pointing out some girl. 'Is she easy? Will she go with me?' Of course a manager can't say.

'You must talk to her yourself,' they would tell him. Or maybe he would say to a manager: 'I don't want to waste my time. Get me a girl who will agree to go out.'

Now, when a girl sat down at his table his trick was to take out five one-hundred-dollar notes and spread them on the table. That was a lot of money. For seven dollars you could employ an amah for a month. For twenty dollars you could rent a small flat for a month. With the money spread out on the table he would look at the girl and say: 'I want to take you out to a hotel to sleep with you. If you are willing take the money and we'll go. If not go away and I'll ask another girl.'

This is an ugly way to deal with a girl. It shows no respect. Worse, it shows contempt. Naturally some girls refused. They had their own pride. The managers didn't like it either because the girls would only give them the minimum to be released for the evening – though, of course, they would also give the manager an introduction fee. But still!

One evening I was at the Chung Wah ballroom and the manager whispered in my ear: 'Lee Kim-bun is here and he's up to his old tricks.' I immediately got to my feet and headed towards his table. If I don't like something I like to deal with it straight away. Lee Kim-bun saw me coming. He knew he was acting in a shameless way. He and his friends immediately got up and left the ballroom before I could reach him. He just scooped the money up and put it in his pocket. I would not have attacked him but I would have lectured him in a loud voice. He would have lost face. If he had dared open his mouth to protest or defend himself then I would have hit him. He knew my reputation.

When I think about his fate and the fate of his brother I think that fate is mischievous. Lee Kim-bun threw his money around for ten or more years and when he died he still had some money left so you can say he was lucky. He didn't know what it was like to be impoverished. His brother, Lee Sai-wah, on the other hand, was a serious and responsible man. He invested his money in the property market. But when the property market collapsed he lost everything. He owed the banks millions. In fact, they didn't chase him because they knew he was an honest man and he eventually repaid his loans when the market recovered some years later but he was never as rich again.

I remember that Lee Kim-bun spent a lot of time in Shanghai. If I have one regret it is that I never experienced life in Shanghai. Everyone who went told me they had such a wonderful, wild, happy time there. The Shanghainese are a more joyful people than the Cantonese, who are more conservative. If you ask a Cantonese girl to have a drink with you she will play hard to get but a Shanghainese girl will do what she can to please you. For the same money you will have a better time with the Shanghainese girl. There is a saying: People may laugh at the poor but no one laughs at a prostitute. That means no one will look down on you if you have money, no matter where the money comes from. For the Shanghainese, money is more important than reputation, but for the Cantonese, face is much more important.

There is another reason why Shanghainese women are preferred. To put it crudely, they have bigger breasts. Before the war it was common for Cantonese mothers to tie a tight bandage or cloth round a teenage girl's breasts to stop them growing. Cantonese mothers wanted their daughters to be flat-chested. They believed that 'big breasts mean cheap girls'. That was the traditional way. But Western films were popular and both Cantonese and Shanghainese girls copied the fashions. I remember when Jane Russell arrived! Wonderful! After that it became very fashionable to have a Western figure.

This Lee Kim-bun fell in love with one of the beauties of the Shanghainese red-light district. What a sucker. He even married her and brought her to Hong Kong. But she had a boyfriend on the side. Everyone knew about it. She didn't try to hide anything. Even Lee Kim-bun knew it and accepted it. The boyfriend of course would have had powerful triad connections. Shanghai at the time was controlled by two gangs, the Greens and the Reds. And both gangs were controlled by the same boss!

During the war Lee Kim-bun stayed in Hong Kong but his wife deserted him and returned to Shanghai. Later, after the war, he paid her off and got a divorce. He lived a few more years and then he died.

One or two cheats that I have known

IN THOSE DAYS there was a lot of cheating. Not just then. Even now. Hong Kong is a natural home for cheats. Cheating is a way of life.

CL Li wasn't a very clever man. I met him though KF, his brother-in-law. CL's family owned the Bank of East Asia. He wasn't stupid but he wasn't extremely clever. He was just rich. That's how he could be cheated easily. Actually he knew he was being cheated and he still allowed himself to be cheated.

There was a man, named Yu 'Lo-chat' – 'Old number seven' Yu – who was a well-known cheat. This Mr Yu was respected by all the other cheats. In this world, anyone with money and power gains respect.

Now it is an obvious fact that anyone who is born with money will have a weakness, some bad side to their character. They will have some habit or some desire that they like to spend money on. They like to have some excitement. Or there is something or someone they hate. Anyone who helps them achieve their desire will be a friend. So it is natural that any rich man will have many unsavoury friends. CL's weakness was that he liked to gamble. He didn't mind losing money as long as he could enjoy his pastime. 'Respected Number Seven' was well known as a master of all the gambling games so sometimes CL would invite him to his house to set up a small casino for the night for the entertainment of himself and a few friends. They all knew Yu cheated but they did it for the fun.

Now, I had some friends at this time who were cheats and they explained how it was done. Let's take poker. The way to cheat at this game is simple to explain but not so easy to do. First you had to mark the cards very slightly. As you look through the cards you have to mark all the aces in one way and all the kings in another way and so on. You do this as you are pretending to count the cards. If it's a new pack of course all the aces are together and the kings. Once you've marked them then the game is easy. You know whether your hand is higher than other people's or not. You know when to bet high and when to fold. Now the way to mark the cards is to make a very slight mark on the back of the card with your finger nail. Naturally a cheat will train his eyesight so that he can see the slightest mark without any trouble. My friend told me that the way he practised this was to set up a table and to drape a mosquito net between the chair and the table. On the table the only light was from a candle. He would sit for hours practising marking the cards and reading them as he dealt out the pack. Once you can see the marks in those conditions you can easily see the marks in a brightly lit room. Naturally if there are two cheats in the same game they will quickly recognise this. They will see each other's marks.

Mahjong? That's not so easy. The best mahjong player I have ever seen was CL Li's uncle. It was amazing what he did. Actually, he wasn't a cheat but he could cheat easily and no one would notice. Now, in mahjong, every player takes thirteen tiles for his hand. Players who aren't very good have to sort their hand into the three suits but most expert players don't rearrange their hands at all. If they did their opponents would learn too much about what they had and what they didn't have. But CL's uncle only had to look at his hand once and he had memorised all his pieces. He then put them face down on the table and played blind for the whole game. When he had a complete hand he just opened it up and there it was. Now that's not cheating. The way he cheated was like this: when he threw out a piece into the middle of the table he would pick up a discarded tile that he wanted at the back of his hand while he was discarding his own tile. I think he did this as a trick sometimes just for fun. He was a rich man. He didn't need to cheat to win.

But let us go back to Respected Number Seven Yu. He was a clever cheat and was an expert at all forms of gambling. But that wasn't the only way he cheated. He was surrounded by a number of associates and helpers. He made use of these people to suck on the rich. How? Maybe he could kidnap some rich young man. Or, better, he would arrange for the rich man to be cheated at gambling. Even if the boy had not come into his fortune yet his father would have to pay. Maybe he would threaten to harm the boy if the debt wasn't settled. Another common way of cheating was to lure a person into investing in some business venture. If this was done cleverly the person would invest over a long period of time and lose everything. My friend Lee Sai-wah met his wife in this way. Yu decided to make Lee Sai-wah a target. He was rich but he wasn't such a strong character that he would try to get revenge. Now where did his money come from? His father made it. He was once a very poor man. He was so poor he was once caught for stealing chickens. All his life, he was always known as 'Chicken thief' Lee. Maybe it was property. Maybe it was smuggling or drugs. I can't remember. But Lee Sai-wah was a gentleman. He wouldn't have tried to get revenge. That is something that cheaters need to judge carefully. Take me. Many people must have thought about trying to cheat me but they never did. Why not? Because of my character. I would beat them to hell if they tried to cheat me. Also I was too clever to be cheated. But Lee Sai-wah was a good mark. Yu fixed up a girl and trained her to do what he wanted. He arranged for Lee Sai-wah to meet her. Soon Lee fell in love with her. Now these cheats are very patient. They can wait years. His plan was for the girl to ask for expensive presents or perhaps later to introduce business ideas. Maybe he even planned for the girl to marry Lee Sai-wah. And he would certainly have succeeded except for one thing. The girl fell in love with Lee Sai-wah. He wasn't bad looking. He was a good man. Who can say what happens in the heart of a woman? So she confessed everything. She told him all about the plan to cheat him and she told him that it was Yu who had set it up. Lee was so impressed with the girl's honesty that he married her anyway. Naturally he couldn't prove anything against Yu so there was nothing he could do except spread the story around.

These cheats are very clever and patient people. There have been a number of bank collapses over the years. It is certain that each one was the result of a special plan by a cheat. How can they do this? It's easy. Bankers know nothing. They only know how to invest money safely and cautiously. They only know how to follow the procedures. But the cheats know how to set up schemes. Now one way is for the cheats to get control over a banker, maybe through a girl or by getting him into debt or by blackmailing him. When they control him they tell him what to do, where to funnel money so that it disappears into their pockets without being traceable. Believe me, they can do this. Naturally they do it slowly. Bit by bit over the years. They don't want it to be obvious. Maybe they will leave the bank weakened so that it collapses a few years later after they have gone. Another way is to take a big account in a bank. Naturally, if I am the banker I will be very friendly to you and offer you some special incentives. After a while, you may say to me: 'My son is an accountant with such and such a bank and he would like to change his job for one with more authority. Can you arrange this?' So naturally I will do what I can to give your son the job. A few years later the son may have risen to a more senior position. Now he is able to influence the bank. Now the cheats can set up false accounts and arrange for money to be transferred to them. If you know something about money and banking it's not so difficult to cheat a bank.

Some people just cheat for fun. There were six brothers who everyone knew as the Six Snakes. They were rich so they didn't have to be cheats. But for them it was a game. It was well known. I'm talking about after the war now. We often used to meet in coffee-shops or at the Jockey Club bar and gossip about who had been cheated by who. It was a common subject. The Six Snakes were quite open about it. I think it was a form of competition between them to see who was the cleverest. They even cheated their own friends. They would boast about it: 'I cheated so-and-so.' They said it quite openly. I remember one famous case. One of the Six Snakes cheated one of his friends of $300,000 by persuading him to enter some kind of smuggling syndicate and then saying the money was lost in some way: the boat had been caught by the police or sunk in a storm. The boy's father was furious. He was a close friend of the family. He went straight to the old man. 'Your damn son cheated my son! He doesn't give me any respect. I have known him since he was a young boy. I have treated him like a nephew. If he had asked to borrow $300,000 I would have lent it to him without any question. But he cheats my own son. He doesn't give me any face!' The father apologised and asked him to calm himself. 'Don't worry. I will pay you back myself. That son of mine is no good!' When we heard the story we all laughed and passed it around. That's how it was then. Cheating was just a game of cunning and cleverness.

One man beats fifteen

MOST PEOPLE THINK CENTRAL is the business centre of Hong Kong but for most Chinese, until very recently, the main business centre was in the district called Nam Pak Hong, which is the area just west of Western Market. Even now, you will find there are a lot of banks and gold merchants there. Here are the big warehouses of shark's fin and salted fish and along the old waterfront road are the big rice wholesalers. Go and look. They are still there. The whole area has hardly changed in the last fifty or sixty years, even longer.

One day, while I was still working at the Hongkong Hotel, my friend Lee Sing-to asked me to accompany him to pay a visit to a girl he had met. I was happy to go with him. We were both well-dressed, smart young men going out to have a good time.

The girl lived on the third floor of a large family-owned rice whole-saling business. To get to her room we had to go into the main hall of the warehouse and ascend an open staircase to the third floor. The ground floor and the second floor were all part of the shop. The third floor consisted of private rooms. This was where the store owner's family lived. I think the girl was a distant relative who rented her own room. At the top of the stairs we came upon an old woman. She asked us who we wanted to see. We told her the girl's name.

'She's not in,' the old woman said. 'Come back later.'

'Please tell her Lee Sing-to called on her,' my friend said, and we started to walk back down the stairs. As we were descending, a man appeared at the top floor balustrade. He was obviously the owner of the warehouse. Maybe we had disturbed his siesta. He looked us over. Now I can tell you we looked smart in our new suits and shiny leather shoes – and we were both young and handsome. I can tell you we felt good. Even our ties were the very latest from America. We were very pleased with ourselves. Any girl would be happy to be in our company. Maybe that's why this man got angry with us. He was just wearing a vest and shorts like all the warehouse workers.

'Hey you!' he shouted. 'Go out the other entrance.'

'What?' Lee said. We didn't really understand what he meant.

'Go back up and take the other staircase down.'

I looked up and saw what he meant. There was another staircase that went from the third floor down to the back of the building. He didn't want us to go through the rice warehouse. But this was too much trouble for me.

'That's stupid,' I said. 'What's wrong with this staircase?' And we continued walking down. Maybe I swore at him. Young men swear. Maybe I said: 'Go fuck your mother.' That doesn't really mean anything. It's just a way of talking. Anyway, whatever I said, he got angry with us and lost his temper. He leaned over the balustrade and shouted down to all the workers on the ground floor.

'Look at these men!' he said. 'They're troublemakers. Throw them out!'

I was surprised and looked round to see who he was talking about. I saw him pointing at us.

'We're not troublemakers,' I shouted. But old Chinese men are very stubborn.

'Throw them out of here!' he shouted again.

'Don't worry. We're going,' I shouted back. But it was too late. Everyone had gathered to watch us. Below us on the shop floor there were a dozen or so coolies and porters. Along the landings above us there were others. They started to shout at us.

'Who are you?'

'What do you want here?'

Lee Sing-to became very nervous. He was not the fighting type.

'We just came to visit a girl,' he tried to explain. 'We're not trouble-makers. If she were here she would be able to tell you we're just friends.'

But no one was listening. The boss wanted to throw us out, it was their job to throw us out – no matter what we said. More porters came in off the street from neighbouring shops. They all carried something, either a pole or a length of rope or a hook for hauling sacks of rice. Porters are a rough and ready crowd. They'll do whatever you want as long as you pay them. And they're used to pain. They're not so easy to defeat. Still, I was a *kung fu* fighter and I was prepared to defend myself. I had no intention of being hustled by anyone. I had my own face to protect. But first I tried to reason with them.

'Go and get a policeman if you want. I have no objection to going to the police station.'

But they weren't interested in right or wrong. They weren't interested in getting the police. They wanted to grab us and throw us into the street and if they tore our suits so much the better.

All this time we had been slowly descending the stairs and we were now on the final landing, eight or ten stairs from the bottom. One of the coolies jumped up and tried to hit me or grab me. I didn't wait to see what his intentions were. I just used one hand to knock him off balance and then I pushed him back so that he fell down to the ground. There was a pause. Everyone had seen how quickly and easily I had knocked the man down. Now Lee was not a fighter and my way of thinking was this: if there's a fight, it's better if I don't have to worry about him. So I told him to go.

'Let him go,' I shouted to the crowd as all eyes were on me. 'It's me you want.'

Lee quickly pushed his way out while I distracted them.

'Why are you troubling me?' I shouted. 'What have I done to you?'

But the coolies just looked very mean. People of this class just wear shorts and canvas shoes. They are all hard muscle and bone. They keep their heads shaved. They work hard all day to earn enough to eat and drink a little. They sleep in the streets. They are the lowest class of workers. Naturally they're not very intelligent. I quickly assessed the situation. If they attacked me one or two at a time I wasn't worried. I had the advantage that I was higher up. My *kung fu* was much better than theirs. I was afraid of no man. However, I was worried that they might close the entrance to the warehouse and trap me. Then they could easily exhaust me. This was a big danger. But I was thinking faster than they were. I saw the problem first. Also I didn't want to get into a fight. I was dressed for a day out with my friends. I didn't want to ruin my expensive clothes in a long fight. I realised I had to get out of the building at once.

There were a dozen or more men between me and the door. I jumped down the eight or ten steps and chopped hard left and right with my hands. I knocked several men aside and the others naturally backed away.

That was all I needed. I reached the door and started to run down the street. They chased after me. I didn't want to be chased too far. I don't like to run away from a fight. Catching sight of a porter's carrying pole propped up against a wall, I quickly grabbed it and turned round. Before the coolies could collect their wits I yelled as loud as I could and charged towards them. They immediately turned and fled. I chased them for about ten yards and then stopped. Everyone in the street who saw this started to laugh and applaud me. Those coolies lost a lot of face. Ten or fifteen against one and they ran away! I had to laugh. I went to put the pole back where I got it and found a coolie sitting there leaning against a pillar.

'I'm sorry I took your pole.'

He just stared at me for a moment, shaking his head. 'Wah! You are wonderful! One man chasing fifteen! Really you are a hero!' I remember his exact words to this day. I just laughed and walked off to go and get drunk with my friends. I had to celebrate this fight where one man beat fifteen.

My mother died one Saturday morning

MY MOTHER DIED ONE SATURDAY MORNING in 1941. At that time we still didn't know if the Japanese were going to invade or not. At least most people didn't know. I can tell you that I did know. I didn't know when but I knew that it would happen sometime. I may not be a genius but I could see what was happening and I didn't try to delude myself like some of my friends. But the real reason I knew was that one of my classmates, Tang Kin-shan, had a good job with the Mitsubishi company. A few months before the invasion all the Japanese companies moved their operations to Canton. He went with them and a short time later I got a letter from him. 'Shen-kei,' he wrote, 'as you know, I am well connected with the Japanese and I know many things that maybe I should not know. I can tell you now, without a doubt, the Japanese plan to invade Hong Kong. I have heard this discussed many times. Maybe you should think about bringing your family up to Canton where it will be safer and more comfortable when the fighting starts. Of course this is for you to decide but please bear in mind what I have told you. Please do not doubt the truth of what I am saying. The Japanese will invade but no one knows when. Even they don't know yet.' I got this letter two or three months before the invasion.

I personally believed Tang but some of my friends just laughed. Lee Sai-wah was one.

'Don't be silly! You might as well worry that your head will fall from your shoulders.' Those were his exact words. I remember Tang once said something about the Japanese: 'They are stubborn and persistent. Once they have decided to do something they don't give up.'

We often teased Tang for working for a Japanese company. It wasn't a popular thing to do.

My problem was that although I trusted Tang my household was not small. I now had three children. The youngest was just crawling. There were my parents, my wife, the amah, the *mui-jai* and myself. How could I uproot all these people. I will tell you the truth, I was happy in Hong

Kong. I had a job. I had girlfriends. I didn't want to go up to Canton. What would I do there? Of course we could stay with my wife's father but that would be no fun for me. I decided we would just prepare ourselves and wait. I wasn't scared of the fighting. I could not imagine what war would be like. I didn't think the fighting would be so bad. We were more scared that there would be riots and that our house would be broken into and looted. So we were in this strange situation of living life normally and expecting any day that war would start. And then my mother died.

This Saturday morning I was at home. From when I was still at school it has been my habit to spend that morning at home. My thinking was this: I fool around every day of the week. I am out from Monday to Friday. There should be a moment during the week when I should rest. So I stayed in on Saturday morning.

One of the tasks that I liked to do at this time was to iron my tie and handkerchief. I refused to let anyone else do it for me. These items stand out so I liked to pay very special attention to them. Of course the amah would try to do it for me but I always waved her away. It's not a difficult job. Just two or three pressings and it's done. It was just something I liked to do.

I had set up the ironing board in the sitting room just outside the door to my parents' bedroom. The flat had two bedrooms. One for them and one for me, my wife and children. Naturally we all liked to sleep together. This arrangement is not so common now but in those days we liked our children to sleep with us until they were five or six years old. My eldest son was a quiet sleeper and stayed with us until he was seven or eight. We all shared the one bed. This is a matter of love. Naturally it was a big bed, over five foot wide and six foot long. The children would sleep on one side, my wife in the middle and me on the other. Now maybe you will think this interfered with our love making. Well, since my first wife and I had eight children altogether it didn't interfere very much! All the children slept very soundly. Of course we were rich enough. We could have given them all beds of their own, even made of gold if we had wanted, but we preferred them to share our bed.

So, on this Saturday, I was ironing just outside my parents' bedroom. My mother was sitting on the bed having a smoke on her water pipe. She would put tobacco in a small tube at one end of the water pipe and light it up while she puffed at the pipe stem. Then she would puff it seven or eight times before knocking the tobacco into a spittoon. After that she would lie down for a rest. I knew the rhythm of her habits so well that when she fell back on the bed after only two or three puffs I immediately knew there was something wrong. I put the iron down and rushed into the room. She was unconscious and her pipe was clenched firmly in her hand. My first concern was that she might cause a fire so I managed to pry it out of her grip. At the same time I called for help. Then I pulled her up to a sitting position and started to shake her and slap her face to get a reaction.

'Come on! Help me! Keep her upright!' I shouted to my wife and the amah and the *mui-jai* who had all run in to help me. I left them to try and bring her back to consciousness.

'Don't let her lie down.' For some reason I thought it would be bad for her to lie down. I didn't know where my father was so I phoned my brother-in-law at the hotel. He immediately called a few doctors and notified my sister who came round straight away. Within about fifteen minutes a doctor who lived nearby came up to look at her. He advised us to send her to hospital immediately, which we did. We took her to the French hospital in Causeway Bay, which was across town from where we lived. It had the reputation of being one of the best hospitals but the chief doctor there told us there was nothing he could do to save her. Eventually my father arrived at the hospital. Then came the famous herbalist, Wong Sing-sum.

I should explain about Dr Wong Sing-sum. A few years before this, my mother had had a sudden collapse. It was a minor stroke. This first time it wasn't serious: she just fell to the floor and felt a bit weak. My father sought out Wong Sing-sum, who was renowned throughout China and even in Japan. He really was marvellous. He understood so many things deeply. I doubt if even modern Western doctors understood even half of what Wong Sing-sum understood.

That first time, he came to our house and examined my mother. Then he told us what we should do for her. We expected him to prescribe some herbal teas but, to our surprise, he told us we should find some thick green bamboo, perhaps four or five inches in diameter. Then we should cut this into lengths of about one foot. Each length should then be heated over a flame and held at an angle so that the bamboo sap would drip down and be caught in a bowl. The bamboo should be burnt very slowly. We were to do this three or four times a day and give her the sap to drink. Of course we were happy to do anything but where could we get the bamboo? I remember this was a problem. In the end my father paid some workmen to go out into the countryside and find the right kind of bamboo and bring it back in a lorry. After only two or three days of this treatment my mother was feeling much better, almost one hundred per cent healthy. But now, on this Saturday a few weeks before the Japanese occupation, Mother had had another stroke. When Wong Sing-sum checked her pulses – in Chinese medicine, doctors check three different pulses – he shook his head.

'I'm sorry,' he said. 'This time I can do nothing. I advise you to prepare her funeral.'

Then he asked us what Mother had been doing before her collapse. He wanted to know what had precipitated the stroke. We could think of nothing out of the ordinary that morning.

'What about yesterday?' he asked.

Then we remembered the tonic soup that my sister had sent round the evening before. The weather had been cool and changeable for weeks. That evening, Mother had made herself a tonic chicken soup with some medicinal herbs. That same day, my sister also prepared a mutton herb broth for her own family and thought it would be a good idea to send some to Mother. She put some in a pot and sent it round with her amah. This was quite late the previous evening. Our idea about health tonics is this: if you are strong and full of vitality you should not take any health tonics at all. It would only overload the system with vitality and cause you to be ill. Young people should not have health tonics of any sort. So when the amah arrived with some more tonic soup, my mother didn't want to give any to my wife or myself – but she didn't want to waste it, so she drank maybe two bowls. We told all this to Wong Sing-sam. He shook his head slowly.

'Her system wasn't strong enough. The tonics forced her pulse to beat stronger and her veins couldn't cope with the pressure.'

That was why she had had her stroke.

In the end, the hospital asked us to take her away. There was nothing they could do for her, they needed the bed and I suppose they didn't want to have a patient die in the hospital. This would have disturbed the other patients. We brought her home and made her as comfortable as possible. It was very sad. We knew we could only wait for her to die. In fact she died two days later, on the Monday at about two o'clock in the afternoon. My father then arranged for scaffolding to be built outside the house. Putting up scaffolding is not a cheap matter and it has to be done quickly. Nowadays they don't do this but in those days it was common to build a temporary bamboo staircase outside the house and to bring the coffin out by knocking a hole in the wall. Now some people say that the reason for this is to stop the spirit of the dead from coming back because when they retrace their route to the house they can't get back because the hole they came out of is bricked up again. I don't know where this story comes from. To my mind this is nonsense. First of all, who says a ghost can't go through walls? No, the real reason is that the coffin is too big to go up and down the narrow staircases inside. The only way to take the coffin in and out is through a hole in the wall. There is another reason for rejecting the story of ghosts. In fact we welcome the ghost back. On the seventh day after the funeral we believe the ghosts of the dead return to their homes for a final goodbye. This is a sad occasion for everyone, especially the ghost so we arrange all the person's dearest possessions, clothes, ornaments, jewellery, food and so on. We then go to our rooms. We don't wish to disturb the spirit. Men and spirits cannot mix. We belong to different worlds.

My mother had the very best coffin. It was made of Liuzhou wood. She had a good funeral. Our family is very small. It was not even a dozen people including her brothers and sisters. But she had many friends and we were rich and we could afford a very fine funeral. I was the chief mourner. I had to lead everyone in the rituals. I was told what to do by the funeral director. We took her to the cemetery and put her in the plot that my parents had bought long before for their use. We were all very sad but we couldn't be sad for long.

A few weeks later the Japanese invaded. We decided the house was too full of sad memories and, perhaps more important, was not safe enough if there were riots. We expected looting so we packed up all our things and moved to the staff quarters of the Hongkong Hotel. These were two large buildings on on the lower side of Wellington Street near the corner with Wyndham Street. Here we thought we would be safer. In fact, as it turned out, it was a good decision.

The Japanese invade Hong Kong

I DON'T REMEMBER MUCH about the Japanese invasion. People say there was a lot of bombing. As far as I am aware the city was largely untouched. One day some bombers came over to attack the naval base at Tamar but most of the bombs dropped into the harbour and one exploded on the empty hillside above the city near Magazine Gap. The airfield at Kai Tak was bombed but next to the airfield were the Whampoa docks and the Japanese didn't want to damage them too much. I can say that most people on Hong Kong Island were unaware of the fighting. In fact, I don't think there was much fighting. The Japanese quickly over-ran the British forces. By the time they reached the main city of Hong Kong the fighting was over. They came over from the south side of the island, through Wong Nei Chong Gap and then down Blue Pool Road to Happy Valley and Wanchai and then slowly, on horseback, they came to Central.

As soon as we knew the Japanese were going to invade we thought there would be chaos and looting. It seemed inevitable. But nothing like that happened. The first thing everyone thought of was to get money out of the banks and to buy food. By the time the Japanese invaded everyone had prepared themselves as far as they could. Now, we just waited. I think we all knew the Japanese would win but we expected the fight to be very hard and long. Actually, Hong Kong fell very quickly. The sound of explosions stopped. We waited. Most of the people hated the British but they also hated the Japanese. Maybe the British were better. Maybe the Japanese were better. Who could say? On the one hand the Japanese were Asians like us. On the other hand, they were famous for being very cruel. The massacre at Nanjing was still a recent memory. What would they do to us? Everyone stayed indoors and waited to see what would happen.

On Kowloon side the Japanese quickly pushed the British back. The Peninsula Hotel was the command headquarters for the British generals. But there were many civilians there too. My brother-in-law's colleague,

Tsui Tim, was the Chinese superintendent of the hotel. As soon as he saw the situation was getting worse and that the fighting was getting closer he ordered the British flag to be pulled down. The British commanding general was furious. He ordered Tsui Tim to put it back up again but Tsui refused. He told the general: 'If we have the flag up the Japanese will aim their guns at this building. There are some women and children here. Also I am responsible for the safety of the hotel staff. I think for everyone's sake this is the sensible thing to do.' And so the flag stayed down. That's why the Peninsula Hotel was not damaged by gunfire.

The Japanese rode into Central a few days later on horseback. They immediately took over the Hongkong Hotel as their headquarters and put the staff quarters under their control as well.

For the majority of the people of Hong Kong food became the big problem. Some people were starving on the streets. The poor people had nowhere to live and no money to buy rice. But it was no problem for my family. My brother-in-law was the superintendent of the Hongkong Hotel. Naturally, we had access to all the food supplies in the hotel. We had caviar, salmon, steak, lobster, anything we wanted. My father and the rest of my family didn't like Western food so much so he would choose food to make Chinese dishes. And there was plenty of wine and brandy. My father was always a heavy drinker and by this time so was I. Every night we had a feast. Each of us drank two or three bottles of brandy a day. My father liked Hennessy. That was the best in those days. As soon as the invasion started, Ho Tim had closed the hotel up and told all the staff that because of the emergency they were all laid off immediately. There was no possibility of paying them off because there was no money on hand. He told them they were welcome to stay as long as they wanted at the staff quarters but from now on they would have to find their own food. If they ate in the canteen they would have to pay for it. He advised them to go back to China. What else could they do? China was better for two reasons. First it was under the control of the puppet government of Wang Ching-wei who had been set up by the Japanese. It was therefore more stable and it was possible to do business there and get work. Also, if anyone went back to their home village in the country they were always certain of getting some simple food at least. Anyone could plant some sweet potatoes. Hong Kong was just a port.

It had little food supply of its own: some vegetables and pigs. All the rice and most of everything else had to be imported. So, gradually, over the next few months, the staff quarters emptied. Not all at once as some couldn't afford to go straight away and others wanted to wait and see what would happen in Hong Kong. We expected violence but there wasn't any.

My father had a safe at the hotel which he had needed for his business. Here he kept money that he had made from the lottery business and other property. I remember we had some jewellery in there including a piece of jade. When I think of this jade piece my heart breaks. It was pure green colour. The very best colour of jade. It was one inch wide and three inches long. I was so poor in those early days that I had to sell it for only $700. Within a year it was worth 500 times as much. If I had just that one piece of jade now I would be rich. I could buy one or two flats at least. But I had no choice. I had to sell it to buy food for my wife and children. My fate has been a hard one. But this was later. Now, at the time the Japanese invaded, I had no problems. I was eating well. I was drinking a bottle of brandy every day and I was making a lot of money.

When everything had settled down a bit, maybe a week after the Japanese arrived, I set up a gambling table in the street just outside the entrance to the staff quarters. I was the only one in Central though I heard that triads were operating tables in other districts. Immediately I started to make lots of money. The reason was simple. People who didn't have enough money were hoping to make a big win and so be able to buy a ticket for China. Other people were just bored because there was nothing to do at all. Other people had most of their hot cash in their pockets so they felt rich. Chinese are gamblers. We love gambling. I just had one set of dominoes so we played *pai kau*. It's quite a complicated game but everyone knows how to play. I paid a few of the hotel staff to look after the table and many of the other staff bet at the table. Some were lucky and got what they wanted but there is one simple rule of gambling: the banker must win and I was the banker. Another group of people who had some money in their pockets were the Taiwanese interpreters who came to Hong Kong with the Japanese. They were quite well off. They also liked to gamble.

Don't think I just made money from the hotel staff. I helped a lot of people at this time. All the hotel staff knew me. They called me 'Kei gaw' – 'gaw gaw' means 'elder brother'. Even though I was younger than them they called me elder brother out of respect. They would come up to me and say: 'Kei gaw, I need some money to go back to China. I don't have enough. I don't like to bother you and I don't dare to ask to borrow some money but you can buy my bicycle. Or my watch or this bottle of brandy.' A lot of them were waiters and when they left their restaurants they would take a bottle of wine or spirits. They didn't drink it themselves but sold it to me. So I would give them say five dollars for a bicycle. That was a lot of money in those days. So I quickly acquired six, seven, eight bicycles. I didn't need so many bicycles but it was a way to help these people. I had so much money. It was easy for me to do. Later I sold them for a small profit. This was small stuff for me. I was making five or six hundred dollars a day.

Of course, once I started up my gambling table several others had the same idea and soon there were quite a lot of tables. When this happened the Japanese issued an order banning gambling. They posted up notices everywhere saying that anyone caught running a gambling table would be executed immediately. I think some people were caught. Everyone else went out of business immediately. Everyone except me! From then on I was the only one in Hong Kong running a gambling business. You could say I had a monopoly of gambling in Hong Kong! How is it I could succeed? All it took was a little cleverness. Now I must explain something. When the Japanese took over the Hongkong Hotel they placed a large banner with the words JAPANESE MILITARY AUTHORITY over the entrance to the staff quarters. I simply pulled the table into the entrance to the staff quarters and carried on. When Japanese soldiers and gendarmes passed by they would see us gambling confidently. Then they would see the sign, hesitate, and then walk on. Naturally, we would bow at them and point out the sign with a smile. It seemed to them that we were carrying on the gambling business with the full authority of at least one senior military officer. My father and brother-in-law thought I was very clever. My wife never worried about what I did. They all knew I could look after myself.

Some people say that the Japanese soldiers were very cruel. That was not my experience. I did not have the impression that they brutalised the people. There were cases, certainly. But I have to say that, from my own experience, they behaved correctly. Always we had to bow low and obey them. If we did that we would be all right. I would say they behaved better than soldiers from other countries. Better than Chinese soldiers even. Naturally, if they didn't like something they would kill you straight away. They wouldn't shoot you. That's not their way. They liked to use their swords. They would just cut off your head. I saw this once or twice. One man was caught stealing something, some food, I think it may have been a duck. He was caught and killed straight away. His body was just left lying in the street.

The gambling business could not continue forever. Not because of the danger but because soon no one had any money. The value of money was dropping fast and the cost of everything was rising fast. The Japanese introduced military yen and made Hong Kong dollars illegal. Still, people preferred to use the Hong Kong dollar on the black market. This was strange perhaps. There was no government to support it and it was illegal. Still, people preferred it. But it couldn't be used openly. Later people started to speculate by buying up high-value notes. You could buy a hundred-dollar note for thirty or forty dollars.

After a few months, the staff quarters stopped being so safe. The soldiers knew that here was a regular source of manpower. From time to time they would do spot checks. What they wanted was labourers. If they had a job, they would come and get as many workers as they needed. They always needed workers because they paid almost nothing, so naturally, no one wanted to work for them. All they would do was supply you with enough food to stay alive. Many workers escaped and walked to China. So when they needed workers they would grab whoever they could find and force them to work for a few days. Only men. They left the women and children alone. I was lucky. I was never caught. But once my father was caught and taken away. When I returned to the quarters from whatever I was doing a few hours later, my wife told me what had happened. I can tell you I was damned angry. I didn't think twice. When I am angry I am like that. I ran down to the Hongkong Hotel where all the senior military officers lived. I charged into the lobby and demanded to see a senior officer.

'Who is the most senior officer here!' I shouted. Really I was furious. I didn't care about my own safety. Naturally I was stopped by the staff.

'What do you want?' a translator asked.

'Your soldiers have taken away my father. Why do you need old men to do your work? If you need someone you should get someone young. Let my father go. I don't mind taking his place!'

'And who are you?'

I told him my name and told him I was the brother-in-law of the hotel superintendent. Naturally, Ho Tim still worked there for the Japanese but he earned very little. The translator calmed me down and promised to look into the matter. In fact, he did do something because my father was released a few hours later. He was very frightened by the experience. I knew that the next time we might not be so lucky. We had to move.

I found a flat on the Wanchai waterfront, just next to the Luk Kwok Hotel, which later became famous because it was the original of the hotel in the Suzie Wong book. So we all moved there and for the next few months we did nothing. Nothing at all. No one had any money. Gradually, the money we did have on hand, our 'hot cash', gave out. It became more and more difficult to live.

It was at this time that our *mui-jai* ran away. She was the one my father-in-law had given my wife when we got married. Her name was Shen Yee. Why did she run away? Who can say? Maybe it was because we were getting poorer and poorer. Maybe she felt guilty to be eating our rice. Or maybe she felt this was a good time to gain her freedom. I can tell you that she was free to go anytime. No one would have stopped her. Actually, by that time it wasn't really legal to have a *mui-jai,* but no one told their *mui-jai*. The girls were illiterate so many of them didn't know. Maybe they did know but were happy to stay with their families. It was a kind of security. Anyway, the fact is, even if it was the law everyone ignored it. Maybe I am old fashioned but I have no objection to the *mui-jai* system if the master and mistress of the house are good. I can say that we always treated our *mui-jai*s well.

Shen Yee disappeared and then, a few days later, a friend of mine told me that she was working in a barber shop. Although there was no work for anyone in the normal way there was always work for a girl in a barber shop. In those days, when you went to a barber shop it wasn't just to get your hair cut. They performed other services, especially massage. And it's common for a customer to make an arrangement to meet the barber girl later for sex. So the girls who work in these shops are a form of prostitute.

When I heard Shen Yee was working in this barber shop I went to see her. When she saw me she looked scared. She thought I had come to take her back.

'Shen Yee, don't ever be scared of me. I don't want to do you any harm. You are free to do what you want. I just want to make sure you are happy.'

She said she was happy there. After that, I dropped in to see her from time to time. Naturally, I felt some affection for her. We had lived together for six or more years. I didn't want any harm to come to her. I saw her maybe ten times and then one day she was gone. No one knew where she had gone. I never saw her again.

For my wife, everything continued as before. She had three children to look after with just one amah to help. But my wife was always very clever about domestic matters.

During these months, the population of Hong Kong dropped a great deal. Maybe, it was only half or a third what it was before. The people who stayed had no money at all. People stayed at home or just walked the streets looking for opportunities. It was a hard time. Everyone suffered. There was starvation. Sometimes you would see bodies on the streets. I remember once, a man stole a cake and just stuffed it in his mouth. He didn't care if he was caught, as long as he had something to eat. One thing that some people ate at this time was wild taro. This was not a good vegetable to eat. I'm not sure what exactly it does. Maybe it is slightly poisonous or maybe the wild taro paste can't be digested so it stays in the bowel until it completely blocks the intestine or the stomach. People knew it was not good but it filled the stomach and stopped them feeling hungry. Many people died from eating too much. At first there is no problem but after six months or so of regular eating it becomes fatal. Another thing, girls and women were afraid of the soldiers but I don't think there was much rape. My wife stayed at home most of the time.

One day my father made a decision.

'What good is it to be rich if you can't afford to eat? I can't stand to see all my grandchildren starving. We must sell some of our properties in Canton so that we have money to buy food.'

So I was sent to Canton to sell some properties. My father was too old and frail. He didn't feel up to travelling.

I took the ferry up to Canton with all the documents and certificates that were needed. I had to have his signature on everything. None of the property was in my name. I sold a few houses so once again we were rich and had enough money to buy food.

When I came back from Canton I found a nicer flat in Village Road in Happy Valley so we moved there. It was very cheap to rent. It was possible to move into some very nice flats and live even rent-free. Many owners who had fled to Canton were just happy that someone was living in their flats. We paid a rent but it was very small. Shortly afterwards, I got another flat for my father as there wasn't enough room for us all. And then I got a third flat which I used for entertaining my friends and that's where I took girls. I didn't like to go to hotels. I didn't want people to comment about me. As for my wife, that was no problem. She didn't care much. She was an old-fashioned woman. She accepted that a man could have several concubines. I never cheated or lied to her. I would always tell her straight what I had been doing the night before: whether I had a good time with a society girl, or a dancer, or a film star or a waitress. She said to me: 'I don't mind if you mess around with girls. All I care about is that you take care of us properly so that we have a comfortable life.' We understood and respected each other.

A man's fate is a strange thing

A MAN'S FATE IS A STRANGE THING. It can change suddenly. One minute you may be poor, the next minute you are rich. It was about six months after the Japanese invasion when suddenly my life changed. Suddenly I was rich. Suddenly I had money in my pockets. I wasn't dependent on my father, or KF. I didn't have to be a broker. I had all the money I needed and more.

This moment was the turning point in my life. Naturally, I didn't realise this at the time. All I knew was that I had as much money as I needed. My father still had to sign all the documents but he left all the decisions to me. While all my rich friends were broke I was suddenly rich. I can tell you that money is nothing. But it is a glorious feeling to have money – money to throw away on pleasure. That is all I thought about. Everyone else struggled to get by. They led quiet lives at home or they escaped to other countries. Only I had the desire to have fun. What else was there to do? It was a bad time to think of business. We just had to cope the best way we could until the situation improved. And I had money to spend. That was one thing. The other thing was that soon I was to have very good connections with the Japanese administration. These were the two necessary components: money and connections. For the next three years and some months of the occupation I led the second most glorious time of my life. My school years were first. Then came the years of the occupation.

Let me explain how it all happened. When I went up to Canton to sell the houses, naturally I fooled around and had a good time. While I was there, I paid a visit to my old school friend, Tang Kin-shan. He was the one who had warned me several months before the war that the Japanese intended to invade.

'You should make some connections with the Japanese,' he advised me. He said he knew of someone who would be a good contact for me, the abbot of the only Japanese Buddhist monastery in Hong Kong – which happened to be in Wanchai, not very far from where we lived.

His name was Fuji-san. Tang gave me a letter of introduction to him. I
thought very hard about taking this step. I was worried that there might
be some negative consequences but in the end I made contact with him.
I wrote him a letter introducing myself and saying I would be happy to
be of use to the Japanese administration. A few days later I got a reply
asking me to visit him for tea. When I met him he was dressed in civilian
clothes, not the robes of a monk. I remember I was surprised when I
met him. His head wasn't shaved as I expected it would be. He had short
hair in the military style. All I knew was that this man had powerful
connections with the Japanese military.

'You would like to be of use to the administration?'

'That is my intention. But I don't know how I can help.'

'You can speak English? Then, please come here every afternoon at
four o'clock and teach me English and I will teach you Japanese. We can
exchange lessons. How would you like that?'

Naturally I was happy to agree, so it was arranged that I would be an
English teacher. I also set out to learn as much Japanese as I could. For
the first few days I just taught Fuji-san but then he introduced me to
some other Japanese who also wanted to learn English. Within a few
weeks I had seven or eight students. I knew very little of my students. I
knew their names but nothing else. I guessed they were senior officers
but when I met them they were not in uniform so I didn't know what
rank they were or which section of the army they worked in. Now, I can
tell you, they all studied hard. They were very serious about learning
English. Fuji-san could speak some Cantonese but soon with my
Japanese and my students' English we could communicate quite well.
Actually, I was very surprised that they wanted to learn English so I asked
them why.

'We are engaged in the Great East Asian War,' one of them explained.
'Our forces will eventually take over Australia and New Zealand. First
New Zealand and then Australia. In order to get a more favourable
posting to these countries we must learn English.'

The others all nodded.

'Also, it is good for promotion,' another one said. 'The more languages
we can speak the better our chances of promotion.'

'We enjoy your teaching,' a third officer said. 'We know you are a
learned literary man and also that you are good at *kung fu.*'

'How do you know all this?' I was surprised as I had never told them about my *kung fu*.

'Your friend Mr Tang wrote to me,' the abbot said.

'Why don't you join our army?' one of the officers asked.

I laughed. 'I may be good at *kung fu* but I know nothing of military matters. I have no experience of warfare or politics or anything of that sort. I would be a very bad soldier.'

Although I joked with them and laughed actually I was scared by the suggestion. If I joined them I would be considered a traitor. I kept this very clearly in mind. They repeated the suggestion several times but I said the same thing very firmly each time.

They went to a lot of effort to show that they appreciated my teaching, and I think also they valued my friendship. They tried to pay me for my tuition because although it was supposed to be an exchange actually we did very few classes in Japanese. Naturally, I refused, saying I was happy to do it out of friendship. Eventually they stopped asking me.

I realised, as any intelligent man would, that my connection with these officers was a sort of potential power. If I needed anything later it would be easy, or at least easier, to get it. One evening, I was out at the time, two military trucks with about a dozen soldiers drew up outside my house. The entire neighbourhood was alarmed. My wife was terrified as you can imagine. Japanese soldiers? There were many stories of Japanese soldiers going to a flat and knocking down the door and raping all the women inside. I never met anybody who had firsthand experience of this but that was one of the stories people told.

There was a loud knock on the front door. My wife was very scared and at first she was too frightened to open the door. But the officer knocked again and called out my name. Maybe I had done something wrong and they had come to arrest me? She realised there was nothing she could do. She looked through the grille and saw they were gendarmes. She knew that if they wanted to come in nothing would stop them.

'Yes?' she asked.

'Is this the house of Mr Hui?'

'Yes.'

'We have come to deliver some rice.'

The soldiers carried several large sacks of rice up to our second-floor flat. Rice was rationed at that time. One man's daily ration was six taels of rice. The Japanese had to import rice from China to feed the population. Everyone would have starved otherwise. In fact, people still did starve. This rice was a present from one of my students.

A few weeks later I was invited to a party at their officer's mess. I can't remember the reason for the party. I think it was because they insisted that I try their *sake*. They knew that I liked to drink and wanted me to taste *sake*. I don't think I had ever had *sake* at that time. I knew all the Chinese and European drinks but not *sake*. The monk came and collected me in his car. I didn't know where the mess was and as there was a curfew all the streets were dark and empty. I could hardly see where we were going. When the car stopped I realised we were outside the front doors of St Joseph's College on Kennedy Road. They had taken over the school and made it their mess. There was a guard at the door and they all saluted me as I entered. When they saluted you, they screamed out loud. I jumped back a few steps but the monk just laughed. The monk was in civilian clothes but all the soldiers appeared in full dress uniform. I was led to a room where there was a long low table. We sat down in the Japanese style. There were a number of women there too. Japanese women. Each one of us had a girl sitting at his back. Her job was to keep our glasses filled and to feed us when we were too busy talking. She would pick out a choice morsel with her chopsticks and put it in my mouth. I can tell you that Japanese women know how to serve.

So we ate and drank and talked and laughed. Now, I have a good head for spirits and this *sake* was good but not so strong. I could drink a lot without getting drunk. But the Japanese enjoy getting drunk and so they drank more and more. It's quite a pleasant drink. It's served warm. We drank for several hours. The *sake* made us all feel warm. It was summer now and quite hot anyway. As the officers got hotter they started to take off their clothes until most of them were only wearing the cloth wrapping, like a baby's nappy, that they wore as underwear. Also, Japanese are very *ham sap* – wet and salty – what's the English word? Randy? Some of the officers liked to touch the women. Only the monk and myself continued to behave in a proper way. I also took off my jacket and shirt but I kept my trousers on! At the end of the evening one of my students turned to me.

'So, my friend and respected teacher, you have tasted *sake*. Was it good?'

'Excellent!' I said.

'Now, have you ever tasted Japanese girls?' They all laughed at this. I laughed.

'I have to admit I haven't.'

'Take one of these girls to a room at the back, Mr Hui. Do what you want with her.' They were all prostitutes. This was their life.

'You can take any one of them. Whichever one you like. Don't be shy. We are all friends.'

I must admit I was tempted. It was true that I had never had a Japanese woman. Maybe she would be different in some way. It might be fun to 'taste' them as the officer had suggested. However, after a moment's thought I shook my head. The fact was they were prostitutes. Even if I didn't have to pay, I was scared of disease. Also, for some reason, Japanese women are not attractive. I don't know why, I shook my head and made some excuse. It was after midnight when Fuji-san drove me home.

One of my students was the second-in-command of the gendarmes, the political branch of the military police. They had great power and authority. They could arrest anybody, even a general, if they wanted. This man's name was Kakei-san. One day, after the class, he said he had a job that he thought would suit my abilities and which would at the same time be very useful for the Japanese administration. He asked me if I would be prepared to take control of the Hong Kong Entertainment Bureau. If I took the job I would be in charge of all the entertainment shows and also I would have control over all the people in the industry: actors, actresses, singers and so on. Kakei-san explained that, if I agreed, this would allow the entertainment industry to be less formally controlled. Obviously, it had to be controlled otherwise the film makers and opera groups might be influenced or abused by anti-Japanese forces. However, the military administration realised that people needed amusements and if they controlled these too tightly there was a danger of alienating the people. That's how he explained it to me. He asked me to think it over. I thought about it very seriously for one or two days before agreeing. One thing that influenced me was that many senior people in the business world were also collaborating with the Japanese. Also, it seemed to me that I would be helping normal life to return to Hong Kong. I assumed the position was a minor one but actually, I discovered later, it was a very senior post.

Kakei-san asked me to give him a negative of my photograph and the next day he gave me a large pass. It was the chop of the military police and the other had the chop of the Entertainment Bureau. Copies of my photograph were sent to all the cinemas and places of entertainment as well as to all the government departments. I remember that shortly after this I went to the Supreme Court building, now it's the Legislative Council building, to see Kakei-san. That was the headquarters of the gendarmes. As I approached the entrance, the guards, there were six of them, suddenly stood at attention and screamed out loud. We always said this sounded like the killing of a pig. It was a loud high-pitched sound that seemed to end in a choke. Then I realised they were saluting me. I asked Kakei-san how they knew I was a member of the Japanese administration. He told me they would have recognised me from my photograph which had been circulated. This was their way of giving me face.

The Japanese were like that. They had a profound respect for authority. For example, the puppet government of Wang Ching-wei, which was based in Nanjing, was headed by a famous revolutionary. He was the number one or two man in the Kuomintang. At this time he was more famous than Chiang Kai-shek. Wang Ching-wei actually was a great hero, the most famous revolutionary at that time. He was famous because he had tried to assassinate the last Chinese emperor. Not many people know about him now. If they do, they think of him as a traitor but my way of thinking is that he helped China retain some form of independence by saving it from being controlled directly by the Japanese. Life would have been much harsher under the Japanese. Because of his position he could demand what he wanted and the Japanese had to give it to him to give him face and to make people understand that he had real authority. Of course, secretly, the Japanese had the real authority. But if China had been under the direct control of the Japanese life wouldn't have been so busy and prosperous.

Actually, these years were quite stable and good for business in China. That was why I was able to sell my property in Canton. There was a market in Canton at that time, but not in Hong Kong. That's why all my friends were so poor. Later, after the war, of course they all had their property intact while I had sold everything. So it was also a curse on me that my property was in Canton. Wang Ching-wei later claimed he had done what he had done to make life easier and to save lives. I believe him.

However, the Japanese were not so very bad to Hong Kong people during the war. I saw some torture. There was some abuse, some cruelty. But overall I can't say that it was terrible oppression. Times were very hard for most people. There were very few jobs. Getting enough food to eat was a problem. We were lucky. My family lived well throughout the war. Since then I have suffered for it. But I thought then, and I still think, it was good for everyone that I and some other people collaborated with the Japanese.

I didn't take the job very seriously. Very few films were being made at that time. The main form of entertainment was Chinese opera. It was part of my job to approve all performances and scripts. This was easy as no one wanted to annoy the Japanese. One of my other responsibilities was to approve travel permits for entertainers to go up to Canton. I was happy to take the title. Why not? I thought like this: you want to make use of me? Fine. Then I'll make use of you. If I can make life easier for people, good. If this makes it easier for me to fool around with girls, fine. If I have some power to use to help people and help me have fun, why not? But, although I was working for them, in my heart my sympathies were not with the Japanese. I was well-known in society and word quickly spread that I had been made head of the Entertainment Bureau. Later, when I began to own horses, people thought I was making a fortune from collaborating. They thought I was rich through my connections. They didn't realise I was spending my own fortune. I don't think they blamed me. Everyone understood that these were difficult times. You had to make the best of your opportunities, as long as you didn't do anything to harm your country and as long as you used your influence to help friends.

One day, quite early on, maybe in the first few weeks of my job, I went to the Po Shing Theatre. Naturally, all the ticket collectors and managers knew me. The performance had already started and there was quite a large audience. I slipped in and sat down at the back. After a few minutes I realised that some sort of confrontation was going on. I noticed that two men sitting at the front were attracting a lot of abuse from a group of men who were standing round the side. At first I thought it was a personal quarrel and ignored it. But then the two men at the front got up to leave. They walked past me to the entrance. I could see that they were scared. I was curious so I got up and followed them. Out in the lobby I hailed them and asked them what the problem was. They explained that they were off-duty policemen who were out of their district. Now, it was clear to me that the other men were triads and that they must have a lot of influence with the local area Japanese military officers or maybe with the Taiwanese interpreters who were well known to be corrupt. Otherwise they wouldn't be so arrogant. However, I had my own power as well. I told them not to be scared. I would take care of everything. They were a bit surprised.

'Please come back in with me. I will take responsibility for anything that happens. If they want to say anything they were just to say: 'This Mr Hui is responsible for us.' Maybe they were used to taking orders or maybe there was something in my attitude that convinced them, I don't know, but they agreed to come back in with me. So the three of us went back in and sat down again at the front. Now the triad members were a bit unsure of themselves so they started to gather at the back of the theatre. I knew they were wondering what to do. Certainly they would try to attack me. I thought to myself: 'If I want to seek a compromise, I had better confront them directly and do it now before they work out a plan.' So I walked to the back where they were waiting.

'Show me your tickets!' I said. Now this is a sort of pun. *'Fei'* meaning 'ticket' also sounds like 'bullet'. Nobody responded. No one said anything and no one moved. I still had the initiative. 'Come on,' I said, 'if your "tickets" are the bullets in your guns let's see them. Pull out your guns. Let me see them. I don't care how many you've got.'

Still they didn't react. I don't think any of them had any guns. I was just testing them. They just looked sullen. Then I shouted at them for causing problems for customers of the theatre. I warned them that there would be big trouble if they did anything.

'All right! Out!' I said and pushed them out. I suppose there were about fifteen of them. They were bemused. I knew that my acting in such an authoritative way when they didn't know who I was would confuse them. They allowed themselves to be pushed out to the entrance. But they stopped here and started to mutter to each other. I knew I hadn't won the fight. They would soon gather their senses and realise I was only one person. They would wait for me and attack me later. Or maybe they would come back. I went up to the manager's office. He invited me for a drink but I told him I had important business. I rang the nearest Japanese army post and told them who I was. I didn't have to explain. They already knew me. I told them to send some support and within minutes the Japanese soldiers arrived in their jeeps. As soon as the triads saw them coming they ran off.

That was the only time I had any problems of that sort. Actually, this question of bullets and guns was something that concerned me. That was why I challenged them in the way I did. I wanted to see if they had any guns. I have always known that it is useless in this day and age for a man to be a *kung fu* fighter. So what? He can easily be killed with one bullet from a gun. Bang. That's it. I would be dead. If one of them had made a move to pull out a gun I would have attacked him immediately. Now, actually, I myself owned two guns. I had been given them by my students. I think they had wanted to get me interested in military things. One of them was a small Derringer. It looked like a small toy gun. The other one was a Colt 45. I loved them both. I loved to hold them in my hands. They were very beautiful. But I never carried them. My reasoning was this: if people came to hear that I carried a gun then they would try to shoot first. But if they knew I never carried a gun they would know they didn't need to use one. If I relied on my hands alone I knew I had a ninety per cent chance of winning but if I carried a gun I had a ninety per cent chance of being killed. So I always left my guns at home.

The biggest owner of race horses in Hong Kong

I T WAS AT THIS TIME that I became the biggest owner of race horses in all Hong Kong. First you must understand that life under the Japanese was very boring. There were very few amusements. There were no cabarets. Just a few nightclubs. Cinemas showed only Japanese films, which were very slow and tedious. The opera however was excellent. First class. But apart from that the only popular form of entertainment were the horse races. Before the war, KF and I used to go riding in the New Territories. KF was very keen and became a very good rider. He was very slight. A natural jockey. In fact, before the war, he had trained at the Jockey Club. All the jockeys in those days were amateurs.

After nearly a year of the occupation KF was broke and hungry. Life was hard for him and Cat. He needed to find some way of earning a living. He was working as a jockey but he couldn't get so many rides. That's why he turned to me. I had good connections with the Japanese and I had plenty of money. He suggested to me that since he knew which horses were the best I should try to buy these and then he would ride them. He could then live on his share of the prize money and a share of my bets. I would make money because I would have all the best horses. I thought it was a good plan. I wanted to help KF and some other friends like the famous jockey Kenny Kwok. Also I liked the idea of owning horses. There was a ready market for them. Owners were quite happy to sell for the right price and I didn't care about money. As I had a lot of cash I was in a good position to buy whichever horses I wanted. Everyone knew which ones were the best but not everyone could afford them. I didn't care how much it cost me as long as I got the best.

It didn't matter how much anyone asked for the horses. If I wanted it I just paid for it. I don't like to bargain. That's not my style. But KF knew how much I should pay. Naturally, I care about not having enough money to support myself, but that's a different thing. Money itself is nothing to me.

Since the British had gone everything had changed and nothing had changed. Before the war only British could join the Jockey Club and be members and own horses. Now, only Japanese could join the Jockey Club and own horses. No Chinese were allowed to own a horse. Not officially. Unofficially, there was no problem. Just like before, if you wanted to own a horse you just gave a small percentage to a Japanese officer in exchange for him agreeing to register the horse in his name. I would give the officer anything from five to twenty per cent of the horse. Now the Japanese brought the horses down from Manchuria. When they arrived all the members of the Jockey Club who wanted to own a horse would write their names on a wooden tally which was put into a box. Lots were drawn and the lucky members would be allocated a pony for a certain price. Now I didn't buy any horses in this way because I wasn't a member. After this sale by lot there would be private sales of the horses. This was how some members made extra money. With good advice from KF and Kenny Kwok, I bought up some of the best horses. Actually, they weren't horses, they were Mongolian ponies. They were short but very strong and they could run very fast. When I go into a thing I go into it all the way. Within only four months I had bought ten. Eventually I had eleven ponies. One of them was called Silver Dragon. Not a big pony but he was fast and had a strong heart. On what I won on this pony alone I paid off all my stable expenses. I had at least five or six big winners. If I wanted to win it would be hard for others to do so. Naturally, my horses didn't win all the time. That's not good tactics. But it cost me nothing to be the biggest horse owner in Hong Kong. All my expenses were covered by prize money and what I made on the bets. The way jockeys made their money in those days was to advise the owners if they thought their horse could win a race. If they thought it could, the owner would bet on it and a certain percentage of the bet would be for the jockey. That's what I did. If I bought fifty tickets, I would tell KF that ten of the tickets were for him.

Race days were spectacular events. The stands were always packed. In those days there was a race every fortnight. Maybe there would be extra races if there was a special holiday or festival. Gambling is in our blood. If you saw all the people gambling you wouldn't believe they were so poor, even starving. I remember the first race after the occupation I was surprised to see for the first time all the horses' and jockeys' names in Chinese, not English. English disappeared completely during those years. The Japanese military were not supposed to bet but no one bothered to hide what they were doing. It was all corrupt. The Jockey Club was run by the military. Everyone made a lot of money.

If I were ever to get rich again I would love to own horses. I can't explain the feeling. It makes you feel electric with energy. On a horse's back you feel like a hero. Every morning, early, at about five, the horses are taken down to the race track to be exercised by the *mafoos*, stable boys, and jockeys and trainers. I used to go down and ride the ponies. This was how I got to know them. KF would be there too every morning getting a feel of the ponies and getting to know them. Horses are very clever. They know if you are an experienced rider. If they think you are a novice they will try to throw you, or rub you against a tree to knock you off. After an hour or so of exercising we would sit together in the club house and have breakfast while we talked about the horses. Then we would all go up to the stables and look at the horses together. We would discuss which horse would win and what our tactics should be.

On the day before a race I would take a bottle of the very best brandy to the stables to give a shot to the horses who were going to run. It was always Hennessy Three Star brandy. Before the war a bottle would cost $18 to $20. During the war a bottle cost about $200. I used to buy it in boxes of a dozen bottles at a time. I myself would drink it with my friends on race days. Obviously it is not a good idea to give too much brandy to the horses so everyone from the *mafoos*, the stable hands, to the trainer would have a glass too. It sounds crazy, doesn't it? Giving brandy to horses, the very best brandy, when people all around me were starving and didn't have enough to eat. But what could I do about that? Nothing. I tell you, if I had my time over again I would do the same. And all those starving people? If they were in my place they would do exactly the same. That's how it is.

Once, one of my horses became seriously ill and I was told there was nothing we could do about it so I told the *mafoo* to kill it, which he did. If I had sold the flesh of the horse I could have got my investment back, the price of meat was so high. But I didn't care about that. I told my friends to divide it up between them and I took some myself. I can tell you horse meat tastes better than beef. You can boil it in water and make a sort of thick soup. Wonderful.

My two great pleasures at this time were racing the horses and mixing with the most senior Japanese officers. These connections gave me a lot of potential power. I was able to help a lot of people, mainly with travel permits. I myself had a six month permit that allowed me to go wherever and whenever I wanted.

Apart from the horse racing the only other real entertainment was opera. The opera stars at that time were really marvellous. I can say they were sensational. I knew them all, naturally. My new position made me a very important figure in this world. The more conservative and old-fashioned sections of society loved opera. I used to go to the shows regularly and if I did I would generally go backstage afterwards. If I was in Canton I would invite them all for a drink at my hotel afterwards and they would all come out of politeness, to give me face.

One day I was approached by the fifth concubine of Tang Shiu-kin. Tang had been very rich before the war but his money was all frozen in property during these years of the occupation so at that time he wasn't very active. Now, this concubine was not an official wife. Also, she was not a quiet, conventional woman. On the contrary, she was a social girl. For a Chinese woman, she was quite tall. She was probably two inches taller than me in her stockinged feet. For these reasons she was suitable for entertaining – especially entertaining European government officers who were useful for his business dealings. I think that's why he set her up in her own flat. He never gave her any title. But everyone in society knows all the gossip and they keep count of everyone else's concubines so we all called her his fifth concubine. For a rich businessman at that time it was common to have five, six or even more, ten or twelve wives. Sometimes they would live together in the same mansion. I suppose foreigners find this strange. Sometimes I am asked 'Don't they fight?'. Usually, they are all very careful to stay on good terms. However, it has been known for the junior wives to gang up on the first wife. This can cause great problems for a family if it happens. Nowadays, rich business-men don't have to have wives, they just set up a girl as a mistress, or they have one or two nights with a girl. These are all carefully arranged beforehand and a contract can be made out. I'll tell you a well-known story. There's an actress, she's still around. She is known as the 'million-dollar girl'. The story is that she had a contract to go to bed with one of the richest businessmen in Hong Kong. He had the custom of giving the girls he went to bed with a signed blank cheque. Only he and his bank manager knew what the limit was. I suppose most girls would write a reasonable amount but this girl wrote 'one million dollars'. Naturally the cheque bounced. Really she was too greedy. Word got around. I suppose the businessman told all his friends. It was a good joke. Naturally, the girl denies it. But usually, it is an open secret who has a contract with who and for how long. Beautiful women. This is one of the perks of being a rich businessman. Everyone has to accept it. His wife especially. That's how it is.

Now maybe Tang was neglecting his fifth concubine because she fell in love with me. Maybe she was just flirting. Maybe she was bored. We met quite often as she was a friend of KF's wife, Cat. In fact, she would often tease me about going out with Cat. It was true that sometimes we would be together without KF, but this was usually because KF asked me to accompany her.

'I see that you and Cat are very friendly. I think she must be your girlfriend,' this woman said to me one day.

'Don't make it sound suspicious. Cat and I are good friends. She is the wife of my good friend. Everything is very correct.'

She laughed, 'I know, Mr Hui, but you have many "girlfriends". Are you always so correct?'

'It's true I have many girlfriends. Why do you want to talk about this?'

'Perhaps you have too many girlfriends.'

'Why do you think so?'

'Because, I think you don't have time even to kiss me.'

I had to laugh. She knew I was a romantic fellow. Maybe she thought she could get me.

'I know you are not a married woman,' I said, 'but you are, how can I put it, "occupied". I don't think I wish to make an enemy of someone by kissing his woman.'

We were talking in a joking way. But jokes can be one way of expressing the truth. She didn't give up for a long time. But in the end she too realised I was a very straight man. Frankly, I knew so many beautiful women and girls, why should I take someone else's?

Now, this fifth concubine and her sister often went to the opera. I would say about four times a week. Maybe every day. I can tell you, we Chinese love our opera. Nowadays there aren't many good actors but in those days even the film stars worked in the opera.

One of the best was a man whose personal name was Fei-hung. He was one of the two leading actors at that time. The fifth concubine's sister fell in love with him, or should I say fell in love with his glamour. The fifth concubine knew of my power so she asked me to help her sister by introducing them and giving her more opportunity to be with the actor by taking her backstage. The actor came to me later. He was a little worried.

'She likes me very much but I am a little concerned. I don't want to make a mistake.'

He was worried that the concubine's protector would not approve.

'Don't be silly,' I told him. 'If she's in love with you and you like her, what else is there to think about?'

And so they had an affair.

Another opera star at this time was the actress Gai Jai Ming. Really, I liked her very much. And she liked me too. I could see that. She wasn't very beautiful but I liked her because she wasn't a silly, vain actress. She knew about life. She had worked her way up in her profession, and the life of a minor actress in the opera world is not easy. You have to be very clever to reach the top of that profession. I liked talking to her very much. I remember I often went to the opera when I was in Canton staying at the Oi Kwan Hotel. After the performance I would invite them back to my suite for drinks. Most of them didn't drink a great deal, but Gai Jai Ming liked brandy. She had a good head for drink. About seven or eight of the actors would come to my suite and they would stay fifteen or twenty minutes and then they would drift away. Why? Because everyone knew that Gai Jai Ming and I liked each other very much and wanted to be alone. Now I know it's strange, but if I love a girl, really love her, then I never touch her sexually. If she's a social girl and she's not occupied or attached and she really wants to make love to me then I can make love to her. If I don't think there's any danger or I don't think she is worthy of my love then there is no problem. But if I am really in love or think I might fall in love later then I don't do anything. I consider everything very carefully right from the beginning. Now, with Gai Jai

Ming, I enjoyed her company and her friendship but I could not trust her feelings for me. I respected her a great deal. So, naturally, I was very proper and made no attempt to take her to bed. Gai Jai Ming was very clever. She knew I knew I could have anything I wanted from her. She was giving me every opportunity but I never did anything with her. I did not want to abuse her. One day she said to me: 'Mr Hui, you really are a gentleman. I know you love me and that you are not just attracted to me physically. You are ruled by your head not your heart.'

'You are right,' I told her, 'you are very clever.' I knew that Gai Jai Ming, as an actress, must have her eye out to catch a rich man. That is why I kept my distance. I never could be sure that she loved me for myself. But she was very clever. She knew what she wanted. And eventually she was successful.

It was after the war. Quite a long time after. In the mid-fifties, KF and I drove out to a beach on the Castle Peak Road. There was a nice hotel nearby, the Dragon Inn, where we could hire a room for a few hours and where they had a good restaurant.

While we were on the beach, we bumped into an old friend of ours by the name of Chan. He was a rich man in the entertainment business. We hadn't seen each other in a long time. We had lost touch. 'Come on. We'll have dinner together,' he said.

'Of course. It's your treat!' we said. We were old friends so we didn't need to be polite.

We all laughed.

So we arranged to meet a little later in the restaurant.

At about six o'clock we went down to the restaurant. Chan was already there waiting for us so we all sat down and started to drink. After about fifteen minutes a woman came into the restaurant. Chan stood up.

'I must introduce you to my wife!'

I turned to greet her and was very surprised to find myself face to face with Gai Jai Ming. We both immediately burst out laughing. Chan and KF were both very surprised. I clapped Chan on the arm.

'Let me tell you my friend,' I said laughing. 'We are old friends. If I had wanted to marry her you would never have had a chance!'

How clever was Gai Jai Ming? She wasn't even a concubine. She was his legal first wife. She did very well for herself. Naturally, although I laughed and joked, it would not be good for me to tell him the truth about our relationship. This would have made him unhappy. I remember we had a very happy dinner. We had a lot of memories to share and a lot of things to joke about, but I knew I had to control myself and not say too much. Sometimes saying the wrong thing can ruin a friendship.

Then I didn't see them much after that. I lost touch with all my old friends when I came to live in Cheung Chau. It was like I left my old life behind me. Of course I was poor and all my old friends still had their wealth. It is difficult to maintain a friendship in these circumstances.

The last time I saw them was just a few years ago, about ten days before he died. I saw them come out of a building in Theatre Lane, and I was so pleased to see them that I rushed forward a few steps before I realised that although I had taken five or six steps they had hardly moved, so I stopped. I thought he must be very ill. I saw then that he was leaning very heavily on Gai Jai Ming's arm. I thought, if he's so ill why is he out of doors? Why does he have to go to his office? Then I understood that he was dying and that he knew it and that he must have to settle some affairs. So I stopped and did not approach them. I saw them struggle the five or ten feet to their car. They didn't see me. I felt he would not want to see me who was older than him and still so strong and full of life. He would feel the bitterness of his own death much more strongly.

Fooling around in Canton

THE OCCUPATION LASTED, as everyone knows, three years and eight months. I was in Canton most of that time. Perhaps nine out of twelve months. I had to stay there to sell my properties. I usually stayed at the Oi Kwan Hotel. I kept a suite there on the twelfth or thirteenth floor. It was one of the top hotels in Canton.

My friends in the Hong Kong gendarmes gave me some introductions to their friends in the military police in Canton so I often fooled around with them. Now, I must explain something. The gendarmes were very powerful. They could arrest even very senior army officers. But the military police were even more powerful. They could arrest gendarme officers. In Hong Kong they were both very powerful. But in Canton the situation was different. The Japanese had set up the puppet government of Wang Ching-wei so they couldn't do anything they wanted. Of course they were still powerful but there was some restraint.

One time I was going up to Canton so I booked my suite in advance. When I arrived at the hotel the staff told me what had happened earlier that day. The Japanese high commander for the entire southern China region, I don't know his Japanese name but we called him Chee-teen-booi, had driven up to the hotel with his staff. They were in American jeeps. All the Japanese military liked American jeeps. He had marched in and demanded a suite. General Chee-teen-booi kept insisting and the staff kept saying that all the suites were occupied. Finally, he discovered that one of the suites, mine, was booked but not yet occupied.

'Who is this man?' he demanded. 'Since this room is empty why don't you give it to me?'

The staff told him my name. They fully expected he would insist on having the room. If he really insisted they would have had no choice. But they didn't want to lose me as their customer. They knew I was good for business. I was a long-term resident and I entertained a lot. In fact I entertained every night. But when General Chee-teen-booi heard my name he paused.

'Hui Tak-kwong?'

It seemed to them that he knew my name. He and his officers got
back into their jeeps and drove off.

Now, this story would not be possible in Hong Kong. If a senior
Japanese officer demanded a room he would get it even if a Chinese man
had to be thrown out. But in Canton it was different. When I heard the
story I was surprised myself. I had never met General Chee-teen-booi
and never did. There were only two generals at this level. One for south
China and one for the north. I didn't think that he would have known
my name. However, shortly afterwards, I heard about the same incident
from another source, which confirmed that he had heard of me. When
he heard my name he wondered if this was the name of the man his
junior officers had mentioned. My friends in Hong Kong had written
to their friends and told them all about me. When Chee-teen-booi got
back to his headquarters he asked his assistants if Hui Tak-kwong was
the great *kung fu* fighter he had heard about. One of his assistants was
my friend Mr Li. He was a few years older than me but we had been
fellow students at Lam's *kung fu* academy. He confirmed that I was the
famous fighter. The general never went back to the hotel to trouble
them.

So, you see, I was very popular and well-known among the Japanese
officers of the gendarmes and military police. In fact one of the com-
manders in the Canton region used to borrow money from me but he
always paid me back within a few months. I often used to go drinking
with my friends in the Japanese army. They liked to drink and talk and
fool around. We drank brandy and *sake.* They were strong drinkers. One
time, we had been drinking all afternoon. Evening came and we were
still drinking. One of them suggested that we get some girls and have a
happy time with them. They all thought this was a good idea. Now, I
had heard some stories about drunken Japanese officers, and I didn't
want to have any trouble. I understood that the girls must be Chinese
and that they might be scared of the Japanese so I said: 'That's okay. But
I don't want any girls to be scared.'

'Don't worry!' they assured me, 'we just want to have a good time.'

'Okay!' I said. 'We will find some girls and have a good time, but first
of all you must give me your pistols.'

Everyone knew that Japanese officers were all very proud of their guns. 'We've all had a lot to drink and we are going to have a happy time,' I explained, 'but if anything happens that annoys you, maybe you will pull out your gun and start shooting. That wouldn't be so good.' They all laughed and agreed. So I collected their pistols and put them in a bag which I carried and we went off to find some girls. Actually, I was surprised they were so agreeable to my suggestion. I suppose it's because they were trained to be obedient. In the Japanese army an officer who was even just one step lower in rank, even a small step, had to be totally obedient to his superior. It was very common for an officer to hit his subordinate. To slap his face. Not just once. Sometimes a dozen times with his full force. And they had to stand there and take it. I saw this myself many times.

On this evening, besides myself there were perhaps six or seven Japanese officers. We went to the western suburbs of Canton where there were, and still are, many large mansions. This had once been a very smart and respectable district but at this time many of them had been taken over and were used as houses of pleasure. Each one was run by a mamasan who organised everything. These places weren't so expensive. Not cheap but reasonable. I was not very familiar with this district but we took rickshaws to one place. I told my friends to stay outside while I did the talking. I was greeted at the door by the mamasan.

'Here I am with some Japanese officers. They are my friends and they want to have a good time. Please do not worry that they will cause problems as I have taken their guns. There won't be any trouble.' I can tell you the mamasan was very pleased.

'What a gentleman you are!' she told me. 'Yes, we have girls. Ask your friends to come in.' So I waved to them to come in. All the girls of the house were there. The officers chose the girls they wanted to sleep with and the girls took them off to their rooms.

'And what about yourself?' the mamasan asked.

'I'm not interested for myself. I will just drink brandy. Remember, if there is any trouble I will sort it out. I know them well. But I am sure there will be no problem.'

'All we care about is our life!' mamasan said. 'Sometimes they are rough. But with you here we are safe.'

She was very conscientious to make me feel comfortable.

'Why do you not want a girl for yourself?' she asked. 'There are many beautiful girls here. They would all be happy to be your companion.' I laughed, 'I have enough women. I don't need to fool around.'

'I see you are such a nice gentleman with a very special taste. There is one girl here who is the most beautiful of all the girls in the district. Her nickname is "Diamond Queen". I would like to introduce her to you.'

'Well,' I said, 'I don't mind to talk to her but I won't go to bed with her.'

'Why not?'

'Frankly,' I told her, 'I am afraid of contracting a sexual disease.'

Of course I could have used a cap but I don't like that. I like to be free. I like to be 'face to face' as they say.

I was introduced to a beautiful girl. She was really very beautiful. So I said to her: 'I would like to invite you to have a drink with me and to talk for a certain time but first I would like to know how much you will charge me?' She just smiled. 'The mamasan has told me what a special gentleman you are. I am very happy to meet you. I will not charge you top rate. If you wish to accept entertainment from me I will charge you just the standard rate.' She invited me to her room and we talked. We were joined by the mamasan and some of the other girls who weren't busy. I stayed up all night drinking and talking to them. Now I am a very joyful person. I enjoy talking. It is one of my great pleasures. It is a special pleasure to enjoy the company of one of these professional girls. They would serve you drinks and food and try to be intimate with you. Their talk is very sweet. They like to praise you. They said to me things like: 'How is it that you are such a wonderful man? You just like to sit and drink and talk in an ordinary way. You are very special, very restrained.'

I enjoyed the company of this girl.

'What is God doing?' I asked her. 'It's very cruel that such a nice looking girl as you, such a clever and intelligent girl, even well educated, I think, that you should have to take up this kind of work.'

'I can't complain,' she said, 'it is my fate. I have my parents and many brothers to support. It's not easy to make a living these days. I am lucky. I can earn good money. These times are not easy.'

Towards morning the mamasan brought me a bowl of soup. Each mamasan has her own recipe but basically it is made from chicken liver steamed in herbs. It is very expensive. It is only for special guests. I like it very much. It is a tonic. The way we see it is that when you have been with a prostitute, you have lost some vital energy and this soup is to help you to regain it. In a high-class house of prostitution this soup is part of the service.

We talked and drank all night. I can do with very little sleep but that night I didn't sleep on purpose. I was responsible for all the guns. There would be serious problems if anything happened to them. At seven the next morning I called the officers and in no time at all they were all dressed and downstairs. They were used to obeying orders. They were all very polite and paid off the girls. When we left the house, I opened the bag and laughed: 'I don't know whose gun is whose. You will have to pick out your own gun.' Most of them had to get back to their duties but two of them joined me for the next day's programme of fooling around.

Actually, it was very rare for me to go to a house of pleasure. Most evenings I would entertain some friends, usually girls, at the dining room of the hotel. At my table there would be two or three men. The rest would be girls. Always more girls than men. Always different faces. I had many hangers on. People who liked to please me. They would introduce girls to me. These were nice girls. Family girls. Social girls. If someone was special I would invite them to dinner. And they all enjoyed my company, not just because I was clever or smart or rich but also because I was a gay and handsome man. I am a joyful man. I like to be surrounded by beautiful and smart girls so that the conversation bubbles like champagne all evening. And all these girls knew it wasn't an easy thing to make me fall in love with them. They knew I had a special lover, Margaret . . . Margaret Ko.

Margaret was extremely beautiful. She was my second great love. I can say she was my greatest lover. I mean that my feeling for her and her feeling for me was greater than with any other girl, even perhaps greater than my love for Leung Chui-yee. We knew each other longer. But, you know, I never slept with her either. She knew I treated my family well. She knew I liked to fool around with other girls. She didn't mind. No matter what I did it was all right. She loved me with all her heart.

I had met Margaret a couple of times before I was properly introduced to her. Although she was very beautiful I thought nothing of it. On its own it can do nothing. I think she had been one of my companions at dinner a few times. But then. . . . To explain everything clearly I must go back a little and tell you about my friend Poon.

Poon's father had established a very well-known preserved fruit company. You could get his preserved fruits anywhere in the world where there was a Chinese community. Once Poon's father became wealthy he started to play the games of the super-rich. There was a district in Western called Shek Tong Tsui which had been famous for its high-class houses of pleasure. This was a long time ago. Even when I was young it was past its peak. Actually they were really entertainment houses. Rich men went to these houses to be entertained by young sing-song girls. These girls were not really prostitutes. These girls were like high-class *geisha*. In fact many of them were virgins. They would sing if requested or play chess or play drinking games or word games. They were very skilled in producing rhyming couplets. Often a rich man would hire one for an evening of entertainment and invite his friends to join him. They would drink and the girl would have to keep the guests entertained. If they produced a line of poetry, she would respond with another line that rhymed and was, at the same time, clever. These girls were specially chosen when they were young and trained up. They were educated and taught how to play the *wu dip kum,* the butterfly piano, a kind of long stringed instrument. It was common for rich men to play games that showed off their disregard for money. They might roll cigarettes in large banknotes and light them with other banknotes. There is a story that one extremely extravagant man cooked himself a green-pea congee, a most common dish, by feeding the stove with bank notes, not just ten- or fifty-dollar notes but large banknotes. I don't think this man did it very often. You can imagine it would need millions. But once is enough to show off your contempt. People would talk about it forever. That world did not last long. By the time I visited Shek Tong Tsui it was just a common red-light district with brothels.

In the old days, it was common for very rich men to fall in love with these girls. They were young and beautiful and clever and, even more enticing, they were unobtainable. To go to bed with one of these girls was impossible. The mamasan had higher ambitions for them. She wanted them to be wives or concubines. In that way she would be better rewarded for her efforts in educating the girls. The mamasan would first need to be shown that you were not just rich, but also generous. This could only be done by the man showing off his disdain for money and by entertaining lavishly. Poon's father fell in love with one of these girls and by the time he married her, and he took her as his main wife, he had spent over $200,000. Multiply that by ten or twenty or thirty times to get the value nowadays. But she was very beautiful. I knew her very well. I met her through Poon who was my schoolmate at Queen's College. Some people said that my friend was not the real son of his father. Of this I know nothing. I am sure it is just malicious tongues wagging. An old man marries a beautiful young girl. There must be some gossip.

Poon's mother also spent much of the occupation in Canton. She stayed in a permanent suite at the Great Asia Hotel. She was a friend of the Ko family and so Margaret came up to Canton to look for work. Mrs Poon advised Margaret that she should look for a rich young man to keep her or marry her. This is a natural way of thinking as Margaret was very beautiful. She was about three inches taller than me, tall, slim with long straight hair. Mrs Poon had a wide experience of men and was very shrewd. I liked her very much and often paid her a visit. I knew also that she liked me. She talked to Margaret about me: 'Don't think of Peter Hui as a married man,' she told Margaret. 'He is a rich young playboy who likes to enjoy himself. He is a kind and handsome man. He has a very attractive smile and as far as I know he is a gentleman. You should try to become his friend.' In fact she was determined that Margaret and I should get together. One day when I went to visit Mrs Poon, Margaret was there. Mrs Poon asked me to stay after everyone else had gone and to have dinner with her and Margaret – just the three of us. Mrs Poon made it very clear to me that Margaret was a special girl who was very suitable for me. I remember that I was drinking brandy and after a few glasses I looked at Margaret and a great feeling of warmth and happiness flooded through me and I remember thinking: 'Yes. She is really perfect!' And from that moment we became lovers, she became my constant companion. I told her to give up her job as it hardly paid anything at all. I told her that I would take care of her expenses. She loved me too. I never gave her any presents and she never made any demands. She was just happy to be with me. Our relationship was very pure, very gentle. From that day on she was always the hostess at my table when we entertained. We were together for nearly three years.

This may seem strange to you but I was very concerned about her reputation. Although she was my constant companion I insisted that she return to her flat every night. I took her back myself. She had a room in a small ground-floor flat in the east of Canton. She sublet the room from a young couple who had a few children. At that time she had no relatives in Canton. Later I met all her family. They all liked me and respected me very much. I know people find this difficult to understand but although we were together for so long and had such strong feelings for each other I never slept with her. Sometimes, yes, there were times I knew she wanted to do it, when I was drunk, we would get so hot, I undressed her and then myself and lay down on the bed with her. But always at the last moment I would say: 'No, better not.' No matter how drunk I am, when I thought of morality I always immediately became sober. I am a gentleman in that way. All my close girlfriends know that. 'Peter is a playboy,' they say, 'but even when he's hot he has self-control.' I was brought up with a strong belief in Confucian discipline. I try to behave in a way that is fitting and proper. I have always had a great respect for women. Don't misunderstand me. It's not that I think sex is dirty. To put it in a rough way I can fuck around with girls and I have no problem with that but if I love someone then I take a very serious attitude and I am very careful of my behaviour. I can tell you it wasn't always easy. Margaret and I would often spend hours cuddling each other in my room. Sometimes, she begged me to make love to her. But what stopped me was the thought that I could not truly afford to take a second wife. The money I was spending was my father's money. I always thought of the war years as a time which could not last. Some day the war would end and normal life would return. When that happened I would not be able to continue leading this life. It wasn't fair to Margaret to ruin her reputation and then leave her like that. Yet how could I marry her? That was how I thought. She accepted it.

Apart from fooling around there wasn't very much to do. My job didn't involve much. I had an office at the Supreme Court building but I was never there. All I had was my authorisation document which was like a large book with two large chops in it, one from the Entertainment Bureau and the other from the gendarmes. It worked like this: if an opera troupe wanted to go from Hong Kong to Canton, they would go to the Entertainment Bureau. There the clerks would say: 'Okay we approve you but now you need to get a chop from the gendarmes HQ.' When they went to the gendarme's office they would be told that they needed my personal approval. If I was in Hong Kong they would come to my house. If I was in Canton they would send someone up to Canton with the documents and I would chop them with my personal chop.

One night, I was taking Margaret home when there was an air-raid. The allies were bombing Japanese barracks on the outskirts of Canton. Whenever there was an air-raid all traffic had to stop and turn off all lights. These attacks were never very serious. The allies knew that the main victims of any attack on the city would be innocent Chinese civilians. It was about ten or ten-thirty. There were very few taxis in Canton. If you arranged it in advance it was possible to get one otherwise you had to take a rickshaw. That evening we took rickshaws. We were about half way to Margaret's flat when the sirens went off. The rickshaw pullers immediately stopped. We got out and I told Margaret to pay only half the fare that we had negotiated. But the driver refused. He insisted on being paid the full fare. 'It's an accident. It's not my fault I can't take you the rest of the way. You should pay me the whole fare.' So we stood there in the dark streets alone. The street was completely empty. The other rickshaw driver was already running off.

'Pay me the full fare!' he demanded.

'Here's half. That's all I'm going to give you.'

'It's not my fault we have to stop. We agreed a price. Come on now, pay up.'

'What will you do if I refuse?'

'I will follow you and shout,' he said, hoping to shame me into paying up. I laughed.

'Okay. Then we must fight. If I win I will pay you nothing. If you win I will pay you the full fare.'

He was surprised. Rickshaw men are strong. They can take a lot of pain. No one would choose to fight a rickshaw driver if he could avoid it. Naturally, he was very puzzled. He looked me up and down. I was a slightly built, well-dressed gentleman challenging him to a fight.

'You have no chance of winning,' he said.

'You think I have no chance? Come on then, hit me first.'

He didn't do anything.

'Come on! I have to go now. We have to go home.'

Still he did nothing.

'Okay. Defend yourself. I am going to hit you now.'

When I said this he started to dance around with his hands up ready to fight. Now, I didn't want to harm him or hurt him badly. He was a family man and he had to work. I decided that the best place to hit him was his shin. This would be painful but it wouldn't injure him. Also, he wouldn't expect me to aim so low. I bent down and hit out hard. Unfortunately, as he was moving so much, I hit him in the knee which is much more painful. He immediately ran off limping, leaving behind his rickshaw.

'Come back!' I shouted. 'It's finished. I've won. Here's your half fare.' I put the money in the rickshaw and took Margaret's arm. We walked off and left him.

'Were you scared?' I asked her.

'No. I know you well. I knew you would win.'

A little later she laughed. 'You know, when you fight you are like an actor in the opera.'

'It's not strange,' I said. 'Everything a fighter does must have a purpose. Movements must be clean and clear. When kids fight they just throw their arms around all over the place but a true fighter is very economical with his movements. Fighting, like opera, is an art.'

Paying debts

Don't think I am a bad man. Maybe you think I did nothing throughout all the years of the occupation except enjoy myself? But I tell you, God is my witness, without my help some people might not even have survived the war.

One person I helped was Cyril Kotewall. The Kotewalls are a long established Hong Kong family. Later I got to know Cyril's father, Sir Robert Kotewall. It was KF who introduced me to Cyril. This was in the first months after the Japanese occupation. All their money and valuables were in the Hongkong and Shanghai Bank and the bank had closed its doors. The problem was that the Kotewalls were British so the Japanese confiscated everything they had. I had a good friend who worked in the bank. That's why KF introduced Cyril to me. Cyril wanted my help to see if they could get access to their safety deposit box. I had a friend whose younger brother worked for the bank and was responsible for admitting clients to the bank. I said I would help and I pushed Chung to do everything he could. He managed to arrange for Cyril to get his box and because of that Cyril was able to survive the occupation. If I hadn't helped him life would have been very hard. But people have short memories.

Let me tell you about the man whose life I saved. One day, a man called Cheng Yiu-kwong came to me and it was obvious to me he was scared. This Cheng had been the manager of a shop in D'Aguilar Street owned by a friend of mine. One day, during the occupation, he came to visit me. He was very frightened.

'Mr Hui, you must help me,' he said. 'If you don't I am a dead man.'

I asked him to sit down and tell me the story. Cheng had convinced the Japanese owner of a knitting factory – it was called the Red Head Knitting Company – that he could arrange the transportation of a dozen or so knitting machines from Hong Kong to Canton. For this he had received a large sum of money. Suddenly having so much money had gone to his head. He had just spent it. Some men are like that. Money is like a drug for them. They have no control over themselves. The man who had given him the money was after his blood. The gendarmes were after him and if they caught him he was a dead man. His only hope was to raise the money and pay it back. Although I didn't have the money I knew I could raise it by going round my friends and getting something from each of them. I assured him I would do everything I could to help him. So, together, we went to Cyril Kotewall's office in Central.

Cyril, naturally, owed me a big favour for helping to get access to his valuables. I told Cyril the story and asked him to lend me some money. Naturally he wasn't happy to do this. However, I assured him that I would pay him back within a month. I was guaranteeing all the loans with money I expected to make from the sale of one of my properties in Canton. Cyril opened his safe and waved his hand.

'Take what you want, but even if you take everything it won't cover the debt,' he said. I told him I intended to collect from a few other people. So I took all of Cyril's cash and with the help of some other friends we managed to raise the amount. We then paid it back. The owner of the machines agreed to call off the police and that was the end of it. All the loans I arranged for this man I personally paid back as soon as I had the money. So, you see how generous I was. But was I rewarded? It must be my fate. I have done many great favours for many people but maybe only one or two have paid me back. This Cheng was a very tricky man. Sometime after the war I heard he had made a very big commission on a deal – something like $200,000. A very big amount. He was a drapery agent. At that time I was very hard up. Some friends who knew the story came to me.

'Does Cheng still owe you a lot of money?' they asked me.

'Yes. He never paid me back.'

'He has a lot of money these days. He's down at Shek Tong Tsui every night.' When I heard this I went to his office. I asked to speak to him privately. Naturally he knew what I wanted to see him about. When we were alone I looked at him very hard.

'Cheng, I can kill you any minute. You are so lucky you are an old friend of mine. Otherwise I would beat you to hell!'

He apologised and asked me to forgive him.

'I know you are hard up and things are not going well for you. I am a bad man. I have spent every cent I made. I am so weak. I deserve to be punished.' He took out his wallet.

'This is all I have left. I can give you a few hundred dollars. That's all.'

That's the last time I saw Cheng. I never got any more money from him. As for Cyril, I once borrowed fifty dollars from him after the war. That's the only time I ever borrowed money from him. I could have asked for five hundred and he would have given it to me. But that's not my way. I am not a greedy man. I don't ask people to repay everything they owe me. I just ask for what I need.

If I borrow money I always pay it back. Unless I know that someone can afford it. Then I don't. But people who knew I was hard up still didn't lift a finger to repay their debts to me, or try to help me. Even my elder sister. She had left Ho Tim because she could not accept that he had taken a second wife. She had all their joint property in her name. She was a dominating woman. She controlled everything. She left him and went to Canton with her daughter and son. Ho Tim had no job and no income. The hotel was closed, taken over by the Japanese. There was nothing he could do. I don't know how he survived. He was a fat man. Before the war he was prosperous and plump. But over the three years and eight months he shrank and shrank. By the end he was just skin and bone. He made a big mistake when he put his property in her name. She owned everything and she refused to give anything to his concubine. She wanted the concubine to die of starvation. I know this because she told me. Ho Tim sometimes came to me and asked me to ask my sister to send some money to him. He needed the money to eat. Once I advanced him the money, a few hundred dollars, but he didn't like to take it off me. He was a very proud man. I respected him for that. When I was in Canton I would visit my sister.

'Elder sister, your husband is in a bad way. He needs some money so that he can support himself.'

'So that he can support his whore!'

'Sister, he is very thin. There is no flesh on him.'

'His whore can starve to death first!'

'Sister, he is your husband. You are living on his property.'

'You can go to hell! Don't mention his name again in this house. If that's all you want to say you can go home and die!'

'Elder sister! You don't mean that!'

But the fact is there was no love between us any more. I cannot forgive her for that. This was a bitter thing. How can you suddenly stop your love for your own brother? But this is what happened to me. We have a proverb: The two most poisonous things in this world are the sting of the honey bee and the heart of a bitter woman.

Proud men are born to suffer. Ho Tim never once asked me for a loan. How he survived the war years I don't know. I pressed him to take money. After the war he got his job back and after a few months he was doing well again. The fat came back. I knew Ho Tim. I knew his character well. When I asked to borrow money from him later, after the war, when it was my turn to suffer, I asked him for a thousand dollars. He refused me. He offered me fifty. Only fifty. For me it was an insult. I thought, 'Should I refuse it?' but then I thought that even fifty dollars would keep me alive one day – would, at least, pay the taxi fare to the office of another friend that I could borrow from. So I took it. I never borrowed money from him again. But he was a mean man. He could never repay his debt to me. He never tried.

The fact is, I buried his daughter and he never once offered to repay me. My sister was quite comfortable during the war years. She was living off the rent from our paddy fields in our home village and she had some other property in Canton. It is strange that sometimes you can know something and not know it. For many years I never understood what had happened to our paddy fields in our home village. I never saw the ownership documents. My father never asked me to sell them and when he died they weren't among his papers. I didn't think about that then. Later, when I remembered the fields, I wondered about it. I asked myself: 'What happened to those fields? What happened to the ownership papers?' These would have been very simple handwritten documents on very thin rice paper. Now rice paper is very strong and durable but it can also be eaten by worms. I thought all the papers had been eaten by worms. But now I understand. Now I know. My sister had control over the fields. She lived on the rents. What a mean woman my sister was that she should cheat her only brother. I am sure she is rotting in hell! She never sent one cent to her husband in Hong Kong. Soon after I started selling the properties, maybe it was the second or third one – and she saw I was fooling around – she raised the subject of the properties. When the subject was property or money she was a sharp woman.

'Ah Kei,' she said to me one day, 'you are selling off our father's properties. Don't you think you should put aside a portion for your brother? He also has a right to inherit his share of the property.' I felt embarrassed at this. My sister was much older than me so I always felt great respect for her. Also, it was true. I had neglected to think of my brother.

'What do you suggest, elder sister?'

'Every time you sell a property, you should set aside half the proceeds for him.'

She was right. I wanted her to know that I was honourable.

'I will give it to you,' I told her, 'when our brother needs the money, you can give it to him.'

She agreed. And so every time I sold a house I gave her half the amount to set aside for our brother.

Yes. I had a brother, a younger brother. He was mentally retarded. Actually, I took very little notice of him. He was much younger than me. I remember when I was seventeen or eighteen we went for a picnic and he was four or five at that time. Now, I can't explain this but he was my true brother. I know that I was born when my mother was in her mid forties, and even this was considered late. How could she give birth when she was nearly sixty? I can't say. I was too busy with my own life to pay much attention to it. Maybe my mother was also surprised. She was a fat woman anyway. I remember she went to hospital for a few weeks and then she returned with my brother. My brother was born more or less at the same time as my sister's son. Now I don't know if he was born retarded or he suffered brain damage later because there was an incident. When he was six or seven months old, he had what we call *gup ging* – maybe you would call it a seizure or coma or something like that. We believe that if you don't take immediate action the child will die. There is only one way to save the child and that is to draw the blood back to the brain. To do this we must place a cloth soaked in boiling water on his head. The water must be as hot as it is possible to make it. This will cause the child to feel pain and he will cry out. First he will be bewildered or unconscious but then if he cries out he will be saved. That is the first step. The second step is to make the child drink some urine from a young boy. Not all of the urine. When a boy starts to pee we don't use the first urine he produces and we don't use the last part. We just use the middle part. This is supposed to help make sure it doesn't happen again. I remember my sister was visiting my mother at the time my brother had this *gup ging*. She helped my mother put the towels on. The water was so hot that where they put the hot towels the skin bubbled up and peeled off and he was never able to grow hair there. He always looked funny with no hair on the top of his head. Now I don't know if he was retarded before or after this event. All I remember was that he was strong but not very clever. I trained him up with some *kung fu* exercises. Later he became a bit wild. It was difficult to control him. Then he died suddenly about six months before the end of the occupation, when he was about seventeen years old. That's the story of my poor brother.

So what about the money that my sister kept aside for my brother? Did I see it again? How evil my sister was! She never mentioned the money. Never. I never saw it again although it was rightfully mine. Now, I will tell you something about how good I was to her and you can judge for yourself. My sister's daughter, my dear beloved niece, died at this time when she was only eighteen years old. I was heartbroken. I remember I had just sold a house. I stuffed a rattan case full of banknotes and went to my sister's house. I knew enough of my sister to know that she wouldn't spend much on the funeral. I know that she always said that she was short of cash. What about the money reserved for my brother? She said something like: 'Well, that's our brother's money. I don't like to touch it.' So I put the case on the table and opened it.

'Sister, take this and give my niece a good burial. Don't give her a poor common burial. I want her funeral to be splendid.' The best cemetery in Canton in those days was the Moonlight Cemetery. I asked my sister to give my niece a tomb there. When she saw the money my sister gasped.

'Younger brother! It isn't necessary to give me so much money!'

I said: 'Come on sister! Take it!'

There were witnesses to this. Some of our village cousins were there at the house with my sister. I didn't go to the funeral myself. I can't remember why. Perhaps I had to go back to Hong Kong quickly. But later I did go to the cemetery and visited the tomb. It was a good tomb.

Some fights

TODAY I WILL TELL YOU ABOUT A BLOODY FIGHT I had with a Taiwanese interpreter. In those days we called Taiwan 'Formosa'. Formosans could speak both languages because Taiwan had been under Japanese rule for many years. Over fifty years, I think. This interpreter's name was Yee Tang. I had heard of him and maybe he had heard of me. Certainly I knew who he was. All these Formosans were corrupt. This Yee Tang especially had a very bad reputation. It was very dangerous to get on his bad side. He had very good connections with the Japanese army so he could invent any story he liked. He was also well known as a fighter. I remember it was said he was very *ham sup* and if he fancied a girl he would follow her home. Then late at night he would go to that house and bang on the door. He would demand to be let in and then rape the girl. He would threaten to make big trouble for the people inside if they refused him. He was a big drinker and an ugly brute.

One night, late, it was dark and the streets were empty because of the curfew. Of course, I had no problems being out on the streets because I had a special permit. I was walking home when I saw him ahead of me. He was banging hard on the doors of ground floor flats and shouting: 'Open up! Bring out your daughters. I want to fuck your daughters!' He was cursing like that. Now this was in Village Road and I knew most of the people on the street. They were my neighbours. I also was a bit drunk. He didn't notice me because he really was drunk. Then he turned to go up to Phoenix Terrace which was twenty-five steps above Village Road. KF and Cat lived there. He staggered up the stairs and started to hammer on the door of the first house he came to, which happened to be KF's flat. I knew how frightened Cat would be. I got very angry. I sized him up. He was a stocky, stout man of about five foot ten inches. Very tall compared to me. But I am not frightened of tall men or big men. When you are small like me almost everyone you fight is bigger.

I called out to him: 'You bloody drunkard! Disturbing everybody! What are you doing? Why don't you just go home?'

He was surprised. He turned and looked at me. He stared at me a long time, threateningly.

'Fuck off!' he said. Naturally, I got mad immediately.

'What do you mean "Fuck off"!' I shouted. 'You want to fuck? I'll fuck you down here!' I wanted him to come down to Village Road because there was more space there. It was too cramped up on the terrace. He saw me and he must have thought he would have some fun beating up a little fellow like me.

'What kind of fighting do you know?' he asked. He wasn't completely stupid. I laughed and waited till he had come down the steps.

'You ask me what I know,' I said. 'It's better that I ask you. What do you know?'

'I know everything!' he said.

'Good!' I told him, 'I like to fight with people who know about fighting.' I wanted him to understand there would be no favours on my side and I expected none from his side. Now, in a situation like this where I have challenged someone to a fight, I generally ask them whether they want to hit me first or want me to try to hit them first.

'Up to you!' he said.

'Okay! I'll go first!' Even as I was talking I hit him hard on the chest and knocked him to the ground. He was stunned how fast it had happened. He just lay there. Maybe he was trying to clear his head.

'I can't wait all day!' I said. 'It's your turn to try to hit me!' But he still stayed on the ground.

'If you don't do anything I'm going to hit you again,' I warned him.

'Come on and try!' he said and got to his feet.

I immediately struck him again. The first time I had hit him with the open palm of my hand but this second time I hated him so much that I used the back of my hand. I brought my arm up from under his arms which knocked them aside and raked my knuckles against his face. My knuckles are very big and hard. Three or four times a normal man's knuckles. Now this is a very simple movement, very elementary, yet, whenever I used it, I always caught my opponent off guard. It's not easy to defend against, especially from a smaller man like me. I can't go over the arms so I must come in from under them. I hated him so much that I wanted to hurt him badly. He fell to the ground hard. I didn't give him a chance to get up but I stamped down hard on his pelvis. This is a very vulnerable point and it incapacitates an opponent.

'Do you want to fight any more?' I asked him.

He shook his head.

'If you say one word to me now, I will kill you.' I glared hard at him and I meant every word. He knew it.

'Don't kill me!' he pleaded. He knew I was well-trained. He knew I could kill him easily and in fact I was still considering it. But I have a weakness. If someone humbles himself before me my anger disappears immediately.

'I know who you are. You probably want to know who I am,' I said to him. I told him my name. 'Now, I warn you. If I hear that you are continuing to harm people I will search you out and kill you. It will be nothing for me to do that. Next time I won't forgive you.'

Naturally, he checked up and discovered I was the teacher of his own senior officers. He never came back to Happy Valley. God knows I have done many things, I have committed many sins, but indirectly I have helped many people. This incident occurred about a year before the Japanese surrender. This wasn't the only time I had a fight with interpreters.

There were a lot of Koreans and Taiwanese in Hong Kong during the war. They had a very bad reputation. Much worse than the Japanese. I think it's always the way. Servants are always worse than their masters. They were the ones who dealt with both sides – the Chinese and the Japanese – so they had a lot of power and they used this power to squeeze everything they wanted out of the Chinese. Not just money! If they knew a man had a beautiful daughter they would use their position to abuse or even rape the girl. As I say, I had several fights with these people, even though they did me no harm personally. I just hated them.

I smuggle my relative into Hong Kong

L ET ME EXPLAIN ABOUT FONG-JEH. She was a sort of relative. Her surname was Hui and she came from the same village so we were related. You can say she was a native-village sister. She was older than me so I called her *jeh-jeh* – elder sister – or Fong-jeh. Fong was her personal name.

She was just a poor country woman. She was a very good companion to my second sister when she was alive. When my dear sister died she went to live with my elder sister to help look after my niece. Now, my sister didn't pay her a regular salary but she would pay all her living expenses and from time to time – maybe twice or three times a year she would pay her a lump sum as a present.

Now when my niece died my elder sister suggested to Fong-jeh that she should go back to the native village. I think my sister wanted to save money. But Fong-jeh didn't want to go back to her native village. There was nothing there for her. Although people in the country always had food, life there at that time was not so easy. Fong-jeh was very unhappy at the idea of going back to Taam Shan. She talked to me about it.

'There are jobs in Hong Kong. I can be an amah. You are a man with many connections. Can you arrange it for me?'

I could see that she wanted so much to go. As Fong-jeh was so close to our family – she was also a very good friend of my first wife's – I felt I should try to help her. It was impossible to get a permit until we got to Hong Kong. But once there, I could arrange that easily. So the first thing was to talk to the smugglers. I must explain that throughout the war there was a lot of smuggling from Hong Kong up to Canton. Mainly it involved medicines. I can't explain why this was one of the main items being smuggled. All these medicine companies had shops and factories in China. It must be that there was a shortage. The factories couldn't produce enough. The smuggled goods were from medicine shops in Hong Kong that had stockpiled goods. Maybe they could sell it for a higher price in China than in Hong Kong. Another very popular item for smugglers was metal tape for strapping around crates and parcels. Again, I don't understand why this was such a profitable item. Naturally, smuggling was a very risky business. If you were caught there was a big risk that you would have your head cut off. Of course there must have been a lot of bribery.

I knew the man who financed one group of smugglers. I explained the problem.

'How much will you charge me?' I asked him.

'Mr Hui, for any other man I would charge a great deal. But for your sister, I will charge you nothing. You are doing this for your relative, not for yourself. I admire that.' But he told me that he could only take me as far as Tsuen Wan, which at that time was just a small fishing village a few miles along the coast to the west of the Kowloon peninsula. Now it is a big city with a highway connecting it to the main urban area. The world of only fifty years ago has disappeared. In those days there was no highway to Tsuen Wan. There was only a narrow road cut into the side of the hills that fell steeply to the harbour's edge.

We sailed from Canton in a junk and early in the morning we were dropped off at the pier in Tsuen Wan. There, we found some young men with bicycles who agreed to take us to Kowloon. Fong-jeh sat on the back of one of the bicycles and I sat on the back of the other. These were strong country boys and we were not very heavy so although the road went uphill for the first half of the journey we were progressing smoothly.

We had gone about a third of the way when a man on a cycle coming towards us shouted at us to stop.

'You! Where are you going?'

We waved in the direction of the city. I remember he was dressed in the black shiny silk clothes that fishing people used to wear. It is a very hard-wearing cloth. We could all see he was carrying a pistol.

We all got off the bikes. He was a hard man. It was obvious he was a Chinese CID officer. Some Chinese worked for the Japanese in this way. I don't blame them. Everyone had to make a living somehow.

'Where have you come from, eh?'

'Tsuen Wan,' I said.

'Show me your permits,' he demanded.

I patted my bags, 'I have a permit here for myself. But my sister here hasn't got one.'

'Then you must come back with me to the gendarme office in Tsuen Wan.'

'Well,' I said, 'you are Chinese and we are Chinese. I ask you very politely please don't do this. Tell me what you want, I will get it for you. Tell me how much money you want. Or anything else. I will get it for you.'

He just shook his head and waved me away.

'No. You must come to the gendarme office! Let's go!'

But I didn't move. By this time I had moved close to him. We were face to face. I said: 'I won't go and she won't go either.'

He was surprised but I continued talking. 'You know and I know that if we go back it is certain death for my sister. Not for me because I have a permit. But the way I am thinking is this: it is better that you die than my sister.'

I could see he was stunned. He had thought he had full control over the situation. He had the authority and the gun and I was just a slight man. We were both very tense at this moment. I stared at him and he stared at me. Then I continued.

'You can do what you like to try to take us back. You can take your pistol out if you like but I tell you straight, you will never manage it. If you try you will be a dead man. You have no chance. If you don't believe me you can try it. Just try.'

We all stood there frozen for a long time. The man had his back to the steep slope that went down a hundred feet or so to the water. It wasn't a cliff but it was very steep. I would knock him down then go down after him and kill him. I would have to, in case he recovered and came after us.

He thought about the situation for a minute. I could see he was calculating everything. Maybe he understood that I knew something of *kung fu* from the way I was standing. I think he was holding his breath because suddenly he let out a long, deep breath. He was scared. He nodded.

'All right. I don't want your money. Since you are a good brother to your sister. I will let you go.' I could see he wanted to get away as quickly as possible. He tried to hop on to his bicycle. But I wasn't so sure of him. I grabbed him by the arm.

'First, you and I are enemies. But since you have allowed us to go I would like to pay you some money. This is all the money I have but I can get more easily in Hong Kong so you can take this. And here is my card. If you need anything please contact me and I will get it for you. I am very grateful to you.' But he waved away the money. He took my card and we shook hands and then he hopped on his bike again and pedalled off towards Tsuen Wan. We stood for a few minutes watching him disappear. When he was out of sight, both the cyclists whooped with laughter.

'Wah! That was wonderful! That was a real scene!' my cyclist said. 'I have read novels and so many stories that tell of these things. But now I have seen it with my own eyes. He had a pistol but you weren't joking. You weren't fooling. What you said! The way you acted! You are a real hero!'

All the way to Mongkok he laughed and joked about what happened telling himself the story again and again. When we reached Mongkok I attempted to pay him for the ride. He refused: 'No, I have already gained a great advantage from you. What happened today I will tell all my relatives and my friends. You had real guts. But more than courage you had the spirit of a killer. Wonderful. I am so lucky that I was there to see it with my own eyes.'

Later I asked Fong-jeh if she had been scared.

'Yes. I was trembling inside from fear!'

Later she told all our relatives that I was such a fierce and heroic man.

Now, let's go back to the smuggling. There was a man who had a small firewood and charcoal business in Canal Road. He was a short stocky man. His family were fishing people who had come ashore. He used to deliver charcoal, carrying it in baskets with a pole over his shoulder. He wore just shorts and wooden slippers. It is a dirty business. He rented a space on Canal Road from CL Li and in fact Li used to complain that he never had enough money for the rent. After the Japanese invaded business became bad. So this man went into the smuggling business. He had connections among the fishing people and he had a good sense of business so he had a very big advantage. He used to load his boats at Shek O, which is now a very popular beach but then was just another fishing village at the east end of Hong Kong Island. I was told this story by a policeman by the name of Lee who was in charge of Shek O. This man had to pay Lee a certain sum for every boat he loaded at Shek O. One day, he had two boats which he was loading and Lee himself was loading another boat on his own account. Lee's boats of course would be safe as long as they were in Hong Kong waters because he was well-connected but as soon as they sailed north of Hong Kong he had no power. He told me that the three boats were sailing together at night up the Pearl River when a Japanese marine police boat stopped his boat. Somehow this other man's boats escaped and managed to get through without any trouble. I remember Lee saying to me: 'That man is a lucky guy!' It's true, he had a reputation for luck. It was said that he didn't lose one single ship all the time he was a smuggler.

When I heard this story I asked myself: Do you believe in luck like that? Of course not. Luck like that does not exist. This man made his own luck, if you get my meaning. He made so much money during the war that he became one of the richest men in Hong Kong. From charcoal carrier to billionaire! Later he made even more money smuggling goods during the Korean war. But that's another story. And who was this man? Henry Fok. Everyone knows him. He went up in the world and I came down. That is our fate.

Japanese and Chinese

JAPANESE AND CHINESE: We are both Asian people. Our culture has some connections. The Japanese use our system of writing. You might think that we would be very friendly. But it is a strange truth that countries that have borders with each other often hate each other while countries that are distant can be friends. It is a universal human characteristic. Our slang word for Japanese is 'turnip heads'. Maybe they have a slang word for Chinese but if they do I don't know it.

So, during the war, I was well-connected with the Japanese – and I don't mind admitting that I was very proud of my connections. It was one of my pleasures to be so well-connected. But I was never so proud of my connections with the Japanese that I thought they were superior to us Chinese. I was never so proud that I preferred the company of Japanese to my Chinese friends. But there were some Chinese, especially girls, who thought the Japanese were superior and they looked down on us Chinese.

I will tell you one story about a case like this. I had arranged to meet a Chinese friend at the Hongkong Hotel. They served Japanese food. This friend was a smuggler. He had a lot of money – at that time, if you had a lot of money it couldn't be clean money, unless you were like me and had your money in Canton – and he enjoyed dining at the hotel. So, late in the afternoon, I rang the hotel to see if he was there. I wanted to arrange to meet him later. The telephone operator was a Chinese girl but she spoke Japanese because most people calling the hotel would be Japanese. Now, I can't speak Japanese at all. Just a few words. So I spoke to her in Chinese. Her reaction was like this: this man is Chinese so I don't have to show him any respect. She spoke to me in a rough way. Naturally I was furious.

'You damn. . .!' Actually I said something much worse, 'If you dare to stay where you are for the next half hour you are a very brave girl. My name is Hui Shen-kei and I am coming to see you. I know where you are!' She didn't say anything. She realised she had made a mistake.

I went straight to the hotel and went straight to the operator's room. Of course, I knew all the offices in the Hongkong Hotel. I went straight into the room without knocking. There was only one girl there so I knew it was her.

'Are you the one who spoke to me so rudely on the phone?' I demanded.

She was too scared to say anything.

'All right!' I said. 'You are a Chinese like me and you are a girl. If I hit you I would feel ashamed. So, come! We will see the manager!' I grabbed her arm tight and pulled her out of the room into the corridor.

'Let go of me!' she shouted, and struggled to free herself.

'You can never make me let go of you!'

There were staff around us and they looked on in amazement. Some of them knew me.

'Sir!' they protested. 'What are you doing?'

I told them to fetch the manager.

The manager came very quickly and when he saw me he bowed. Like all Japanese he was very polite. I understood that my position was not so good. I had gone into a private part of the hotel without permission. This could not be defended easily. So I pulled out my authorisation papers. He could see immediately I was important. When he saw the big chop of the gendarme office he bowed even lower.

'Can you speak English?' I asked.

With a bit of English and Japanese I explained the whole situation to him. When he understood he went red in the face and pulled the girl aside. Then he smacked her across the face. Not just once, many times. Now, I began to regret what I had done. I felt that she had received enough punishment. She had certainly learnt her lesson.

'Enough!' I stopped the manager's hand. 'Please forgive her. She's just a young girl. She was impolite once. That is all. Please teach her to be polite and I will be satisfied.'

The manager bowed low again and promised to teach her politeness.

Now, just across the road from the Hongkong Hotel was a bar run by one of the Landaus who run Jimmy's Kitchen. The Landaus are Jewish. Maybe they were German. Anyway, it is certain they weren't British. They weren't put in the camps and they were allowed to run their business as usual. But of course the only customers with money were Japanese officers and one or two rich Chinese like me, but generally speaking most Chinese didn't like to mix with the Japanese. I didn't mind because I didn't care about anything except having a good time, and there was one thing that attracted me to Jimmy's bar and that was the girls.

Jimmy's bar had some of the most beautiful girls in Hong Kong. They were Eurasian girls. The Japanese made a point of not putting Eurasians in the prison camps. You can say that was a good thing. My very good friend was a girl called Phyllis. She was beautiful. I knew her before the war. We often passed each other at the Hongkong Hotel. We got to recognise each other but I don't think we ever said anything to each other then. We were what you can call nodding acquaintances. She was a blonde, in fact she looked a hundred per cent European. Before the war everyone I knew considered her beautiful. So when I first saw her in the bar I was surprised to see her there. And when she spoke Cantonese I was a little bit taken by surprise. It was very strange in those days to see someone who looked European speak natural Cantonese. Phyllis worked in the bar as a hostess and naturally the Japanese officers were very attracted to her. This was the only way a girl like her could make a living during the years of the occupation. Naturally the bar did good business. There were five or six girls like Phyllis who worked there as hostesses. They made their money from the drinks they were bought. At the end of the evening . . . well, they were free to make more money that way if they wanted, and they all did. It was normal.

One night I was there having a good time with Phyllis and another girl. It was after midnight and the curfew was on. I was never worried by the curfew. I had a special permit – actually, it was just a letter – that informed whoever read it that I had special permission to be out at anytime of the day or night. In fact I didn't have to go out at all. Just round the corner from the bar was the Metropole Hotel. This was just a small hotel on the upper floors of the same building. One of my students, Kakei-san, rented a room there on a permanent basis and he invited me to use it whenever I liked. I often stayed there. It was very convenient. Naturally I always rang my wife to make sure she wasn't worried about me.

So I was drinking and laughing and joking with Phyllis and another girl. There weren't many people there, maybe three or four. Then another officer arrived and sat in the corner away from us. I didn't take any notice of him. He was just another Japanese officer. But as soon as Phyllis saw him she waved a greeting to him and spoke to me: 'Peter, I must explain to you that I am being kept by an officer and he has just come in. He seems to be a bit angry. I think he's jealous of you. I think he is also a bit scared of you so I don't think he will do anything. After all you must be someone to stay in a Japanese pub after midnight.' She spoke in Cantonese so that he wouldn't hear her. I just told her not to worry. I was used to this. I knew that people didn't know if I was Japanese, Chinese or mixed. They just knew I was somebody and they kept their distance.

After a few minutes the waiter came over with a note from the officer to Phyllis. She nodded to him and spoke to me again. 'Peter, I can't show you this note because he is watching me but he has asked me to go and join him.'

'Okay,' I said, 'you can go but not for another ten minutes. I still want to enjoy some more of your company.'

I can tell you that I liked Phyllis very much and she was a little in love with me too. She often came up to the hotel room after work and spent the night with me. I kept Phyllis for another fifteen minutes and then she went to join her lover.

A few evenings later I bumped into Phyllis and I asked after her man. 'Has he forgiven you?' I joked.

Phyllis laughed.

'He was so angry and jealous. That's why he keeps me. He doesn't like the idea of sharing me with other people. He wanted to know everything about you. He asked me so many questions. I just told him: 'Listen, I warn you. That man is Peter Hui. Don't ever trouble him. If you do cause trouble with him you will certainly find yourself in trouble.''

I liked Phyllis. She was a very nice girl. Maybe you say she was just a prostitute but I tell you if you haven't lived in such times you are not fit to judge. She was a good girl. After the war, she did well for herself. She married an American naval officer.

Torture

I DID SEE THE JAPANESE torture people twice. Both times it was at the old Supreme Court building, which was the gendarmes' headquarters. The first time I saw it I was with Kakei-san. We passed a room where I saw a man stripped naked. A piece of string was tied to his big toes and he was hung upside down on the wall. Then he was whipped. I also saw them turn on a water hose and push the end into the victim's mouth. Naturally no one can stand this for very long. You can't breathe. If you try to breathe you will choke. Naturally the man struggled and then he fainted very quickly.

I can say it disturbed me to see this. I turned to Kakei-san: 'Is this really necessary?'

He saw the effect it had on me. He took my arm and we walked on. 'Not now. Not here. I will explain this to you later.'

It was some days or weeks later that I got an invitation from him to have lunch.

I was a bit nervous. He was a very powerful man. He had never invited me so formally before and he seemed very serious. We had our lunch and then went up to his room.

'Mr Hui, the other day, you were upset to see us torture a man.'

I nodded.

'I must explain to you something. We belong to the political branch. If we find something suspicious we must do everything we can to get all the information we can. If this means we must torture people then we must torture them. This is our training. This is our discipline. If we show any sympathy for our victims it would not be good for us. When we were being trained it was made very clear to us. We must be prepared to torture anyone. Our friends, our relatives, even our fathers and mothers if necessary, even our loved ones. That is our training.'

I nodded. There was nothing for me to say. If I protested too much he might turn against me. I naturally didn't wish to provoke his anger.

I had power only because he was behind me. But torture was not something I could accept.

'But still,' I said to him, 'It is not so good. It's not so human.'

He understood that I was a gentleman. I had no experience of military matters or politics.

'In times of war, we must do many things that are not so human.'

This also was true. We never discussed this subject again.

I saw torture another time. I heard the screams. I turned my head and hurried past the room. These were cruel times.

A fight . . . and a lucky escape

I THINK IT WAS SOMETIME IN 1943. I was drinking with two friends, KF and someone else. I had just come back to Hong Kong with a lot of money in my pocket from selling some of my properties. I was very happy and I insisted on taking them to an expensive restaurant in Tsimshatsui. It was a very exclusive restaurant but I had plenty of money in my pocket. What did it matter how expensive it was?

The girls there were mainly Chinese but there were some Japanese girls and some Eurasians. We went there to drink. In fact we had been drinking a lot that day already. Naturally, some of the girls came to sit with us. They made their money in commissions on the drinks they had and on how much they could persuade you to buy. Of course, if you thought a girl was demanding too many drinks or you didn't like her you could just ask her to leave. When we entered the restaurant we were all in a good mood and we had a few girls join us. One of them spoke some Japanese. We were just joking around and having fun so I started to have a conversation with her in Japanese. I spoke a little Japanese. Not very much but some. Naturally her knowledge of Japanese was much better than mine as she mixed a lot with Japanese officers. When I forgot a word or didn't know a word she laughed at me and she said: 'If you ever meet a Japanese you should stop talking!' I got rather angry at this and stopped joking with her. Really, she was very impolite. Maybe she didn't want to sit with us but she had a job to do. If she didn't want to sit with us she should have gone away. She was very proud. Shortly after this she said something else that was a little insulting to my friend. I think she assumed it didn't really matter what she said as the restaurant was owned by gendarme officers. She thought I would never dare do anything to her. But I felt a rush of anger rise up in me. I scolded the girl loudly: 'You're a Chinese girl and you think you're superior to other Chinese!' Then I was so angry that I slapped her hard across the face. She screamed and ran off crying. I think she must have been frightened by the expression on my face. I can be very furious. Now, still this wasn't so bad. Hitting a woman. It must happen sometimes when people get drunk. You can say I wasn't a hundred per cent right. A man shouldn't hit a woman. My only excuse was that I was seventy per cent drunk. But still, at this stage, everything would have been all right if I had apologised, paid up and left. It would have been a small interruption to the evening and maybe a small lesson to the girl not to be so impolite.

Now, Japanese are very polite people. I have to say that. If you have any problems with the Japanese you must always be very proper and very polite. Then everything will be okay. The manager, who was Japanese, came over to my table and bowed to me and was very polite: 'Yes, Mr Hui? Did the girl do something wrong? If she did I must apologise.'

Now, I didn't say anything at that moment. Inside me I still felt a terrible fury at the girl. Also, although I mixed with Japanese I can say that, psychologically, in some part of my mind, I hated the Japanese. I found I could not control myself. I stood up and hit the manager too. He staggered back a few paces but he didn't fall down. He was a short, stout man. Many Japanese are quite stout. He said nothing then but immediately left. The staff all saw what had happened and seven or eight of them started to approach me. My friends were very frightened and immediately left the table. I too suddenly became aware that the situation was serious. I had hit the manager of a restaurant run by senior Japanese gendarme officers. They would want their revenge. Maybe I should have run. I could have escaped. But that is not my way. I am a *kung fu* hero. I am not afraid to die. I had started a fight. I had to go through with it. That is the discipline of a *kung fu* man. I prepared myself to die fighting.

Very quickly the number of staff increased from seven to over twenty. I could see that they all knew something of martial arts. I was very alert to this. First of all, they started to circle me but when anyone came close I would hit them and then run round to the other side of a table. There was a raised area, a sort of stage, where the band played. There wasn't a band there that evening but the drum set was still up there. I jumped up on to the stage to give myself the advantage of height. They threw a few ashtrays at me but it was easy for me to fend them off. I had the thought of kicking the drum into the crowd of people below me so I gave it a big kick. My foot went through both sides of the drum but the drum itself didn't move. I was very surprised but then I realised that the drum was bolted to the floor. However, they saw I knew how to fight and they backed off a bit. They were not keen to fight me individually. There were some other musical instruments on the stage and I picked them up and threw them at the waiters. I remember the trumpet ended up very bent after I had thrown it. I had calmed down a lot by now. I had no wish to hurt anyone seriously. There were steps up to the stage on either side and I saw that some of the waiters had got up to the stage and I saw that some of the waiters had got up behind me so I jumped back down on to the floor and continued to fight as before. Naturally, they couldn't catch me at all. They stopped to think about how to catch me and they conferred with one another. Finally they came up with a plan and started to form a circle round me. I said to myself: 'You damn silly fools!' I wasn't at all worried because I understood that it doesn't matter how big a circle is, I would still only have to fight one or two people at any one time. But I was too full of confidence and I didn't think it through. When the circle closed in on me they suddenly all jumped on me – just like in American football. There was nothing I could do. Suddenly I was on the floor under a pile of bodies. I am sure there were at least ten bodies on top of me – over a thousand pounds. I thought I was going to be squeezed to death. Then they got up carefully, one at a time. They grabbed hold of me and carried me off to an office at the back.

Now, really, I was so lucky. My friends had managed to contact one of the senior Japanese officers who was our friend. They explained what had happened and the officer phoned the restaurant to say that I was just drunk and nothing must happen to me. After about ten minutes an officer arrived and arranged for me to be released. Reluctantly they allowed me to go. Naturally, I never again went back to that restaurant.

Now, I wasn't aware of this at that time but there were a few other tables of Chinese having dinner at that restaurant who witnessed this event. Many years later, when I was doing my tailoring business, I was introduced to a tailor called Yung Lam. We became quite friendly. The first time we met he immediately recognised me: 'I know you! You are a wonderful hero! I saw you fighting the Japanese at that restaurant in Hillwood Road. You had so many chances to escape but you never tried to run away. You just kept standing there and fighting. Even though you are such a short man, you have the heart of a hero.' Whenever I met him he would tell my friends: 'Look at this man. He is truly a hero. He is greater than any hero in any novel!'

A chicken thief

I WAS IN SHAU KEI WAN VISITING the sergeant of the gendarme office. He was very keen on horse racing. We were talking about horses and gambling when some Japanese soldiers came in dragging a Chinese man with his arms tied behind his back. They brought him into the station and told the sergeant what he had done wrong. I understood from what they were saying that he had stolen a hen or something. The sergeant just nodded and pointed to the kitchen. I realised suddenly that he intended to kill the man. Why else take him into the kitchen? They planned to take him there to chop his head off. It was very strange. The sergeant wasn't angry. It was all very ordinary. I followed them into the kitchen and when I saw I was right I spoke to the sergeant.

'Come on. It seems to me this is a very small thing. Stealing a chicken? In the old days, before the occupation, this would be a petty offence. Not even a crime. Please, I ask you. Don't kill this man for such a small offence.'

The sergeant paused and thought for a moment. Of course he had the power and the authority to kill this man and many people were killed for such a small crime. But I was a senior person too. Maybe he did it out of respect for me.

'All right. Let him go!' he ordered the soldiers. They untied him and waved for him to go. That's how it was with the Japanese. They could kill you or they could let you go. They didn't worry about fining you or putting you into prison. All or nothing. Black or white. The prisoner understood that I had saved his life. He bowed on the ground in front of me and *kowtow*ed. Do you know what a *kowtow* is? That is the way, in the old days, everyone had to greet a senior official. You kneel on the ground and bend forward until your forehead hits the ground. To show strong feelings you can hit your head hard. That's what he did. Two or three times he banged his head on the ground. I said: 'Come on. Don't do this. Go now!' Then he ran off. No one else saw this. Just the Japanese and myself. But God knows. God keeps a record.

How I broke the bank at a casino

IN THE LAST MONTHS OF THE JAPANESE OCCUPATION a number of casinos opened in Hong Kong. One was in a big teahouse in Yaumatei. Up till then the Japanese had forbidden them but now they needed money. The war wasn't going very well and it wasn't so easy to get the money to pay for the occupation. Soldiers needed to be paid. Everyone knew the tide of the war had turned against Japan. There had been defeats in the Pacific. Italy had been invaded, Germany had been defeated at Stalingrad. It was obvious the Japanese would eventually lose.

Anyone with money was welcome to go to these casinos: the Japanese themselves, people who worked for the administration, collaborators, smugglers, visitors from China. Anyone. That's when I broke the bank at one of these casinos. I had just sold a few houses in Canton so I had a lot of money. Now before we went into the casino my friends urged me to be sensible. They knew my character. I was carrying probably about thirty taels of gold. You know, in our traditional way, we didn't have coins, gold or silver coins. Instead, the gold or silver is shaped like a boat or a hat. That's the old Chinese way. But at that time the gold I had was in irregularly shaped lumps each of which had been stamped with its weight by a reputable gold dealer. You could get one-, two-, three-, up to five-tael pieces. Five was the maximum. My friends told me I had been drinking and although I wasn't drunk, it wasn't a good idea to gamble everything. If I carried all my money I might be tempted to bet everything I had. I understood that they were being sensible so I took out my money and split it up. I kept twelve taels to use for gambling. That would be my limit. I gave them the rest to carry for me. At that time it was common for rich people to carry gold on them. By this time, the Japanese military yen was virtually worthless. Gold was used for most large transactions. So we went into the casino and we were welcomed by the management.

I sat down at one of the tables where they were playing *dai sai*. This is a very simple game. There are three dice. The banker shakes them up in a wooden cup and then you bet on 'high', that is the dice total over ten points, 'low' is ten or under. If the dice comes up three of a kind then the banker wins. It's a very simple game. If you win, you win what you bet. Now, I tell you, I am a gambler. And it's a strange thing but I am always very successful at gambling. I took out six taels of gold and placed it all on my first bet. I bet on 'high'. I won. So now I had twelve taels on the table. I bet it all again. Again I bet on 'high'. I won again. Now I had twenty-four taels on the table. Everyone in the casino became aware of what was happening. They stopped what they were doing and came over to watch. I suppose they all thought I must have been a smuggler to have so much money and be so reckless with it. What was I going to do? I could hear them thinking to themselves that it was time to stop. I had been lucky twice in a row. I must lose eventually. The odds were against it. I was enjoying myself thoroughly. What did it matter to me if I did lose? Only six of the twenty-four taels on the table were mine. That's all I would lose. So I doubled up again.

'Wah!' they said. 'You really are a big gambler!' That's what the casino manager said. Everyone was quiet as the man rolled the dice again. Again I bet on 'high'. It was unbelievable. I won again. Now I had forty-eight taels. Almost the price of a good building in Canton. Again I pushed them all on to the table and made my bet. The croupier was sweating a bit now.

'Mr Hui. Maybe you should stop now,' he suggested.

'I don't want to stop! Continue!' I said.

He shook his head in admiration.

'I can't take responsibility for such a large sum. I must ask the general manager first.'

So I told him to get the general manager and in the meantime to give me some brandy. Everything in the casino stopped for about twenty minutes. No one wanted to miss anything. Finally, the general manager arrived.

'Mr Hui,' he said, 'I would like to ask you to take back your bet. You have won a very good sum. Please be satisfied. The fact is if you bet again and win I don't have enough money to cover your bet. Naturally, I can send to another casino for the money and we will get it but my bosses will be very unhappy with me and they will blame me. So, for my sake, could you please do me a big favour and take back your bet.'

What could I do? I knew him and I was friendly with him. He was a close friend of Ho Tim, my brother-in-law. I understood it would not be a friendly act to continue to bet. So I said to him: 'Don't worry. I will stop. No need to explain. But I am doing this as a favour to you and you must remember this favour all your life because I am certain that I will win a fourth time. And although I am taking back my bet I want you to throw the dice again. I would bet again on 'high'. We can see if I would win or not.' He agreed to this so I withdrew my bet. The man with the dice rolled them again and then opened the cup. It was 'high'. Once again I would have won. Everyone standing round saw this. They were all very impressed. I can tell you, they will remember it all their lives.

Now, the fact is I am a good gambler. I understand gambling. If I win, I win a lot but if I lose, I lose just a little. I am a real gambler but I don't like to spend a lot of time gambling. I never bet more than four or five times. Why do most gamblers lose and I win? It is a matter of courage and strategy. I can say that most gamblers only dare to lose. They never dare to win. My way of gambling is this. I divide my money into three or four stakes. Then I bet one stake. If I lose then I bet another. Maybe I will lose four times. Then I am cleaned out. So I finish. I have only lost what I can afford to lose. But if I win then I add the winnings to the bet and bet again. If I win I will double it up again. If I still win, then I will pause and ask myself: is my luck going to stay with me? If I feel lucky I will double up one more time. If not then I will take my winnings and start again with a single bet. That's my strategy. But a loser. What does he do? When he wins he puts his winnings in his pocket. He doesn't dare to double up. But when he loses he doubles his bet to try and get his money back. So they double up when they lose but they are afraid to do that when they are winning. That's why I say they only dare to lose. They don't dare to win.

All the opium in Hong Kong

THREE MONTHS LATER PEACE CAME. The Japanese surrendered. I remember all the soldiers in the street just broke down and cried. Many Chinese took the opportunity to throw stones at them. The Japanese didn't retaliate. I remember some soldiers camped out on the race track. In fact they killed all the horses and ate them. All my racing horses. Victory! Silver Dragon! And all the others. Killed and eaten. What did it matter to me? My father was ill and I started to realise that I was very nearly ruined.

In the last few weeks of the occupation my friends asked me what advantages I had extracted from my Japanese connections. At first I didn't understand what they were talking about so they explained. It seemed everyone was taking over Japanese property. Buildings and flats and so on that were Japanese would have to be handed over to the British or the Americans or whoever took the surrender. So it was of no use to the Japanese to hang on to these possessions. They were signing over ownership of all this property to anyone who wanted them. Girls who were mistresses of senior officers were getting flats and other property. Maybe I could still save myself. I went to see Fuji-san, the abbot.

'Fuji-san. Everyone knows the Japanese will surrender soon. Some of your friends have signed over their flats to their girlfriends. Now, I am short of money. Actually, I don't mind admitting to you, I am ruined. I have been a good friend of the Japanese. What can you do for me? If you don't give it to me, you will have to give it to the British administration,' I said.

'Don't worry,' he said, 'I can help you. You will get something. We have a lot of things stored in the Kowloon godowns. I can get you some of this stock of goods.'

When he said this I remembered that there was a lot of raw opium there. In fact all the raw opium in Hong Kong was stored there.

'Just give me the opium,' I said. 'Forget about anything else, just give me the opium. That will do me fine.'

'I will arrange this if I can,' he promised, 'I don't think there is any problem.'

'I will need a permit so that I can get it out.'

'I'll see what I can do,' he said.

A few days later I called on him and he handed me papers stating that I was the owner of all the opium and a permit to take it out of the government godown.

'Good luck!' he said. I wished him luck too. That was the last time I saw him.

Now, imagine this: I owned all the opium in Hong Kong. We are talking about tons of opium. Just imagine it. Can you believe it? Tons of opium. It was like a wonderful dream. I was near ruin and now I was rich again. Now I was richer than I had ever been before. I can't believe it myself now. What was I thinking of? All I knew was that opium was a valuable commodity. If you owned a lot of opium you must be rich. That was my way of thinking. So obviously I was rich. But the problem is that raw opium is not an easy thing to store. And at that moment everything was collapsing and it wasn't easy to get things arranged. How could I transport it? There were very few trucks. There was little petrol. How could I get into the godowns? The guards didn't co-operate with anybody. There was no morale. For about ten days after the Emperor announced the end of the war there was a state of vacuum. The British and the Americans hadn't yet arrived. Chiang Kai-shek's army was just across the border and everybody expected them to take over and liberate Hong Kong but for some reason they didn't. If they had I am sure I would have been all right. I understand how to deal with Chinese. It would have been a simple matter involving some money. But they didn't. Also I was worried about my father. He was very ill and weak. I had to worry about getting food to eat for my family. I ran around to some friends and arranged five or six empty flats to store the opium. But there was still the problem of transportation. However, I wasn't so worried. I had the papers in my pocket. Everything was legal. The British were a people who respected the law. So when the British took over I waited for things to settle down.

Then, one day, I presented myself at the godown with my papers. I wanted to establish my claim to ownership at the earliest opportunity. Now, the status of opium in those days was that it was legal to buy it through the government monopoly. Perhaps I was inexperienced, a sucker. Perhaps there was some way I could have got hold of the opium earlier. I must have been living in a dream. But what could go wrong? I asked myself. I was the legal owner. I could prove it. Wasn't that enough? I presented my papers to the sentry and he took me to see an officer who also inspected the papers. He was very polite.

'Yes, Mr Hui. Your papers are satisfactory. I accept that you are the legal owner,' he said. 'However, I must inform you that the British administration has confiscated your opium, so I cannot release it to you.'

That is when the dream burst. I was stunned at first. Completely stunned. I had placed all my hopes on the opium. Now I regretted that I had been so greedy. There were a lot of other goods in the godown I could have owned. I could have owned everything. But I had said 'Just give me the opium!' The words started to haunt me. I was nearly broken in two. I had no money. I had spent it all.

Now my father was dying. He had always been a strong drinker and he suffered badly from gout. At the end he couldn't even move his legs. He became unable to control his functions. I had to pay for his medical expenses. For the very first time in my life I had to worry about how to earn a living and how to get money. Food prices were unstable again and there were big shortages. The Americans had to bring in rice on their ships. If they hadn't, everyone in Hong Kong would have starved to death.

A few weeks after the surrender my father did die and I had to pay for his funeral expenses. It was then that I sold that jade that I regret so much losing. I was so worried that I couldn't sleep. I would roll from side to side all night worrying about how I could cope. I had to pay the hospital bills, buy a coffin. I even had to worry about how I could afford to buy the incense sticks for my father's funeral.

In fact I had no money to pay for all these expenses. I owed the doctor, the hospital, the coffin maker. I didn't buy the best quality coffin. Just a medium quality one. I even owed the man who sold me the incense sticks. They all trusted me and in fact I was able to pay them back within a month. I still had a little property but I knew that I wouldn't get much money from that. I calculated that our average monthly expenses at this time were about seven or eight taels of gold. I had six children by this time. I had no support from my wife's family. They were in Canton and they had their own financial problems. So I went up to Canton to sell my last piece of property. This was a large godown about the size of three playing fields, well placed between the railway station and the river. It earned a lot in rents but these weren't enough for our needs. Maybe it was possible to live on less than I spent, but once you have been rich like me it is impossible to control your spending. It went through my hands like water. I sold the godown in *dai yeung,* that was the name of the Chinese currency. I changed this at a loss into Hong Kong dollars. I calculated that I had enough to pay off my father's funeral expenses and then support me for about two-and-a-half months. It never occurred to me to ask my father for the deeds to the land in our home village. We had three or four hundred acres. I don't know what happened to the ownership deeds. If I went back to my native village perhaps I could have got some elders to say that the land belonged to my father but of course they didn't know if I was the true owner of the land. If I had my deeds and the Communists gave me back this land I would be a millionaire again. But it's not worth thinking about this. During the war we did hear that the large house we owned had been pulled down and all the bricks sold. One of my clan sisters told me this but I just said: 'Let them go ahead. These are hard times and they are all poor.' I knew we had no intention of going back to live in the house. Why should they not get some profit from it? So I sold my last properties in Canton. Now, I was stripped raw. I had nothing. Not even my father. I still hoped I could somehow succeed in overcoming the problems and get back on my feet. I was a clever young man. I was only thirty-one years old. I knew all the rich people. What could stop me? I had no doubts it would come right in the end.

The summer the war ended

T HE EUROPEAN WAR HAD ENDED. The Americans were getting closer and closer. Even the Japanese knew it. We all knew it was the end.

And for me too it was the end. I had had three years of fooling around. Now it was over. Peace would come and normal life would start again. I wasn't very worried. I would have to work. Something would happen. I had many friends. I was still young, only thirty-one. I was intelligent. I would get involved in some business. But it was all very uncertain.

Margaret and I had been together for two years. I tell you truly, I loved her more than I have loved any other woman. I have loved many, each in their own way. But Margaret was special. And I know that she loved me too. But I couldn't afford to keep her any more. I had a wife and six children to look after. I told her I couldn't marry her and that I was giving her permission to go after anyone else she wanted. It happens that there was a young man who was very much in love with her. Sometimes he was a guest at my dinner table. They were from the same district. They left Canton to get married. Her husband was a man with a lot of courage. He was a man like me. He depended on himself. He was not a triad but he was involved in a lot of shady business: smuggling and so on. You can say he was a sort of gangster.

The Japanese had surrendered but the British still hadn't returned. What was going to happen to Hong Kong? Chiang Kai-shek's army was not far away. There were rumours that he would seize Hong Kong and take it back for China. There was a lot of excitement. Also some fear. There was not much food left. People were hungry again. Then the American navy arrived. People rushed to the waterfront to see them steam in. So Chiang Kai-shek had decided not to take Hong Kong back. Then there were rumours that the Americans would take over and then there were other rumours that the Americans would hand Hong Kong over to China. But eventually it became clear that the British were back in control. People had different feelings about that. Some were pleased. Some weren't.

Everyone liked the Americans. They came with rice and for a while everyone got rations of rice from the ships. Every day there were long queues at the dockside. Then sometime in September there was a big victory parade. We watched the soldiers march by. We didn't know what to think. It was a time of strong feelings. Excitement. Change. Peace again. But there were no jobs still. It wasn't so easy. And these big Americans with their loud voices acted as if they owned Hong Kong. They had plenty of money.

Then came October tenth. This was the day that the Kuomintang celebrates the October Revolution that brought down the Qing dynasty in 1911. Naturally we all had a big celebration. This was a day that we Chinese could feel proud of. I was drinking in the bar at the Hongkong Hotel. I was with KF and Li Ping-wah. The streets were crowded with people. There was no time to arrange official events so everybody went to the streets to celebrate. I remember on that day there were over seventy ships in the harbour: destroyers, battleships, supply ships, aircraft carriers. They were all flying flags. There were sailors everywhere. All the restaurants and street stalls were crowded with sailors having a good time. There were firecrackers. I remember we bought strings of firecrackers and lit them and threw them to the ground. Everyone was doing the same. The noise was wonderful. This was in Pedder Street, right in the middle of Central district. There was no traffic. More than half the crowd were sailors. They were also lighting firecrackers and throwing them all over the place. Everyone was happy. Setting off rockets. Having fun.

Suddenly, we saw that a crowd had formed at the side of the road. Something was happening. There was a rickshaw man and an American sailor. The sailor was sitting in the rickshaw and he was holding a towel around the rickshaw puller's neck. He seemed to be pushing and pulling him. No one knew what was happening. I remember it was a warm day and the rickshaw man had no shirt on. I suppose it was his towel that he had over his shoulder so that he had something to wipe his face from time to time when the sweat got in his eyes. Maybe the American thought it was funny to treat the man like a horse.

The crowd was quite thick and we were on the outside trying to see what was happening. Naturally it wasn't any good to jump up as a lot

of the people in the crowd were tall sailors. So I bent down and twisted
and turned my way through the legs until I got to the front.

'What's happening? I asked.

'The rickshaw man is refusing to take the sailor,' someone told me.
Now everybody was happy and this seemed like a small thing. Maybe it
was a communication problem. So I went up to him thinking that I
could interpret for them.

'Why are you treating this man like this?' I asked. But the sailor just
ignored me. I felt insulted. My good mood immediately left me.

'If you want to mistreat this man then you must fight with me,' I said.

This time the sailor looked at me. He was surprised.

'Come on!' I said. 'Come and fight!'

I think he was drunk. Some people get mean when they get drunk.
Maybe he wasn't very intelligent. Anyway he saw I was challenging him
and maybe he wanted to have a fight so he got out of the rickshaw. I
saw he was a big man, over six feet tall. He didn't say anything. Naturally
I backed off a few feet to give myself some room. He didn't smile or joke.
I think he was puzzled. I was so small and he was so big and yet I was
challenging him to a fight. To him I was just a small, very slight,
well-dressed Chinese man.

'Okay,' I said to him, 'You had better get ready because I am going to
knock you down!' So he lifted his arms like a boxer. I suppose he was
wondering to himself how I could knock him down. I showed him. I
bent down suddenly and with one arm I grabbed his lower legs and with
the other arm and my shoulder I pushed him hard backwards. It was so
sudden that he fell back hard and I heard his head crack on the road. I
stood up and waited to see what he would do. He lay back for a few
minutes and shook his head. He rubbed the back of his head. It must
have hurt.

'Come on!' I shouted to him. 'Get on your feet and we'll fight again.'
There was a big crowd watching us. I suppose they were all surprised
and amused to see such a short Chinese fight with such a big American.
But with *kung fu,* size is not the main thing. Speed and knowing where
to hit are the key points. The big American got to his feet and I could
see he was angry. He had lost face.

There were at least two or three hundred people in the crowd and
most of the people at the front were American soldiers. The Chinese

who wanted to see were elbowed out of the way. They were too small to see over the sailor's shoulders. There were some kids there and they crawled through the legs of the soldiers to the front. At the back of the crowd people shouted: 'What's happening?' and the kids shouted back: 'He's knocked down the American sailor. The sailor has hit his head,' and so on.

The sailor got up and came towards me punching. But I was too quick on my feet. He couldn't hit me. My main worry was that the other sailors in the crowd might impede me or crowd me in but they didn't. It was a fair fight. Once I had knocked him down I wasn't so angry with him but I knew that I must knock him down again and control him otherwise the fight would go on too long. If I just dodged his punches I would never win.

There is a *kung fu* movement called 'A Buddhist Monk Exposes his Cloak to the Sun'. When the sailor came towards my left I ducked low and chopped upwards so that I hit him in the side of the ribs just below his arm. Naturally this made him stagger to the other side. This blow requires strength and you need to be well-trained to get the timing and the angle right. If you hit too early or too late in the movement the strike loses its power.

He came towards me. I circled away so that he was on my left side. Then he moved in to punch me. I dropped low and then chopped upwards. I kept using my right hand. It is very difficult to defend against an attack like this from below. I repeated this tactic seven or eight times. By this time the fight had drifted across to the other side of the road. We had worked down towards the tram tracks on Des Voeux Road. Everyone was very surprised that I could simply hit him again and again in the same way. But although I knew I was hurting him he was a strong man and he kept coming towards me. I was beginning to get impatient. I decided I must knock him down again. So I decided to use a *kung fu* trick.

As his legs weren't close together I couldn't knock him down in the same way as I had done before. This time, when I ducked, instead of hitting him, I grabbed hold of his left leg and pulled it up while, at the same time, I pushed hard against his chest. He lost balance and fell over. This time I fell on top of him. I immediately changed my hand position and forced his chin back. He tried to twist and turn but because of my position I was able to keep him firmly in this position. He grabbed hold of my neck with his hands and tried to strangle me. But it is not so easy to strangle someone if you don't know how to do it. You can't do it by squeezing the whole neck. I can demonstrate this easily. If I put an egg in your hand you won't be able to squeeze and break it, even though it is such a weak thing. Now when his hands came round my throat I suddenly realised what I had to do to end the fight quickly. I was pushing his chin down with my left hand so my thumb was on the right of his throat. If it had been the other way I could easily kill him. The left hand side of the throat is much more vulnerable than the right. The windpipe is on the left and the gullet is on the right. I quickly squeezed the right side of his throat. One squeeze and he collapsed. He went limp. I didn't dare to keep squeezing for long. I didn't want to hurt or injure the man. I released him.

'Do you want to fight again?' I asked.

He shook his head. 'No!' he rubbed his neck. I knew it was painful as this is a weak point. The problem was I was still lying on top of him and I was worried he might be tricky and try to hit me as I got up. So I grabbed his arm and turned it and pushed him strongly to one side as I levered myself to my feet. In fact he had no fight left in him.

By this time my blood was hot. Fighting does that to me. I shouted to the crowd: 'Okay. Does anyone else want to have a fight? Come on. I'm here. You can come and fight me!' Nobody dared. I saw three or four of his friends pick the man up and carry him away. He was hurt and very tired.

I stood there for a while with my friends. The crowd slowly dispersed. We decided to go down to Wanchai to continue our drinking and eating. There weren't any trams. It was several months before the trams started operating again. We went back to the line of rickshaws in Pedder Street and we each got into one. When we got to Wanchai the rickshaw driver and his two friends all refused to take our money.

'You have done a lot for me!' he said. 'I am the one who was being pushed around by that sailor.'

Even the government needed cash

I WASN'T THE ONLY ONE that was short of money. Even the government was short of money. When peace came and the British returned to Hong Kong, they didn't have enough cash to get the economy going again. So what did they do? I'll tell you.

I have already told you that one of the most profitable businesses during the war was medicine: Tiger Balm, Tse Ku Tsui and all the others. All of these medicine companies had so much money that they all speculated by buying up Hong Kong $100 notes. They could buy $100 notes for thirty or forty dollars. Why? Because $100 was too big. No one had any change for it. It wasn't easy to use such big notes to buy everyday things.

All the medicine companies had large, imposing mansions on the Long Bank Road in Canton. That's the road that goes along the side of the river. It's the best area in Canton. This is a fact. When things go badly, the medicine business does well.

So the British government approached all the owners of the big medicine companies for money to restart the economy. The home of the owner of Tse Ku Tsui was near Victoria Park opposite the polo ground. One of the younger sons of the family told me this story personally. One day, shortly after the war was over, the government sent a lorry to their house to collect all the notes they had. How many did they have? No one knew. Not even the owner of Tse Ku Tsui himself. He had sixteen trunks full of one-hundred-dollar notes. Millions upon millions of dollars. Just sitting in their house. How many hundred-dollar notes can you put in one trunk? Imagine it. That was just one company. The government went to all the medicine companies. That's how they got the cash to start up again after the war.

Margaret truly loves me

ABOUT A YEAR after I last saw her, I heard that Margaret Ko was back in Hong Kong and working as an assistant in the Arts Tailor shop run by Mr Kwan. Before the war I often had my clothes made by him. He was well known as a fashionable tailor for the rich. His tailor shop faced on to the entrance to Ice House Street. At that time I had some business connections in Henry House so I often passed by the shop. Although I knew she worked there I never stopped, or even looked to see if she was there. You can't let the past keep a hold on the present.

So, Margaret often saw me pass by the shop. She had asked her friends to contact me, to tell me she was working there. Her friends told me that her husband had disappeared. Later she had heard he had been killed. Where? How? Why? She didn't know. Those were turbulent times. Now she had to work for a living. I also heard that one of Mr Kwan's friends and customers was chasing Margaret but that she was refusing to have anything to do with him. These mutual friends told me Margaret was miserable that I was ignoring her. But what could I do? I was barely earning enough to get by. How could I marry her? How could I start up our relationship again? Better to forget it, I told myself.

Now one of these mutual friends was a well-known underworld character. He was a contract killer. I knew a lot of people in that circle at that time. This man was Wong Kum-choi. He and I were good friends. Actually, I can tell you a very funny story. Wong was quite famous at this time because of a job he had been hired to do. There was an opera star in Canton. A very famous opera star. You can still find his records if you look for them in the music shops. He was a famous singer but not yet at the top of his fame. He was having an affair with one of the concubines of a wealthy businessman. It is very common for opera stars to have affairs with the wives of rich men, especially if they are not the favourite wives. In this case the rich businessman got to hear of it and was furious, so he hired Wong to kill the star. Now Wong was a clever man. He wasn't just a rough man who relied on his strength and courage.

He was a cool man. He waited until the opera star was in the middle of a song and then he stood up, took out his gun and shot him. Right in the middle of a performance. It caused a wonderful scandal.

Everyone knew Wong had done it. Several of my friends told me. In fact Wong himself told me. Now this is the funny part of the story. In fact Wong missed. He only injured the opera star. As a result of the publicity, the singer became richer and more successful than ever before. So actually he did the opera star a big favour!

Wong was never caught. One day he came to see me at the hotel.

'Margaret still loves you,' he said. 'How can you be so cruel not to go and visit her? She wants to talk to you.'

'That's all finished with.'

'Whenever she sees me, she asks me if I ever bump into you,' he continued. 'She asks me if you are angry with her. She asks me why you never go to see her. She sees you passing by but she's too embarrassed to come out and call after you.'

Eventually I gave in. So one day I went into the shop.

There was a silence as we stood looking at each other. There were too many things to say. This wasn't the right place or the right time.

'When do you finish work?'

'At six.'

'I'll be at the Gloucester Coffee Shop.'

She nodded and I left.

When we met we talked. We talked about everything. We talked about the past, the future, the present. I told her I loved her. I told her I would always love her. I told her I knew she loved me. That was very clear to see. I told her I was broke. I had to struggle to support my family. I had another baby. Now I had five or six children. I must be very potent. Sometimes it seems that every time I make love I make a baby. Margaret told me she couldn't have a baby. A doctor had told her she had some sort of problem. Something about her tubes being too deep. She had told me this before. I could have married her and she wouldn't have given me more children. That didn't worry me. I had so many children. Margaret cried as we talked. She kept trying to hold my arm, my hand in hers. 'It's useless to dream,' I told her. 'I am broke. I can't afford to keep you. In the end it will only cause you more pain. If I start up with you again it would end with you hating me. I can offer you nothing.'

The fact is, the only thing that counts is money. Without money, life is full of hardship and who can stand that for a long time? I was very clear in my own head and I was determined not to change my mind. Margaret clung to me and cried and did everything she could to make me change my mind.

'Margaret,' I said, 'I know that someone is chasing you. He has asked Mr Kwan to help him attract your interest. I also know that you have been ignoring him. Don't be silly. He's a rich man. As far as I know he is a kind man. He can give you a good life. He loves you very much. You should get to know him. If you like him you should marry him. Then you will be happy.'

I had been told about this admirer. Mr Kwan told me himself later. His friend did spend many hours in the shop chatting and making himself pleasant. Eventually Margaret realised there was nothing left between us. She accepted his invitations and not long after I heard they got married.

But that is not the end of the story. One day I was walking in Central when I became aware of a car slowly driving behind me. I looked round and saw it was a Rolls-Royce but I couldn't see who was inside because the glass was darkened. So I looked at the number plate. Then I understood. It was a well-known number. I knew then that Margaret was inside the car and she wanted me to know she was looking at me. This happened not just once but several times.

Truly she did love me and I did love her too. Money and happiness. It's not easy to have true happiness without money. Later I heard she had seen some specialists and they had corrected her problem, and she finally had three or four children.

Her husband was very good to her and to her brothers. He employed one and helped the other to finish his education in America. I am sure that Margaret will say to me now that I was right. I did her a big favour. If she is still alive she will still remember me. She will think of me until her very last hour.

The Shan Kwong Hotel

THIS WAS THE WORST TIME OF MY LIFE. I had no money. Not a cent. I had a wife and six children to support. Where could I get money? As I prayed over my father's coffin in the graveyard, I prayed for help. I asked God to be merciful to me as I also was a generous and merciful man. I had helped others in the past so I asked God to help me too.

How I survived the next few months I cannot tell you. I don't know how. I sold everything I could sell and I borrowed everything I could borrow. It was a hard time. I can't even think of this time at all. It is all black in my memory.

It took many months before Hong Kong slowly began to recover. It wasn't so easy. If you had some connection with the government and you were involved in some essential business then the government helped you to set up again. If you had run a taxi service before the war then it lent you the money to buy new taxis and to get a garage space fixed up. The bus and ferry companies were the same. If you were in the construction business, and the government knew you, then it was easy to get the sites you wanted at a very reasonable price. But that didn't help me. Naturally I spread the word that I was desperate for money. I told all my friends. I told everyone I met. I just hoped that in this way I might be given a job that I could do. But everyone had the same problem. These first months after the war were just as bad as the war years for people without money.

One day, I was invited to meet someone who used to be wealthy, but like me he had been ruined during the war years and he was now working with a gang of cheats. So I went and talked to him and the result was an invitation to join the gang. I knew a lot of rich people. I could easily induce them to invest in the gang's fraudulent schemes. Or I could tell them who would be a good target. I told you, it's very important to know who will accept being cheated and who will try to get revenge. You must know the character of the person you intend to cheat. I listened to the offer and then I said I would have to think about it.

I thought about the offer very seriously. They were talking about a lot of money. I talked it over with my wife. Something serious like this has to be discussed. Eventually, I came to the conclusion that there were two things I should be worried about. I didn't care about my name and I didn't care that I would be cheating people. But I was worried that they would cheat me too. Also I was worried that if there was a disagreement and I left them then they might try to kill me because I knew too much. So the next time I saw them I said I would do it but only on condition that they gave me $20,000 in advance. I think they were a bit surprised. They too said they would have to think it over. In the end nothing happened. I think they too were scared that I was going to cheat them. Maybe they thought that I was the same as them.

So I was still struggling to pay the rent and earn enough to feed my children. We decided that one way to take care of our basic needs was to let out one of the rooms in our flat. So we put out a notice that we were looking for a sub-tenant. Happy Valley is a nice area and it wasn't difficult to find someone to take the room. Our new tenant was an elderly man, nearly sixty. He was quiet and he had no bad habits. I often spent an hour or so in the evenings talking to him. He knew my situation well. One day we were talking he said to me: 'Mr Hui, you have some experience in the hotel trade. How would you like a well-paid job?' It turned out his sister was the wife of Mr Tai Tung-pui, a very rich man closely connected with the Ho Tung family. I knew of Mr Tai by reputation but I had never met him. He belonged to the generation older than mine. He was a close friend of the famous philanthropist, Tang Shiu-kin. My tenant told me that Mr Tai owned the Shan Kwong Hotel in Happy Valley. Naturally I knew it well. I walked past it several times a week. It wasn't a big hotel. Just a three-storey building. The problem was this. When the Japanese invaded it had to shut its doors. There was no business. All the staff left. Mr Tai himself went up to Canton to spend the war years there. However, the doorman of the hotel did not have any money or anywhere to go to. So he stayed at the hotel. After a while he came to realise that he could make a little money renting out rooms to Japanese officers who wanted to have a 'happy time' with girls. So, the doorman opened up the hotel again and it was soon known as a place where officers entertained girls. I think it was also a brothel. He hired more staff and soon made a lot of money. A fortune. Through his connections he arranged for the hotel ownership to be put in his own name. Now the war was over, Mr Tai wanted the hotel back but the doorman refused to hand it over. Mr Tai couldn't go through normal legal channels to get it back because the law and order situation wasn't so settled. Everything was still managed by the military authorities. Also, it was possible he might lose the case. The hotel was now registered in the doorman's name. Tai Tung-pui was a gentleman, he wasn't able to handle a situation like this. He wanted to get rid of the doorman but he didn't want to get involved with triads. He had tried offering the doorman several thousand dollars – a lot of money in those days – but the man had refused. So Tai Tung-pui asked his friends and relatives if they knew how he could solve the problem. My sub-tenant suggested that Mr Tai would be happy to employ me as manager of the hotel if I could get rid of the doorman. Naturally I was very happy to accept the offer.

I met Mr Tai Tung-pui at the hotel and he agreed that I could be manager of the hotel if I could get rid of the doorman. The doorman was obviously not happy to see me. But to start with he didn't care. He was in a strong position and he made it clear to me that he had no intention of leaving. So I thought about the problem. What was the best way to do things? Naturally I would have had no problem throwing him out into the street if I wanted – but then he might go to the authorities or he might have triad connections. I needed to solve the case once and for all.

I knew that he certainly had triad connections. Anyone dealing with girls in this way must have good connections with both the triads and the police. If he went to the triads then the problem would become more serious. But I happened to know the leader of the local triad. Either the triad gang would support me or they would support the doorman. That was the only way to solve problem.

The triad gang that controlled most of Happy Valley was known as the Fierce Tiger Group. The leader of the gang was sometimes called 'Tiger'. He was very smart, very clever. How did we meet? Ah! It was before the war. I was with some friends and we had gone to a bawdy house. We were drinking and chatting with the girls when one of them made a comment that was a bit insulting to one of my friends. I didn't think twice. I just slapped her face. The girls were furious and the mamasan started to scream and shout at me. Now everybody knows that a brothel must be protected by someone: whether it is the police or a triad group. This is common sense. So I said to the mamasan: 'Shut up your screaming and go and get your protectors. Tell them Hui Tak-kwong is here. He has hit one of your girls but he is not a coward. He can fight men as well. He will not run away. Go and call your protectors and give me a drink while I am waiting for them.'

'You wait and they will teach you not to slap girls!' the mamasan said and went to call her protectors. Naturally my friends were scared.

'Now, don't worry!' I told them. 'You can go. This has nothing to do with you. I will stay and sort out this business!' So they went and I stayed. Time passed and no one came. After thirty minutes my patience was gone.

'Where are your damned protectors?'

The mamasan had nothing to say.

'I am not a coward but I can't stay here all day,' I said. 'I'm going. If you want to find me, I work at the Hongkong Hotel. You can find me anytime.'

And so I left.

'Wait, you haven't paid for the drinks.'

'That's your business,' I told them. 'You were rude to my friends and you have kept me waiting here for half an hour.'

Sometime later, I was approached by an associate of Tiger's. He asked me if I wanted to meet his boss. I said I was very happy to do so. Why not? So we met for dinner one evening. We got on well. He knew of me. When he'd heard my name at the brothel he had just laughed and sent nobody. He knew it would damage his reputation if his fighters couldn't defeat me. So, after that, we met from time to time. When the Japanese occupied Hong Kong all business in Central district closed up. But there was still some business in Happy Valley. This was a comfortable area where many wealthy people lived. Naturally, where there are wealthy people, there must be people serving them: shops, laundries and so on. So triads can also make some money too. Tiger took his group from the Gough Street area to Happy Valley.

So now, I went to talk to Tiger. I explained the problem of the doorman.

'It is true that he pays us and we have been protecting him,' he told me. 'But if you want to take over the hotel I will be on your side. What do you want me to do?'

'Just tell him to leave the hotel and don't make any trouble for us. I can deal with the rest.'

'That's easy to do.'

So the doorman had no choice but to go. As he was leaving I saw he had a big bundle of towels and sheets and so on. He still didn't understand about me. He thought I was just a small man who had used my connections with the triads to get him out.

'What's that?' I said. I confronted him face to face. 'You won't take one thing from this hotel. If you try to take anything I warn you I myself will beat you to death. Don't think I couldn't do it!' Naturally he didn't dare to take anything. All the other staff left immediately. They understood that a new manager must start everything fresh.

Mr Tai was amazed. 'Only four days and he's gone!' he said. 'Wonderful!'

Getting new staff was no problem. In fact Mr Tai had a lot of relatives that he needed to help so he employed them in the hotel. I was the manager. Now I didn't need to worry about money. My sub-tenant understood the situation and after a few months he left and got a room in another flat. He was a nice gentleman and, naturally, I will always be grateful to him.

Now let me tell you about the hotel. It was three storeys high and built in the side of the hill so it had two entrances: one on the ground floor to the hotel and one in the basement area where the restaurant and kitchen were. On the first floor there were seven or eight rooms and on the second floor there were another two or three rooms and another large room that I sometimes used as a restaurant area when we were full downstairs or else as a place where customers could come and play mahjong.

I knew a lot of rich people and naturally many of them owned horses. As the Shan Kwong was near the race course it was natural that we soon became a sort of club for the rich. Men would entertain their families at the Jockey Club but when they wanted to have fun and fool around they came to the Shan Kwong Hotel. Our restaurant was not very big so it was quick to fill up and a full restaurant is a noisy place. We Chinese like noise. It is more joyful than silence. So the rich people enjoyed coming to the Shan Kwong. If they wanted to have a happy time they could rent one of the rooms easily. If people saw them come in to the hotel they would think they were going to the restaurant. It was easy for them, when they were leaving the restaurant to go up to the main entrance and, when they were out of sight of the people in the restaurant, they could quickly slip upstairs. Mostly that's what our rooms were used for. If wives wanted to contact their husbands they would ring round all the top-class hotels. But they would never think of contacting us. We were a second class hotel. But, in fact, I set the rates at just a little below the rates of the top-class hotels. Why? Because our customers were all rich and because we were the only hotel in Happy Valley. There was no competition.

So now I was making a lot of money. Not just from the salary. I had two shares in every department so I got a share of the tips and also I got a return commission from the kitchen, from the food suppliers. I also made money in another way. It often happened that three friends would need a fourth person to play mahjong. Naturally if they had the idea to play mahjong earlier they would arrange for a fourth person but many people are like me. They just take things as they come. If they want to do something, they want to do it immediately. Our staff were always happy to encourage our customers to play mahjong because then the tips would be bigger. Why? Look at it this way. If you eat dinner and the bill is $100 then you will leave a $10 tip. If you have been playing mahjong and you win $1,000 then you will be happy to leave a $100 tip. So the staff often tried to encourage customers to play mahjong. Rich people like to bet big amounts. Otherwise it isn't exciting for them. So they would ask me: 'Mr Hui, please can you come and play mahjong with us? We need a fourth person.'

'I am not a good player,' I told them. This is true. I am not a good player. I don't have the patience to play mahjong for too long.

'Please, Mr Hui. Do us a favour.'

'I can't afford to play with you,' I said. 'You are rich. I am not rich.'

'You can take the money out of the till!'

'What? You want me to steal from the hotel?'

'We were just joking Mr Hui. We will finance you. If you win then you can pay back the amount you started with. If you lose it, it doesn't matter.'

So I would play with them. Every month my winnings in this way were more than my salary.

Mr Tang Shiu-kin, who later became a big philanthropist, was a regular customer at the hotel. He came two or three times a week.

I had first met him before the war. KF had persuaded me to go to a cocktail party hosted by Mr Tang. I went reluctantly. Most of the people there were very conservative and they were older than me. I knew I would not enjoy a party like that. But KF insisted and I promised to go for ten minutes. I remember I told him: 'If you want to stay longer that's your decision but after ten minutes I am leaving.' I had better ways of having fun. So KF introduced me to Tang Shiu-kin and we had a drink together. We both drank brandy and he toasted me. Then, while I was there at the party, I saw Mr Tang circulate around his guests and with each group he had a toast. In the time I was there I saw him finish eight or nine glasses of brandy. He was like me. He knew how to drink.

Now, one day I had to confront Mr Tang. You must understand that in any restaurant the most important place is the kitchen. No manager will allow a customer to go into a kitchen. One day I saw Mr Tang get up from his table and walk directly to the kitchen door. I followed him in.

'I know that you are a good friend of Mr Tai, the owner,' I said. 'I hope I have served you well. Why do you need to come in here to look? I am sure you understand the kitchen is barred to customers.'

He just nodded amiably. 'I'm sorry,' he said. 'I just wanted to make sure the cook has our order.'

'If you have any problems you can come to me.'

That was all we said. He went back to his table. Maybe he knew who I was. Why not? Everyone gossips. Sometimes when we talked there was a look in his eye that said: I know who you are.

Sir Robert Kotewall also came from time to time, but not to the restaurant. He was one of the most famous people in all Hong Kong at that time. I think his family was Parsee but he spoke and wrote fluent Chinese. He was a very intelligent and well-educated man. He was also at this time quite old. I remember the first time he came he asked me to show him round so that he knew where all the rooms were. He is the only man I ever arranged girls for. Everyone else had to make their own arrangements. Even Sir Robert often made his own arrangements with high-class girls. He would telephone me and ask me to arrange a room for him. That way he didn't have to stay in the entrance. He could go straight up to the room. Since he was the father of my friend Cyril, I was happy to do small favours like this for him.

How Mr Tai and Mr Tang were both saved by a piece of jade

N OT MANY PEOPLE KNOW THE STORY of how Tai Tung-pui and Tang Shiu-kin escaped death. Mr Tai told me the story himself when I asked him about it. It was in December 1941 when the Japanese invaded. The Japanese army crossed over the narrow gap between the mainland and the eastern end of Hong Kong Island. Then, instead of coming straight down the north coast of the island, they went to the south and then cut back across the middle of the island at Wong Nei Chong gap, just above Happy Valley.

When the Japanese invaded most people expected the harbour waterfront to be a battleground. Actually it was very safe.

There was a very rich man called Fung who decided that the safest place to stay would be at his villa in Blue Pool Road, which had a strong wall all the way around it. He invited a few of his close friends to stay with him. Among his friends were Tai Tung-pui and Tang Shiu-kin. Tai ordered the waiters from the Shan Kwong Hotel to cater to the house party. So, while the Battle of Hong Kong was being fought, these three families and some others were enjoying themselves. For them it was a party. What did the invasion have to do with them? Whether it was the British or the Japanese, what did it matter? The important thing was to stay safe until it was all over and then they would see what to do.

The Japanese invaders didn't march down the main roads. Instead they came along the narrow trails around the mountains. They were tough soldiers who had a great deal of experience of war. The British were quickly defeated. They were no use. Some were too drunk to fight. It was a big scandal. Everyone knows this.

One of the first groups of Japanese soldiers came through Wong Nei Chong Gap and then came down the hillside. This brought them close to the top of Blue Pool Road. From their position they surveyed the hillside with binoculars and they saw a large walled villa with a lot of waiters in white jackets and bow ties, serving food and drinks to well-dressed ladies and gentlemen. I suppose they thought that all the waiters looked like soldiers. That was what Mr Tai assumed later. That's what he told me. But maybe in the heat of battle soldiers need to commit violence.

This group of Japanese soldiers surrounded the villa and set up machine guns. The people inside had no choice. They had to let the Japanese in. I imagine it like this. All the men in bow ties and dinner jackets standing still, holding glasses in their hands, white with fear, grinning, bowing. Maybe they were drunk. All the women, all well dressed, were seated or standing. Everybody stood pale and frightened as the dirty, sweaty Japanese soldiers silently entered with their rifles ready. The sight of this luxury must have made the Japanese angry. They were fighting while these people were having a party. The Japanese officer in charge ordered the men to be taken outside and killed. Just a little way from the villa was a storm drain, a water channel about ten feet deep that ran straight down the hillside down to Happy Valley. There wasn't any water in it then as this was in the dry season. All the men were lined up at the edge of the storm drain. Then the soldiers started to stab them with their bayonets. Bullets were too precious to be wasted. The soldiers stuck their bayonets into the men and then kicked the body down into the drain as they pulled the bayonet back out. From the villa they could all hear the cries and screams of the women as they were raped. Every girl and woman in the house, from the age of thirteen to fifty, was raped. I knew some of these women later. Some of my friends married them.

As for the men they accepted their fate. No one tried to run away. Where could they run? They would just be shot. Shot or stabbed, what did it matter? Mr Fung, the owner of the villa, was stabbed and killed. His body fell down. Then it was Tai's turn. He just faced them bravely. The soldier stabbed him in the left side of his chest, in the heart. But Mr Tai had a wallet in his inside jacket pocket and inside the wallet he kept a piece of jade. The tip of the bayonet hit the jade piece and was deflected to the side where it made a gash five to six inches deep but missed the heart. So Mr Tai was still alive when he was kicked down into the water channel. Next came Mr Tang. He turned his back to the Japanese soldier and waited his turn. I suppose he had decided that his only hope was to fall forward. The soldier stabbed him in the back. But Mr Tang also had a jade piece which he wore in his belt at the back. Again the bayonet was deflected into the flesh of his buttocks. Then he too was kicked into the channel.

Of more than thirty men only these two survived. Naturally they just lay still until it grew dark and they were sure they wouldn't be seen. Mr Tai was more seriously injured but they both managed to get away. They walked down the water channel until they got to the bottom of Sing Woo Road. Then they called out for help. There was no easy way of getting out of the channel. Luckily, the Japanese had not yet reached Happy Valley. Some passers-by managed to get some ropes and they pulled Mr Tai and Mr Tang up to the road.

Mr Tai showed me the scar once when I asked him about the story. I also talked to Mr Tang about it. It was a very sad story. We have a superstition that if anyone escapes near death, then, sooner or later, they will make a fortune. Both of them did make big fortunes in the property market.

The whole department was corrupt

MR TAI FILLED THE HOTEL with his relatives and gradually they stopped giving me proper respect. They would not obey my orders. I got furious with them but of course Mr Tai would not back me up against his own relatives. Eventually, I just quit.

I didn't have a job again for several months. I hadn't saved much money. It was another hard time for me. Then, one day, I bumped into police inspector Chin. He had been a regular customer at the Shan Kwong. He and I were friends. I told him what had happened.

'I know a good job for you!' he said. 'You can speak excellent English. You should become a government interpreter. The salary is not much. Two to three hundred. But don't worry about money. You can earn plenty. We need a few interpreters in the police department. I can tell you, you will not regret it. And the work is not so hard as in a hotel.'

So I agreed to put in an application. I had many friends in the police. They all did very well. Why shouldn't I? In those days it was well known that the government was corrupt. Maybe not a hundred per cent corrupt but at least ninety-five.

So I took the exam. There was a small room where we were examined in spoken and written English and Chinese. The room could only contain about thirty-five people and there were over a thousand applicants for the jobs available. It took about six weeks to test everybody.

When the results came out I found I had come first in the exam. So someone contacted me and told me to report the following Monday. Naturally I was very pleased. One thousand candidates and I came first.

So I became the interpreter for Mr Binstead, who was the senior officer in the traffic section of the Royal Hong Kong Police Force. This was a key position. There were eight sections in the traffic department but they all had to report to Mr Binstead. So everything came through me. My work wasn't just interpreting. I was also in charge of all the top-secret dossiers and confidential files kept in Mr Binstead's office. Only two people were allowed to go into his office. I was one and Chief

Inspector McGuinness was the other. My job was to make all the entries to the files. It was also my job to look up past records. In fact I can say I was the only person to look at the files.

My post was a very sensitive one. Why? Because the whole department was corrupt. There were several sections in the department – accidents, licences, tests, vehicle inspections, repairs, traffic offences, traffic direction (we didn't have traffic lights in those days so at busy junctions there was always a policeman directing the traffic) and so on – and they all had to come through me. Each section had its own interpreter and he would get a share of the corrupt money in his own section but I got shares from all the sections. Naturally, everyone had to trust me. That's why they chose me. I could be trusted. Some of the inspectors knew my background. I had met some of them even before I joined the department. Some of them knew me because my brother-in-law, Ho Tim, had introduced us.

How could the Traffic Department make money? Easy. Everyone wanted to drive so first of all there were the provisional licences. Maybe if you were well-known or a European you could get a licence simply by applying for it. But most people would have to pay under the table. It is very easy to cause problems for applicants. We could ask for medical records to prove they had no eye defects or heart problems or history of epilepsy or something like that. Which driving instructor are you going to learn with? Bring us proof that he is a qualified instructor. Or if they insisted, you could explain there was a waiting list and they would be informed when their turn came up. Most people would take the hint. Either they would pay directly to us or we would sell the licences to a garage or a driving instructor and he would sell it on for a profit. Then there was the driving test itself. Everyone knew how much it cost to pass. There was a standard rate. Then there were accidents. If you had three serious accidents, you would lose your licence for a few months. For a private motorist maybe this wasn't a big problem but for a taxi driver or a lorry driver whose living depended on it, this would be a big problem. Then there was the car inspection section. If they thought your car was unsafe they would require you to take it to the inspection centre for a check. Naturally, there would always be a problem. Then you had a choice of having it repaired privately or at the traffic section's own repair yard. Of course, if the traffic section repairs the car that guarantees that the problem has been repaired. If you had the car repaired privately they would be certain to miss something. Extra trouble. Extra money for the department. Or you might be charged with overloading, or speeding or driving dangerously or driving a vehicle in a dangerous state of repair. If a policeman wants to catch you for something, it's easy. My salary was $240 a month but most months I was there I made over $30,000.

I was very quickly made to understand how I could make money and of course I was happy to go along with everything. Mr Darkin was responsible for licences. Naturally he couldn't market these himself. No Chinese would dare do business like this with a senior European officer. So he told me that if I could sell any licences he should receive $5 for each one. The rest could go into my own pocket. I started to sell them on at $25 each but later I increased the price to $30 and then $35. I never had to look for customers. They all came to me. I never allowed anyone to buy more than six at one time. Except once. It was Chinese New Year, I had forgotten to arrange money for the holiday and all the banks were closed. My wife asked me: 'What are we going to do? We need at least $200 for lucky envelopes and we need money for the food and drink.'

I said: 'Never mind. I will get the money straight away.'

So I went down to a garage I knew. The owner greeted me and invited me into his office to have a drink. I explained that I needed some money and asked him if he would like to have forty licences for $1,200. Naturally he was very happy to have this offer. He could sell them for double the price and it was useful for him to sell a licence with a car. That was a common arrangement at that time. He went straight to his safe and gave me the money immediately.

At about the same time I got an invitation from Sergeant-Major Tsui. He invited me to have lunch with him. Suddenly I was getting invitations to have lunch and dinner from many people I didn't know. But Mr Tsui, I already knew, was an important man. He was in charge of all the traffic police. Now I must explain something about the traffic control section. Everyone in this section was hired from Shandong Province in the north of China. They had a special life-time contract. I think the reason was that they were taller than Cantonese. Cantonese people are very short normally. But the people from the north of China are tall. For traffic police they needed tall men so that the cars could see them clearly. So I met Sergeant Tsui at a restaurant near the Macau ferry pier. We had a good lunch there. Mr Tsui was a rather fat man. He enjoyed his food. After lunch he handed me an envelope. I was surprised.

'What's this?' I asked.

'Please Mr Hui. Please take it.'

Naturally I had to see what was in it. I opened the envelope and found it contained $3,000.

'What's this for?'

'It's your share,' he explained.

At first I told him I couldn't accept it. I was still new and didn't yet fully understand how deep the corruption was. But Mr Tsui insisted and explained everything. There were a number of collection points. Any taxi or truck passing these points had to pay $5 a day. If there were any problems then these would be covered up or sorted out. Of course, since I was the one in charge of the dossiers, I had to be included in the distribution.

'Mr Hui,' he said. 'We know that you are a gentleman and come from a very respectable family. Your manner says everything. But this money is not just for you. It's for all the traffic police. We have families in Shandong Province. We need to take care of them. If you refuse this money everyone would be scared. Who would then dare to accept any money? But if you take it then we will know that everything will continue as before.'

I still hesitated. Naturally I didn't want to seem too eager.

'Mr Hui, we were all just like you. We didn't want to take all this money. But the drivers begged us to take it. If we started looking for problems then they would have to pay us hundreds of dollars. For them it is cheaper to be insured.'

And so every month I received an envelope from Mr Tsui.

I didn't know exactly how the money collection worked. There was a fixed time and place for the collection. Normally, if there was an accident, the report would come to me and I would discuss the matter with the inspector to decide what action to take. Everything came to my desk: offences, accidents, repairs and so on. The sergeant passed the reports on to me. If the accident concerned someone who had paid up then the report would be thrown away or changed so that it wasn't so serious. Sometimes, I was asked to change the records afterwards. If someone wanted a serious case to be changed then he would find out that I was the person to talk to. I would charge him $600–800. If it was a recent case then I would just charge $600 because it would be quite simple. But if it was an old case then it would be more difficult. The ink would have soaked into the paper. It was not so easy to delete the old record and substitute another one. Then I would charge more. Another thing I remember was garages. These were very tightly controlled. It wasn't allowed to have too many garages in each district. If you wanted to have a garage site approved it would cost about $6,000. Of course, a garage is certain to make money so people were happy to pay this amount.

Soon it became known that I was the person to see if anyone had any problem at all in the traffic branch. They would look for me in the nightclubs or they would come to my home. I remember one driver who had been told to report with his car to the police station the following morning. He found me at about two o'clock in the morning when I returned from the nightclub.

'Mr Hui, tomorrow my car will be impounded. Can you help me?'

'Maybe I can and maybe not. If I can't then your car will be impounded and that will cost you a lot of trouble. If you want to solve it then it will cost you $400.'

Most often they would put money in my hands immediately. The next morning I would go to Central Police Station and go to Mr Senior's office.

'Here's the name of a driver and here's the car number and here's $200.'

He would give me a thumbs-up sign. Then the driver would still have to get his car repaired but he wouldn't be fined or suspended or given any trouble. That's how it worked.

Now there were nine senior inspectors in the traffic section. I had met three or four even before I became an interpreter. They all knew I had once been a rich man. Of all the inspectors only one was not European. The ninth was a Shandong man. He was in charge of accidents. He had been a senior inspector a long time before I arrived but he was jealous of my power and the fact that all the European officers showed so clearly they respected me. He didn't know why they respected me and he tried to put me under his thumb whenever he had the chance. Usually, the way he did this was to make me do all his translating work. As he was a Shandong man and as the official language of the office was

English he would pretend to need an interpreter to translate Cantonese into English. Actually, some of the drivers maybe couldn't speak Cantonese either. Perhaps they could only speak a dialect like the 'Ng Yaap' – five districts – dialect or Hakka. Although I don't know Hakka I can understand Ng Yaap dialect because my first wife came from there. So when he needed an interpreter he always called out across the office: 'Mr Hui, can you come here please and do some interpreting.' I got mad as hell at him but he was senior to me. At first I had to obey. There were seven or eight interpreters in the office but he always asked me to do his work for him. One day, McGuinness commented on this.

'Why is it you always ask Mr Hui to do your interpreting for you?'

I knew from this that I had the support of the other inspectors and that although they respected me they didn't give much respect to this Chinese inspector. Once I understood this I decided to get him off my back. The next day, he once again called for me to do some interpreting. I was busy making entries in the dossiers. I lost my temper.

'Damn you!' I shouted at him. 'Why do you always pick on me? Can't you see I'm busy? Get another interpreter. Just fuck off!'

Naturally he was stunned. Everyone heard me. Even the driver who was at the inspector's desk waiting to be grilled. He didn't understand English but he could see from my attitude and the silence that followed that I was angry.

Later I was renowned for telling people to fuck off! The inspector lost a lot of face.

After that the inspector kept away from me. But he was a fool to annoy me. He also had to ask me for favours. One day, he came to my desk and asked me to help him to change a record. Inside I was laughing at him. 'So you have to ask me for a favour. Now you pretend to respect me!' I thought to myself. 'It will be very expensive!' I charged him a lot of money to do the favour. Of course he had to accept. Maybe it was a favour for a friend or a relative. If he couldn't help he would lose even more face. So he had to pay me anything I asked. He didn't ask me for a favour often but when he did I made him pay more than anyone else.

One of the people I helped at this time was James Wu Man-hong, the elder brother of Gordon Wu who is very famous these days for building roads in China. I don't know Gordon Wu but I got to know his elder brother James Wu and I also knew their father Wu Chung. I knew the father first from before the war. His was an interesting story. I didn't know if it is true but several people told me the same story. Wu Chung was just an ordinary taxi driver. One day he picked up an American visitor who was carrying a big bundle. He dropped the man off and then went back to his garage to finish his shift. As he was checking the car over, he noticed that the American had left the bundle in the back seat. He opened it up and found it contained bundles of high-denomination us dollars. He didn't tell anyone about this. Instead he took it home. He didn't know what to do. He gathered all his family together and explained what had happened. He then asked them for advice. Eventually they all agreed that he should keep the money hidden for a while to see what happened. Then he should wait for a few more years until he could find something to invest in. It would be suspicious if he was suddenly found to have a lot of money. But it would be silly to return the money.

So that's what they did. They invested in a garage and gradually built up two taxi companies: one on Hong Kong Island and one in Kowloon. That's the story. Maybe that was a story they told to hide the real truth. There are stories and stories.

I met James Wu because he was running the two taxi companies: the New Taxi Cab Company and the Central Taxi Cab Company. He never paid me any money but he always arranged for a case of brandy to be delivered to me at the time of the major festivals. James Wu was a very clever and respected businessman. Later he became the senior appointed member of the Legislative Assembly. I remember one evening I was invited to a dinner to celebrate something. I was playing cards with Wu Chung and a few others. I was winning a lot of money. I had won about $1,000 in cash and $2,000 in IOUs from Wu Chung. He said to me: 'Don't worry Mr Hui, before we go to dinner I will get you the cash.' I laughed. 'Mr Wu, everyone knows you are rich. Don't worry. There is no hurry. I trust you.' But I never got the money because James Wu passed the table and saw the situation. He said to his father: 'Why don't you let me sit in for you for a while. I will play for you.' And he then won back all the IOUs. He was a very clever man. When I saw that he was winning it back so quickly I laughed: 'Mr Wu, you have won back all the IOUs but I am going to hang on to this cash. Let's go and drink some brandy.'

I remember once a very beautiful girl came for some help. I can't remember what it was. An accident perhaps. Anyway, when we had finished our business she handed me her card.

'If you have time, you can come and be my guest.'

Of course I was polite and took her card but people were always giving me cards and inviting me to dinner. So I thought nothing of it. Then a few weeks later the phone rang and it was her. She said: 'Mr Hui, is something the matter?'

'Why?'

'You haven't contacted me.'

She was a very beautiful girl and was not used to being ignored. So I invited her for a drive to Repulse Bay. I didn't have a car but that wasn't a problem. I borrowed one and we went for a drive. But it was not a good day. In fact it was raining very heavily. We drove to the beach and parked on the sand. We talked and kissed and so on and then we tried to do something more but the problem was it was a small British car. We couldn't do anything in the front seat because the gear stick was in the way. To get into the back seat wasn't easy. It was only a two-door car. So I had to get out in the rain. When we were ready I couldn't do anything. Now this is the way with me. For me to enjoy being with a woman, everything must be perfectly arranged and comfortable. Doing something in a car! That's not for me. Even though I am a slight man and this girl was also very petite but still it didn't work. But she was an intelligent girl and we had a laugh. A few weeks later she rented a hotel room and everything went fine. She was really a nice girl. Maybe something would have developed between us. But very soon after this I had to flee to Canton.

Small Tong, 'Get Rich' Lee and the Greens

I T WAS WHILE I WAS STILL WORKING at the traffic office that my friend Chan 'Number Eleven' came to see me. He was a bloody spendthrift like me. He had already sold his share of his inheritance to his older brother, Number Seven, and then he had spent that. Now he was broke.

Like a number of my friends before, during and after the Japanese occupation, he had gone up to Shanghai. If I have a regret it is that I never went to see Shanghai at this time. People said it was wonderful. The girls were wonderful. The nightclubs were wonderful. It was the greatest city in the world, they said. At least it was equal to Paris. Many young men went to Shanghai from Hong Kong and they only came back when they had run out of money. For fooling around there was nowhere better. Rich young men who only thought of fooling around were natural suckers and it was easy for them to borrow money to throw around and then find they were in serious debt without any way to pay the money back. That's what happened to my friend. When repayment was demanded he always said 'Next week, next week'. Then he had got scared and had come back to Hong Kong where the triads couldn't get him.

In those days Shanghai was controlled by a triad boss called Do Yuet-sang. There were two triad gangs in Shanghai at that time: the Reds and the Greens. In fact, although they were two different gangs, he was the boss of both of them. When Chiang Kai-shek finally became head of the Kuomintang and he wanted to visit Shanghai, he first sent an officer to see Do Yuet-sang to ask if there would be any problems. And when he arrived in the city the first thing he did was to go and visit Do Yuet-sang and pay his respects. His gangs were more powerful than an army. In fact, the Communists in Shanghai were defeated badly because Do Yuet-sang sided with Chiang Kai-shek.

But Do Yuet-sang had no power base outside Shanghai. He could see that the Communists were winning and because he was their enemy he had to set up bases in Hong Kong and Taiwan. He chose Lee Chui-fat to be the boss of the Greens in Hong Kong. So Lee came down with some gang members from Shanghai to set up in Hong Kong. Even before the war quite a few Shanghainese underworld people had been to Hong Kong. Mainly they were looking for suckers to go to Shanghai. So the loan sharks in Shanghai who had lent money to Hong Kong people asked these gang members to chase up their debts.

One day, Chan 'Number Eleven' received a call from some gang members. They demanded that he repay the money he owed and threatened to kill him if he didn't. But his family had disowned him. They refused to lend him any more money. His friends also. Either they had thrown away all their money, like me, or they refused to lend him any money. He didn't know what to do.

He was shaking and trembling badly. They had told him to bring the money to the billiard hall on the top floor of Entertainment Building on the corner of D'Aguilar Street and Queen's Road.

'Don't worry. I'll come with you,' I told him, 'I'll explain everything and if they don't accept the situation then I will fight them.'

'Kei-gaw, these men are killers! One of the men who will certainly be there is Tong. Everyone calls him Small Tong. He's a killer. I have seen him kill a man with my own eyes. It was in a nightclub. He broke a bottle and stabbed it into the man's face. Ah Kei! They are going to kill me!'

We took the lift up to the top floor. Chan was shaking with fear. I said: 'Come on Eleven. Don't be scared. I will win, believe me!'

We entered the hall and Chan pointed them out to me. They were playing at the end table. There was no one else there. I walked straight up to them.

'Mr Tong,' I said. 'My name is Hui. I am here to represent Mr Chan who is my good friend. There is no doubt that my friend is in the wrong. He borrowed money from your friend and he didn't pay him back. Now we are here to try to solve the problem.'

'This debt has been owed for many years!' Tong said.

'There is no doubt that Mr Chan was wrong to do this. But he is a spendthrift like me. He doesn't understand how to keep money in his pockets. If he has money he must spend it. I know this too because both of us were born into rich families and we both threw away our money.

We spent it having a good time. Now neither of us has any money. Mr Chan is poor. He has no money.'

Tong listened to me impassively. He was short but strong. A typical Shanghainese.

'Mr Hui, I must explain that our friend who loaned Mr Chan the money has been very patient. When we asked for the money back, Mr Chan said: "I'll pay it back next week" or "Just give me a few more days" and then he ran off. We feel he was making fun of us. He was treating us like suckers.'

'I understand,' I told him. 'If I were in your position I would also be very angry. But I can explain it simply. Chan was not making fools of you. The fact is Chan is not a brave man like me. He was frightened so he just said anything to get rid of you. In fact it is not easy for him to raise the money.'

Tong shook his head: 'Now, this is the last chance. Mr Chan must pay us back all the money now. We can't spare him any more time.'

'How long can you give Mr Chan to raise the money?' I asked.

'Two weeks. That's all.'

Now the sum of money involved was not small, several tens of thousands. Chan was ready to agree to this and run. He was nodding his head. But I knew Chan couldn't raise it in two weeks. It was best not to pretend.

'I can tell you straight now that Mr Chan cannot raise this amount in such a short time. There is no way he can do it. So this is what I suggest: Mr Chan is my good friend so I will stand guarantor that the money will be paid up in full sometime. But neither of us has any money now. But in two weeks time we will pay you back something – say one twentieth or one fiftieth and then we will pay back the rest in instalments. This is the only way to do it.'

Mr Tong looked at me hard.

'We must discuss this.'

There were seven or eight of them. They went into a corner and talked together in low voices. Then they all came back.

'We have discussed this and our decision is this: within two weeks time you must pay back not one twentieth or one tenth but half. The minimum we will accept is fifty per cent.'

Now I got angry and I knew the expression on my face showed them very clearly that I was serious.

'Tong,' I said, 'I don't want to talk any more. I am the only one here to protect Chan and I only have these hands. There are seven or eight of you. So listen to me very clearly. I am telling you straight. We cannot pay you back half the amount in two weeks. I am not lying to you. We will pay back the debt to you little by little when we can afford it. If Chan hasn't got money then I will pay it back myself. If this answer is not acceptable to you then we must fight. Maybe you will kill me and maybe I will kill two or three of you. That's my final answer.'

Tong immediately put his hands up to calm me down.

'Just a minute, Mr Hui. Let me talk to my companions.'

Once again they went into the corner to discuss the matter. I was ready to fight to the death. I knew Chan was ready to run at any time. Soon Tong came back alone.

'Mr Hui. You have proved to us that you are a good friend of Mr Chan's. We trust you. Your courage shows you are a straight and benevolent man. We accept your arrangement. Within two weeks come back here and pay us what you can. We trust you but not Mr Chan.'

Two weeks later Chan and I went back to the billiard hall. They were all there. I handed over some money in an envelope. It wasn't much. A few hundred. Maybe a thousand. I can't remember. Tong took it and put it in his pocket. Then he invited me to go to a restaurant. I thought 'Why not?' It is always good to get to know your enemy.

Actually, Tong and I soon became friends. He told me he admired me for what I had done for Chan. They were impressed with my courage. In Shanghai there are many killers and top fighters with a lot of courage but in Hong Kong there are very few. Maybe I was the only one. I was ready to fight to the death anytime. He could see that. He took the envelope out of his pocket.

'This isn't Chan's money. It's yours. Am I right?'

'You are very wise,' I said. 'You understand the whole situation. I made a promise. Don't worry. I will pay it back bit by bit.'

He passed it back to me.

'Mr Hui. I hope you and I can be friends. Let us forget this matter.'

So that was the end of Chan's debt. After that Tong and I met several times. Really we did like each other. Our character was very similar.

About the fifth or sixth time we met another man came to join us. Tong introduced him as Lee Chui-fat. I soon discovered that Lee was the boss of the Green gang in Hong Kong. His headquarters was the Ritz nightclub in North Point. That area, even today, is a big centre for the Shanghainese community in Hong Kong. At that time the Ritz was the best nightclub in all Hong Kong.

'Please come to the Ritz and be my guest. Everything will be on the house!' he said.

I knew the Ritz well. I was often taken there by people who wanted to gain something from me because of my position at the traffic office. So I said to Lee: 'Thank you for your invitation but I would like to suggest that we do it like this. I often go to your nightclub but usually, nine times out of ten, I don't pay. I am invited there so you won't do me any favour if you pay the bill. Let's do it like this. If I myself plan to take some girls to the nightclub and have a good time I will call you and tell you in advance. Or if I myself call for the bill then you can do what you like but actually I don't often eat at the Ritz. I am very happy to pay the normal price but if you like you can give me a discount. But it would be a big favour to me if I can settle up monthly. Generally, I just like to drink brandy. So I suggest that once I drink from a bottle then you just put my name on it and keep it for me. At the end of each month we can count up the bottles and I will pay for them at cost price. If that is acceptable to you I would be very happy. I have to earn a living and so do you.' So we agreed to do it in that way.

I went to the Ritz maybe five evenings out of six. It was a very joyful place and I had many friends there. I got to know Tong and Lee Chui-fat very well. Now Chui-fat means 'build up wealth' so maybe you can say his name meant 'Get Rich' Lee. So Lee's parents wanted him to have a good and rich fortune. But in fact, although he was doing well at this time, his fate was very unlucky. Even worse than mine.

I soon got to know that Lee was involved in smuggling. He did very little to hide the fact. He had too much confidence. The Ritz nightclub was on the waterfront road. Every night at two or three in the morning he loaded his boats just across the road from the nightclub – right in the middle of the harbour. It would be very easy for the police to catch him. Certainly, the marine police needed to be paid off. Relations between the police and triads is always close. Lee probably thought that he had solved the police problem by paying them off. But one evening there was an incident at the nightclub and Lee made a few enemies in the CID and they were determined to fix him.

Actually it was a small incident but I can say that Lee's men were stupid. But it was also very funny. One evening there was a beauty competition at the Ritz. All the people going to the nightclub that evening had to pay to enter. Four plain-clothes policeman wanted to get in and look but they didn't want to pay any money. The gang members took them aside and locked them into a broom cupboard for a few hours. Naturally, they were very angry. They decided to get their revenge.

I heard about this at the traffic office. They were going to get evidence to connect him to the smuggling ring. No one knew that I had a connection with him. As soon as I heard it I went to see him. I told him what I knew. He just smiled. He wasn't worried. Maybe he thought Hong Kong was like Shanghai.

'Mr Lee, whether you believe me or not I must tell you that the police have been keeping an eye on your smuggling operation. They know all about it. The reason they haven't done anything is that they want to link you to it. That's why they haven't made any move so far.'

He was a brave man. He wasn't worried by a little risk. Certainly he had no intention of stopping his smuggling line just because the police knew about it.

'If you insist on continuing this business then you must move your boats away from the Ritz.'

This was good advice and he took it. He made sure there was nothing to connect him to the smuggling. However, after some time, the police realised he was too clever to be caught easily. As they couldn't get any evidence against him, they recommended to the governor that Lee should be deported and so he was given twenty-four hours to leave Hong Kong.

Lee didn't have enough time to sort out all his affairs. He was a smart man but when your business is complicated there is not much you can do. He had to hand over the Ritz nightclub to one of his associates. He settled money on his wife and concubines and he gave away the different parts of his business to members of his gang. Then he left for Taipei. When he went he had very little cash. That was a major problem. The fact is, in business, all your money is tied up in projects and people who owe you money – when they hear that you have to leave within twenty-four hours – just have to disappear for a day and that makes it very difficult to collect anything. So Lee left Hong Kong with very little money. He just had to hope that his associates would continue to support him. But naturally his position was not strong. He could not come back to Hong Kong in person. He had to work through other people.

Now, what happened was this: Lee kept demanding money from his associate. He thought he could trust him but he turned out to be a cheat. He sold off the nightclub and the other bits of business and used the money to buy political favours in Taiwan. Everyone in the Kuomintang, every senior political figure in Taiwan, was totally corrupt. If you wanted a position in the government you just had to give big bribes to the right people. While his associate was doing this, he was telling Lee that he was having problems collecting money so he couldn't send him very much. Naturally Lee discovered what was happening. At first he didn't believe it. Maybe he didn't trust his informants. Sometimes it isn't easy to know who you can trust. He decided to come back to Hong Kong to find out for himself.

I got word that he was coming to Hong Kong and I told Tong that if Lee Chui-fat wanted he could stay at my flat. Actually, I didn't realise that Lee was already in Hong Kong staying at a flat in North Point. Naturally his associate wasn't happy to have Lee back in Hong Kong to reorganise his business so he tipped off the police and Lee was arrested. Tong came to me to see what I could do. I looked into the case and saw, firstly, that it wasn't so easy to fix. Lee had too many enemies. However, the charges against him were not serious so I suggested that they should just let the law run its normal course. A month later it was all sorted out and he was deported again.

The situation for Lee became very bad. He had no money and in Taiwan they only respect a man with money. As life became more and more difficult for him he became more and more obsessed with getting revenge. Tong remained loyal to him and I know he visited Lee's wife from time to time to make sure she was all right. Maybe it was Tong who told Lee that the associate was buying favours in Taiwan. His plan was to sell up in Hong Kong and start up again in Taiwan. The man had been given a senior job in the government.

But he made a big mistake. Taiwan was where his big enemy was. Maybe he thought Lee would just have to accept the situation. Lee had no friends there while he did have friends. He had bought friends with Lee's money. He was powerful and Lee had nothing. It was a big mistake. One day Lee Chui-fat contacted him while he was in Taipei and begged him to meet him. They arranged to meet in a narrow lane. I don't think Lee planned to kill him. I think he was still hoping his friend would give him some share of his money that he could start up a business with, some of his own money. The associate was too greedy. He refused or made some excuses. Lee understood that he had been destroyed by the man in front of him. He took out a dagger and started to stab the man. He was completely crazy. One or two stabs would be enough. Certainly five of six stab wounds would be enough to make sure the man was dead. But he kept on stabbing and stabbing. I think he stabbed the man fifty or sixty or even seventy times. On and on. He made no effort to escape. This is not the killing of a professional assassin. This is the killing of a man who has been destroyed and doesn't care what happens to him. This was in 1950 or 1951. It made the front pages of the newspapers in Hong Kong. I felt very sad for him.

After this, my friend Small Tong went to Macau and got a job in the security section of the casino. Many years later, when Stanley Ho took over the monopoly, Tong remained with the casino. In fact, he was still there when I last saw him. He had a very senior position.

Tombola King of Canton

IF I HAD STAYED AT THE TRAFFIC OFFICE I would have been rich. But something happened and I had to resign. I was only there nine months. What happened? I got involved in a traffic accident!

It was after midnight. I crashed into a car driven by some Europeans. I think they were important people. It was my fault. I was completely drunk. I shouted and threatened them. Then I drove off. Unfortunately there was a traffic policeman nearby. He recognised me. So I was reported. I had to resign. But it was funny. When I came up before the magistrate, it happened that I knew him. He was a nice man. I had done him a favour during the Japanese occupation. I had got him some work. Naturally, neither of us showed we knew each other. He listened to the prosecution but then he said it was an unimportant case and dismissed it. I was very lucky.

It was the spring of 1949 when I left the traffic department. So, I decided to go to Macau. But things had changed. I found I was bored. I couldn't gamble or fool around with girls because I had no money. There was nothing to do there so, after a week or so, I left Macau and went up to Canton.

I went immediately to the Tai Kung restaurant. This was being managed by someone I knew from the Hongkong Hotel. After the Communists took over, it became Dung Fong Hung – The East is Red restaurant.

When I got to the restaurant, I found my friend there and greeted him. 'I am here in Canton for a while,' I said to him, 'you must give me a job in your restaurant or I will just stay in your staff dormitory and do nothing.' He laughed and told me I could start work any time. So I became the assistant manager of the restaurant. He was happy to leave everything in my hands. He knew he could rely on me.

Naturally, I soon met many of my old friends. I also made many new friends. Since the Tai Kung restaurant was the best in all Canton, the people I made friends with were people with power and money.

I had been working there for only a few weeks when my friend Tsui Jaw-kei came in.

'Mr Hui? What are you doing here? I thought you were working for the traffic office!'

I told him the whole story.

'This is marvellous!' he said. 'You are the perfect person to help me.' He explained that he too wanted to set up a restaurant in Canton and needed someone to manage it. He had made a lot of money in the last few years. During the war he had got by as a hawker of clothing items, laying out his wares on a camp bed in the streets. The Japanese allowed street hawking. Business wasn't good but he got by. When peace came, he and anybody else who could import goods from abroad made a lot of money. Now he owned the Jamfair Department Store in Hong Kong. He wasn't extremely rich but he was very comfortable. Now he wanted to run a restaurant in Canton.

'The restaurant trade is very precise,' I told him, 'you must know from the start what you want. Do you want to go up-market or down-market?'

Mr Tsui didn't hesitate. 'I want to set up the best restaurant in all Canton. Even better than the Tai Kung. I don't care how much it costs.'

I agreed to help him.

A restaurant is not an easy business to set up. In the first place, a good site is essential. Then you have to fit out the kitchen and get suitable staff. There are always licences you need to get. It takes time. Eventually, we found a suitable site in one of the best suburbs in Canton. I had it decorated at great expense and set the prices at the same level as at the Tai Kung. We called the new restaurant the Jamfair. While all this is easy to say, in fact it took months. By the time it opened I was already involved in other business ventures.

Unfortunately, the restaurant didn't have time to get back its investment before the Communists came. But, at that time, we didn't give any thought to the Communists. Our way of thinking was that Guangdong Province was safe in the hands of the Kuomintang. We never expected that the Communist victory would be so quick in coming. In fact the restaurant did good business when it opened. I had done a good job setting it up. But you can't fight against fate.

Mr Tsui wasn't the only person I met who wanted me to be involved with business. One group of people that I met were the bandits from the southern estuary – my own home district. There were four gangs and they controlled all the waterways and had control also over all the districts in between. I had met one of these bandits as a young boy, 'Teacher' Tuen. Through this connection I soon made friends with many of the bandits. One of them said to me: 'Elder brother, you are a smart and educated man. Canton and Hong Kong. These are places where it is possible to make money. If you have an idea for a business venture then come to me. I can back you up. Not with money but with goods or services.' I hadn't been in Canton long so I had no idea of starting up any business. I promised I would think about it. The fact is that anyone doing trade between Canton and Hong Kong could make a big profit. It was difficult to get many of the basic necessities in Canton: brushes, towels and other items of that sort. I thought about it and we discussed it but it was a difficult business to get started. I was very busy and it would require that I go down to Hong Kong again and find someone to act as my agent and find a place where we could store goods. Also I needed to clear a number of police and customs formalities. I was very busy with the restaurants and I couldn't spare the time. I discussed this with my bandit partners. They were very keen to go into partnership with me to do this kind of business. They worked out a way to do it was to ship rice down to Hong Kong. There they would make maybe five or ten per cent profit. Not much. But with this money they could buy up a lot of basic households goods and make forty per cent profit on the return journey. I remember we calculated it like this: We would start with rice valued at $2 million. This would be sold for $2.1 million in Hong Kong and this would become $2.8 million on the return trip. We could do six trips a month, thirty-six trips a year. I was to get fifty per cent of the profits for my share of the work. We didn't bargain. That's not my way. So I asked the pirates: 'How much do you want to give me?' They thought about it and said: 'Well, elder brother, we have no power in Hong Kong. We are dependent on your connections. It seems to us that we should divide the profits equally.' I found this acceptable.

First of all the bandits had to get the boat and the rice organised. This would take some time. They wouldn't buy the rice from the farmers but they would take the rice and promise to pay them for it later. So the bandits didn't need any start-up capital.

Later I did go down to Hong Kong and managed to set up everything. It took me nearly a month. It was about August that year before we managed to get it organised. But we only had time to do one trip. One trip! Naturally I made some money from that but if I had been able to keep doing it for one year, just one year, I would have been a multi-millionaire. Imagine it! $400,000 profit for me every trip. Multiply that by thirty-six. I tell you I am so unlucky. Every time I am about to make a fortune, bad luck attacks me. Truly, God must want to punish me.

So that was the transportation business. But I also had another business. I became the Tombola King of Canton.

Let me tell you about the tombola business. It all started when I met Mr Poon Yung. Like everyone else in Canton with power and money, he came to the Tai Kung restaurant. I noticed very early on that a group of men appeared at about the same time every lunch time and sat down at a particular table. They were dressed in civilian clothes but it wasn't hard to see that they were senior military officers. Also it was easy to see who was the most senior among them. He was older than the others and they all deferred to him. After they had come several days in a row, I placed a 'Reserved' notice on that table. When they came the next day, they were a bit surprised to find the table reserved. But I explained that I had reserved it for them. Now, why did I do this? Because I understand what it is like to be a respected customer. I understand the value of small things. When you have had that experience you understand everything about how to serve people.

I understood that this gentleman was powerful and important but cultivated and well educated. He did not like to show his power. I did not know who he was or how powerful he was. I only knew that he was the sort of person that I would like to do small favours for.

When he saw that I respected him but did not know who he was he was very impressed. After a few weeks, he invited me to sit and have a drink with him. We talked. We became friends. It became a habit. When he came for a meal we would sit and talk together. I told him of my life and experiences and he told me something about himself. Maybe I told him more about myself than he told me about himself. In fact he didn't talk very much about himself. It was from his subordinates that I heard he was the right hand man of General Yu Hon-mau, who was the right hand man of General Chiang Kai-shek.

One day Poon Yung said to me: 'Mr Hui. I know that you are from Hong Kong. But perhaps you will decide to stay in Canton. I see you are a man of ability. Perhaps you would like to set up your own business. If you have any ideas in this line please tell me. Maybe I can help you. Whatever business you like. Just tell me.'

Actually, I had no ideas for starting up my own business at that time. But once he had suggested it I thought about it. I looked around. The restaurant business was good but it required a lot of capital. The only business that I could see that would be very profitable and which wouldn't require much capital was gambling. It was illegal to run a casino at that time. Chiang Kai-shek had sent officers to Canton to stamp it out. But one form of gambling was still allowed. Tombola, a game like bingo. Each person has a card with some numbers on it. The numbers are called out. The first person to get a row of numbers wins. There were, at that time, three tombola houses still running. They were doing very good business. Chiang Kai-shek allowed tombola to continue as he thought of it as just a children's game. He didn't think this was real gambling.

It was generally understood that it was impossible to get new licences to operate a tombola house. But this was the only sort of business I was interested in. So the next time I saw Mr Poon I said to him: 'Mr Poon, you said you might be able to help me set up a business. I have been thinking about it and it seems to me that I would be interested in setting up a tombola house.' His answer surprised me. He just said: 'Good idea. Why not?'

'I will need a licence.'

'We will do it this way,' he said. 'You find a premises and rent it and start up business and then you will get the licence.'

Now, I was very doubtful about the whole affair. Mr Poon was a senior government and military official. But how much power did he really have? I was asking for something everybody said was impossible. But he showed no surprise and didn't give any sign that this was a problem. What should I do? Was he taking me for a sucker? But he hadn't asked for any money in advance. Maybe I would spend a lot of money and at the end there wouldn't be a licence. But after thinking about it for a while I came to the conclusion that there would be no problem. I trusted Mr Poon. He was not the sort of man to cheat or trick me in this way.

Also there was no profit to him if I failed. So I arranged for a few financiers to become my partners. I offered them sixty per cent and I kept forty per cent for myself. They were happy to agree. I then looked around for a site.

A tombola house can be anywhere. If you open one, people will come. However, there was a teahouse on the corner of a crossroads in the centre of Canton. It had closed down because business was poor. I went to see the owner. Actually, he wasn't himself the owner. He was the tenant, but he wanted to sublet it. He was very suspicious of me. How could I manage a profitable business when he himself had failed?

'Mr Hui, we have just met and I am new to you so you don't have to trust me but actually I can tell you that you don't have to worry about me. I am very surprised that you are willing to pay such a large rent. My own experience is that this is not a good site for a restaurant. May I know what line of business you intend to run here? You are new to Canton. Maybe I can help you.'

I assured him I had all the help I needed and apologised for not being able to tell him.

'I should warn you that Canton is full of bad elements. Many people will want to take advantage of you. Don't trust people.'

I thanked him for his concern and invited him to the grand opening.

'When I open my doors for business you will know!'

'Is it legal business?'

I assured him it was.

But still he was suspicious so in the end we agreed that we would have a verbal contract: just his word and mine. And we agreed that I would pay him every day. The rent was very expensive. I seem to remember it was $300 a day. Then I arranged for the teahouse to be redecorated.

On the opening day, the landlord came round. Naturally he was very curious. 'Mr Hui! A tombola house! You need a licence for that and the government isn't giving out any more licences. Everyone knows that. Have you got a licence?'

'Don't worry!' I told him. 'It will come!'

'How much did you pay them? Who is arranging this for you? Are you sure you can trust them?'

He went away shaking his head. He thought the police would close me down immediately. In fact a few days later a man in government uniform, a high-ranking civil servant, came to see me and handed me a licence.

'Mr Poon Yung asked me to give you this in person.'

I saw that it was a properly stamped licence with a big red authorisation stamp.

Before I opened the tombola house I had to get good staff and the easiest way to get good staff was to steal them from the three tombola houses already operating. That was a simple thing to do. I found that the girls were paid seven dollars a day so I advertised that I would pay them nine. I had no problem hiring suitable girls. Their job was to sell as many tickets as they could to the customers for each round. I also gave them a commission: for every 200 tickets they sold I gave them ten free tickets that they could sell on their own account.

For the first two weeks I offered a special extra incentive for people to come to my tombola house. For each two-dollar entry ticket I offered customers a bottle of aerated water – fizzy orange or lemon – that had a retail price of between three and four dollars in Canton at that time. I had a good connection with a senior officer in the railway company. These fizzy drinks could be bought in Hong Kong for just under a dollar. I arranged for them to be brought to Canton on the Hong Kong-Canton Express. I didn't have to pay the regular freight charge. In fact it wasn't very much. This was arranged through one of the financiers who knew the head of the railway. We also arranged for some well-known singers to come up from Hong Kong to entertain the customers between games.

From the very first night, the tombola house was packed and stayed packed until we had to close up a few months later when the Communists came. In fact I could have filled it ten times over. We always had to turn hundreds of people away every night. I suppose there was standing room for about five hundred people in the room and as we were on the first floor up, there were also people all the way down the staircase. Everyone was mad to gamble. We sold the tickets for one dollar each and most people would buy a handful. The prize was $1,000 for each round. This was a lot of money in those days. My calculation is that for each round we would sell $2,000 to $2,500 worth of tickets. If I sensed that we were selling a lot of tickets for a round I would increase the prize to $1,200. This was a way of stimulating sales. Once a night we had a special 'Snowball' where the ticket price would be increased to two dollars and the prize would be doubled or more than doubled.

I must explain something. At that time no one trusted the local Canton currency so all business was done in Hong Kong dollars.

We had one round every half-hour, so between eight and midnight we had nine rounds. You can calculate how much money I made every evening: maybe twelve or fifteen thousand. Naturally I had to pay expenses out of this and also to pay my partners their share. But how could they know how much I was making? They had to trust me. In fact I didn't give them sixty per cent. I gave them less than that. But they were happy. They were making a very good return for their investment.

As soon as I saw what a good business it was, and that Mr Poon Yung was someone with a lot of power that I could trust, I immediately thought about opening a second tombola house. First of all I had to see if he would support me again. I went to see him.

'I am thinking of opening a second tombola house. Do you think there would be any problems?'

'You are a very capable man, Mr Hui,' he said. 'There will be no problem getting a licence even if you want to open a third or a fourth or a fifth.'

I was very pleased to hear this. I saw that I would be rich again very quickly.

For my second tombola establishment I found a small godown of about 1,500 square feet. This was larger than the first one. But I had to do some work to decorate it and furnish it. This time, when I advertised for girls I had over two hundred applicants. Naturally, I only needed about twenty. It took me over a week to make my selection. Naturally, I chose the most beautiful ones. I saw maybe fifty girls a day for four days. I asked about half of them to come back. Then on the fifth day I had over a hundred girls. I sifted this down to fifty, then down to thirty and then down to twenty. The girls I finally chose saw how valuable their job was and how well paid it was so naturally they worked hard. I never had any staff problems.

And so, from the day my second tombola house was open, I was earning more than double what I was earning before. I sent some of this money to my family in Hong Kong. I knew many people from Hong Kong who came up to Canton on business. I would give them some money and they would make a phone call to Hong Kong to arrange for the same amount to be given to my wife. Naturally, I didn't send all of it home. Not even half. So much money! I could afford anything I liked, so I started to live in a most extravagant way.

In Canton there were some 'flower boats'. These were fishing junks which were very nicely decorated and each boat had a number of girls attached to it. At that time there were only about ten boats left but in the old days, in the days of the Qing dynasty, the flower-boats of Canton were famous throughout China. For the next few months I never went back to my rooms at night. I stayed every night on the flower boats. At midnight, after the tombola houses were closed, I would take a rickshaw down Long Bank Avenue, along the right bank of the river, until we came to the flower boats. There we would have dinner, snacks, brandy, laughter, the company of beautiful girls. These girls were all free agents. They had the right to accept or reject any customer. And for me, it was all free. It didn't cost me anything. I paid for the food and the drink but I didn't pay for the company of these girls and I didn't pay for the accommodation. Naturally, if I slept with a girl then I would have to pay her. But for me to stay the night on the junks cost nothing. At the beginning naturally I did pay. They didn't know who I was and they didn't know me. But later they saw I was a powerful man and that I had a sweet tongue. We became friends.

Each boat had only two or three girls. Some were plain and some were beautiful. There were perhaps thirty girls in all. I chose to stay on the biggest boat and every night I would invite my favourites to share a snack with me. Normally, it was very expensive to spend a night on one of these boats. A whole evening would easily cost $500. That is why there were so few boats left. Most people couldn't afford it. Once the girls understood that I was going to come every night some of them refused other offers so that they could have dinner with me. Every night I had the best seafood and the best brandy. I was served by the most beautiful girls. I was making a fortune and every night I was having a joyous party.

A man comes up to Canton from Hong Kong. Within three or four months he is operating two of the most successful tombola houses. He is also managing the top new restaurant in the city. He spends every night on the flower boats. Naturally, such a man must attract people's attention. People will ask: who is this man? How is it that he can get such opportunities? How much money did he pay and to who? But I can tell you this. I never paid Poon Yung one dollar. So, why did he do this for me? No one else has ever done me such big favours. And yet I hardly knew the man. He hardly knew me. How can I explain it? All I can say is that it happened because Poon Yung liked me. Sometimes these things happen. I always regret that I wasn't able to see him more and to give him a present or give him something back, in return. But after I opened the tombola houses I hardly saw him. He was so busy and I was so busy. When I tried to get hold of him, he was usually out. His junior officers always offered to send him messages but I told them I must see him personally. They all knew that I never gave him any money or any present. But, between two human beings there is something that can happen. A kind of recognition. I impressed him as a capable man. And he liked me. Can you explain why you like one person and not another? Can you explain why you love one girl and not another? How can you explain these things? I will remember him forever. What happened to him in the end? I think he went to Taiwan. After Canton fell to the Communists, I never heard of him again. But his influence was strong. I know the other tombola houses were visited every night by the police looking for tea money. But no one ever came to me. They knew I had powerful protection.

One day, I was at the restaurant when two men approached me and introduced themselves. I have forgotten their names but they were members of the plain-clothes branch of the police.

'We know that you are a powerful man and well-connected but Canton is a complicated place and you may benefit from our protection.'

I understood what they were saying. It was a form of squeeze. If I gave them something I would soon have to give them more.

'Everyone knows us and,' he patted his jacket, 'we have guns.'

'Thank you for your interest in me,' I said. 'If you want to help me I accept with pleasure. But let me tell you something. I will not pay you one cent. You are welcome to come with me for dinner and drinks every evening.'

They agreed without any argument. Why not? I was a novelty. I would entertain them on the flower boats. What other benefits might they get if they stayed in my company? These two were joined by two more from another police station and after that another two joined us. After a month I was continually accompanied by six of the best-known policemen in Canton. Of course, I was carrying a lot of money so it made sense to have someone to accompany me. Every night I put the takings from one of the tombola houses in a money belt that I kept round my waist. It bulged out with the notes. I looked pregnant with money. One of my employees, a man I trusted, kept the takings from the other house. We deposited it in the bank at nine the next morning. I never slept a wink. All night I drank, ate and laughed with the girls.

One night we did have some trouble with the triads. Not big trouble. In the end I forced the head of the 14K triad to apologise to me. I have to laugh. Now the 14K are famous everywhere for their ruthlessness and violence but then it was different. The 14K was founded just after the Japanese defeat by a Kuomintang general by the name of Kwok Siu-wong. At first it wasn't bad. It consisted of retired soldiers who banded together for their own security. They chose the name 14K because fourteen karat gold is harder than eighteen karat gold. We Chinese prefer pure gold which is very yellow and soft. But fourteen karat gold is hard and they wanted to give the idea of being a hard organisation but also a wealthy one. Later when the Communists came they fled to Hong Kong. They ceased to be under the leadership of one man. They fought with local triads for control of territory. The name 14K became very bad. The worst, most violent crimes were always committed by the 14K. Maybe that was the reputation they wanted.

But to go back to Canton. One night three men tried to get into the tombola house without paying the entrance fee. Not a big deal. They didn't expect to be refused. They just told my staff that they wanted to come in free because they were members of the 14K. My staff sent someone to tell me. I was in my office supervising the distribution of tickets. I was mad.

'Where are they?'

The man pointed to the group at the back of the hall. It was already crowded. I could have forced my way through the customers but I was so furious that I leapt on to a table and jumped from table to table across the room. Then I jumped down in front of them. Everyone could see what was going on. The three men looked scared. They hadn't been looking for trouble. But this was not something I could let go. If I showed any weakness the problem would get worse.

'They've got guns, boss,' one of my bodyguards told me.

I immediately raised my hand and threatened the leader of the three.

'You want to shoot your way out? You can try. But I warn you. I will certainly kill two of you before you get me!'

'Please, please. We don't want to cause trouble.'

'Hand over your guns then.'

So they handed over their guns.

'Now, I am going to take these guns to the police station. If you want them back you can get them from there,' I told them.

'They don't belong to us, sir! General Kwok will be very unhappy about this.'

'You tell General Kwok he can have the guns back if he comes and apologises. Then I will give him the guns back. Now get out!'

My bodyguards threw them out.

That night when everyone had gone I hid the guns in my office. The next morning I took them to the police station. I knew the district superintendent. He was happy to keep them for me and gave me a receipt.

The next evening, as we were getting ready, a very well-dressed young man came to the tombola hall and asked for me. He introduced himself as Mr Kwok's secretary and proceeded to apologise that General Kwok couldn't come in person but that he was there as his representative. He was a very polite, soft-spoken man. I liked him.

'Mr Hui,' he said, 'I must apologise for the behaviour of our men last night. I hope you can forget it. It would also be a very great favour if you could return our guns to us.'

Naturally I didn't want any enemies but I also wished to emphasise my position so I told him that I didn't require to see General Kwok in person but that if I received a note giving an apology and an explanation I would be satisfied. I would then be pleased to arrange for the guns to be returned. We agreed to meet the following morning and to have tea together.

So we met. He handed me a short note from General Kwok. It was enough. We enjoyed our morning tea together and then I went with him to the police station and we collected the guns.

And so business continued. But I already knew that time was short. The Communists had won big victories in the north. Now they controlled most of China. They were going to come. We all knew that. I had been introduced by Poon Yung to Mr Yip Siu. Mr Yip was the head of the Military Department, the Wai Ssu Jung Bo. All the other departments came under it. Even the provincial governor was advised by this department. Mr Yip was not a military man. He was an administrator. That is how I came to understand just how powerful Poon Yung was. He never told me his job but I saw that even Mr Yip showed him great respect. He had to bow to Poon Yung. As I was Poon's friend he had to respect me too. And naturally, in the same way, all the staff at the Wai Ssu Department had to show me respect too. Now this was an important connection for me because as soon as it became clear that the Communists were going to come I went round to the Wai Ssu offices every day to pick up the latest reports. They had a radio link with the front. I stayed with the junior officers and listened. I heard everything firsthand.

Let me explain something about Guangdong Province. It is shaped like a triangle. Both sides of the triangle are mountainous and it is difficult country to cross. But at the apex of the triangle, at the point where the two sides meet, there is a pass. This is the site of the town of Siu Kwan. This is the main route from Canton to Beijing. We have a saying that anyone who wants to go north to take the imperial exams must first go through Siu Kwan. Just to the north of Siu Kwan is a place called Chui Kong. This was the site the Kuomintang settled on for their last major battle with the Communists. If they could hold this site then they could hold all of Guangdong Province. Naturally the first people to know what was happening in the north were the agents of the Wai Ssu Department. It was August when they heard that the Communists were coming. There was a great battle at Chui Kong and the Kuomintang were defeated. Now the Communists could not be stopped. It was only a matter of time before they reached Canton.

But the Communists took their time. Now that victory was inevitable they didn't want to have to fight if they could avoid it. So they started to negotiate. They said to the Kuomintang: 'We are all Chinese. We see no point in continuing the bloodshed. Brother should not continue to kill brother. You must know that we have won. We will come slowly and tell you in advance where we will come. If your officers hand over everything in an orderly manner no one will get hurt.' For the next two or three weeks I spent many hours every day listening to the radio. I knew when each town changed hands. The Communists would take up positions. They would contact the Kuomintang officer in charge. There would be a hand-over of keys. Then the Kuomintang would withdraw.

There is a place called Wong Sa close to the western edge of Canton. I was there, on the roof of the headquarters building. We could see the city spread out. We could see Wong Sa, not so far away. The Communists were already there. When I heard that news I left the headquarters for the last time. I went straight to the tombola houses and told the employees that they should go home and wait. Then I went back to my own flat which I shared with an old friend from school who was working for the Kuomintang customs.

The Communists did not come in straight away. Maybe they had to give time for the Kuomintang to evacuate the city. Everything was closed up. The city streets were empty. Everyone was nervous. No one knew what to expect. I went out every day. I don't like to stay in. I need exercise. Besides, I was curious. Some teahouses stayed open so I spent a few hours each day in various teahouses chatting. I was in a teahouse when I saw my first Communist soldiers.

There were ten or a dozen of them. Young men. They came into the teahouse and asked to see the manager. Very politely they asked the manager if he could spare them some rice, and perhaps some salted fish of if he didn't have that some Chinese onion bulbs. They were very courteous and they explained that they only wished to borrow these supplies. They would make a special note and arrange for it to be returned. Since they were soldiers and they could have taken everything they wanted by force the manager was very surprised. He said he could let them have some food. The soldiers thanked him and then asked if there was anywhere they could go to prepare their food. They were all thin, pale-faced men. The manager led them away to the back. I was very curious. These were the first I had seen.

'They are very courteous,' I commented.

The cashier nodded.

'They come in here and ask to borrow food. Will they return it? Who can say? But when you look at them you have to feel sorry.'

It was true. They looked hard. They had been fighting for years for no money and just enough food to survive on. Their uniforms were shabby and some didn't even have shoes. Others had straw sandals tied on with string. Yet their discipline was marvellous. Everyone came to respect them. There was no problem for women. Later, I heard from the teahouse manager that everything they borrowed they returned. It was the same thing with lodging. Groups of soldiers would go from house to house knocking on doors and asking the occupant if they had a spare room. And so it went on. There were no big army camps. The army was quartered on the people of the city.

I asked the teahouse manager if he minded my going back to talk to these soldiers because I was curious. The kitchen area of any restaurant is generally prohibited to customers. But the manager just waved for me to go where I wanted. They were in the yard at the back of the kitchen. I greeted them. Naturally, they couldn't speak much Cantonese and I didn't speak any Mandarin but we managed to make ourselves understood. They had walked to Canton from Siu Kwan in only three days. I had done this journey myself some time before. It had taken me five hours of easy travelling on buses. I was very impressed.

I was stuck in Canton for the next two months. The railway was closed. The train drivers had fled to Hong Kong and it was some time before the rail link was started up again. I spent this time quietly. I would see soldiers marching around the town but more commonly they went round in casual groups. I would often get into conversation with them. The more I saw them the more impressed I was. It took a while for the city to return to normal. The Communists ordered the shopkeepers to open up again for business but at first only about a quarter of them did so. Then the others gradually opened up. But still it was quiet. There wasn't any night-life. But I noticed that soon the streets were much cleaner. It was small things like that that impressed me.

On the first of November the railway opened again. I had got myself a ticket so I went down to the station. I saw immediately that there was no chance of my going. Hundreds of people flooded into the station, climbing over gates and fences. Even though people didn't have tickets they forced their way on to the train carriages and refused to budge. There were only half a dozen Communist soldiers there. There was nothing they could do. I suppose their attitude was that anyone who wanted to go should just go. I decided I didn't want to fight my way through the crowd so I went home. The next day, out of curiosity I returned to the station. I expected to see the same kind of scenes. But everything was under control and there was no problem for me to get on a train. I hadn't brought a suitcase as I hadn't expected to be able to leave. But as there was no problem I got the train and went back to my family in Hong Kong.

A few weeks later I had to return. I had to settle up all the business matters relating to the restaurants. The Communists asked me to open up the restaurant and the tombola house again.

'Naturally, you can't operate a gambling casino but you could have a nightclub with singers. That would be acceptable.'

But I knew that I couldn't make either business succeed. A top-class restaurant caters to wealthy customers. Who would come to my restaurant? And even if I did good business I would have to hand over most of my takings to the Communists. They were very polite and respectful. But when I explained that I wasn't going to keep them going, they informed me that I could not sell off the furniture as it now belonged to the state. So I returned to Hong Kong again. And although I had made so much money I was soon completely broke again. This time it wasn't so easy for me. I didn't know it then but the next few years were going to be very hard.

When I stepped off the train at the Kowloon terminus, that day early in December of 1949, I was not unhappy. I accepted my fate. One day I was rich, the next day I had nothing. I had no worries. I knew people. Something would happen. And in the meantime I had money. I was in no hurry to get work. I didn't even think of it. I look back at that moment. It is like a photograph in my memory. I was happy and rich. The railway station was just a hundred yards from the Star Ferry to Hong Kong. December was still warm with a touch of coolness. I walked from the station to the ferry, got on the ferry and crossed the harbour and then. . . .

My short career as a gangster

I WOULDN'T HAVE MET KEI if Wong hadn't run away from his father's home to marry a second wife.

Wong was an old friend of mine and his father was a very wealthy medicine wholesaler in the Nam Pak Hong area. Wong had fallen in love with a girl and insisted on taking her as his second wife despite the opposition of his father. His first wife, naturally, had no say in the matter. So Wong had to move out of the family house and set up home with his second wife. He had no idea about how to make money. He had no experience of life. He had to borrow money from his friends. But a rich man doesn't understand money. Things went from bad to worse. He drifted about and soon met a number of petty criminals. From time to time, he contacted me and I helped him out with some money but the fact was I was broke myself. Sometimes we met for morning tea. One day he introduced me to four men. One of them was Kei. I can't remember the names of the others. Kei was the leader.

They were from Canton but after the Communists arrived they had come down to Hong Kong. They too were broke. Wong had told them something of my story so they were very impressed with me. Actually, they were looking for a leader. They respected me for my education, my understanding, my intelligence and of course for my *kung fu*. I told them about the war years. Kei had belonged to the Siu Kwei Tui – the Small Ghost Troops. The Siu Kwei Tui were children who had been given military training by the Chinese army and then divided into gangs. They were given the job of going secretly into Japanese army camps and killing as many Japanese soldiers as they could. They would sneak into the camps on dark moonless nights armed only with knives. It was so dark they couldn't see anything. Everything had to be done by touch. Before they went into the camp they would take off their trousers. This was how they could tell who was one of them and who was the enemy. When they came upon somebody, they would touch their legs. If the person was wearing pants they would stab him. These Siu Kwei Tui were very famous at that time and they were very successful. They really scared the Japanese. It was impossible to guard against them all the time.

Why did the Chinese use children for this job? Two reasons. They are small and quick and light on their feet so it is easier for them to do the job. Also, being children, they weren't so scared of death. They never thought of death. They were noted for their bravery and patriotism. Kei was one of these. He was a real hero.

Naturally, as we sat around drinking tea, our conversation turned to the question of money. It was an important question.

'We have no choice,' Kei explained to me, 'if we don't commit a robbery we will starve.'

'You should try to think of some other way of getting money,' I advised, 'robbery is not such an easy thing to do.'

'We've got three guns, Mr Hui, and we know how to use them. If there are any problems we will just shoot and run away.'

Guns? With guns of course, robbing some company wouldn't be difficult. But still it wasn't simple. I explained it to them.

'Even with guns, there is a big difference between a safe robbery and a dangerous robbery. If you do it wrong, if you go into the wrong kind of company, or if you go at the wrong time of day, then you will have a lot of problems but no reward for your efforts.'

'You are right Mr Hui,' Kei said. 'What do you suggest?'

Actually, the more I thought about it, the more I could see that robbing a shop or a company might be a very easy way to make some money. If . . . if it was done in the right way.

'Perhaps I can help you,' I said, 'but one thing you must promise me. You must never hurt people.'

'We don't want to hurt anyone,' Kei assured me. 'We just want to make enough money to support us. That's all.'

'Then maybe I'll help you plan some robberies.'

Kei insisted that I should consider myself the leader of the gang.

I thought about the matter seriously and decided the best plan was to start with something small and easy and then to go on to something even bigger. I had a long-term plan which I believed would make us millions. But first, something small. The man I chose was quite a well-known fortune teller. It amused me to steal from him. If he was a real fortune teller he should know that we would be coming to attack him! Of course, all fortune tellers are just conmen. Perhaps they have some wisdom but I doubt it. They just shake their coins in a tortoise shell and roll them out to see the result. In fact they can't see the result, they have to feel it, as most fortune tellers are blind. That was another advantage. He wouldn't know who was robbing him. He wouldn't be able to identify the men. We waited until evening then I sent them up to the fortune teller's office. We discussed whether I should go or not. Kei insisted on this point.

'Mr Hui, you are not experienced in this work. We have some experience. You plan out the robberies and we will do the work.'

They went off to rob the man and later they returned with a few thousand dollars. It was easy work and now they had some money. Naturally, we had a good dinner with a lot of brandy to celebrate.

Now, there was the question of how to divide the money. I said this was an easy decision: everyone should get an equal share. But Kei insisted that as I was the leader, and as I had planned everything, I should get half. Also, they knew my overheads were high. I had a family to support. We argued until finally we agreed that I should take a quarter. I should explain that Wong also did not go to rob the fortune teller. It would have been dangerous for him to go as he had no experience. He would certainly have done something silly and the others might have got caught as a result. It was too dangerous. Still, he was part of the gang and got his share.

So our first robbery was successful. Now that we had taken care of our immediate needs we could look for someone with more money. But it must be absolutely safe. I stressed this point many times. It must be safe. No one must get hurt. I thought about the options and eventually decided that the Hok Ming Shoe company in Central would make a very good target.

Shops then were more or less like now, staying open until nine or ten at night. We decided to attack the shop just before nine. This was the best time for several reasons. They would have collected all that day's takings. The staff would be tired. They would be thinking of going home. Maybe some would already have left. Everything worked out according to plan and soon Kei arrived at our meeting place with $3,000. Everything had gone exactly as I had said it would.

I decided we needed to do one more robbery before going on to the big job I had in mind. So for the next robbery, I hoped to get $10–15,000 from an office in Central. I chose an import-export company on the fifth floor of Kayamally building, just across the road from the Hong-kong Hotel. An office is different from a shop. If you wait for an office to close they will already have deposited the day's takings in the bank. I knew that this company did most of its business in the morning. So I arranged that Kei and his gang would go into the office just before lunch. I chose this office because I knew the layout. The office was run by two brothers and they only had two staff, so there would be a maximum of four people there.

The first part of the robbery went smoothly. Kei pointed his gun at the brothers. They opened the safe and handed over the cash. Then Kei and the gang left. Now Kei was very brave, but he wasn't very intelligent. He should have tied up the staff. Maybe I should have thought about it. Maybe they didn't have anything to tie them up with. Maybe they didn't even think about it. They took the money and calmly left the office.

They were on the fifth floor of the building. They had the choice of taking the lift or walking. They decided against taking the lift. It would take too long to come. Also they might be trapped in it. So they walked down the stairs. Maybe they didn't want to run and attract attention.

Meanwhile, in the office upstairs, the brothers immediately phoned Central Police Station. The police were alerted and by the time Kei emerged from the building into Queen's Road, there was a policeman checking the crowd for anyone looking suspicious. They saw Kei and his friends and started to follow them. Kei had gone about a hundred yards when he realised he was being followed. They started to walk more quickly. Kei realised the police were after him, so, when they got to Theatre Lane, Kei told the others to run. He took out his gun and started to shoot at the police. The crowds scattered and the police took cover. They started to fire back. Kei only had six bullets in his gun, but the next day, when the newspapers reported the story, it was front page news. Robberies, especially armed robberies weren't so common then. They said that over thirty shots had been fired. Luckily no one was hit. When Kei ran out of bullets, he gave himself up and was arrested. Unfortunately, Kei was carrying most of the money they had stolen.

We had arranged that we would meet at their boarding house after the robbery. They shared a room with some others in a lodging house on the waterfront of Central district. Wong and I went to the room and waited for them. Two of the gang were already there but Kei and the one with the other gun still hadn't arrived. After a while, the third one came and told us that Kei was shooting it out with the police. He wasn't a coward. He just took his chance to get away. We all hoped that Kei would be able to escape. Naturally, we were very nervous and concerned. Then I heard a noise from the street outside. It was the high-pitched sound of police shouting and ordering people around. How did they get there? I didn't know. I knew Kei would never say anything. Not so quickly. But somehow they had found out something. I told the others to leave. I waited for another few minutes and then I thought to myself: 'Why are you waiting here in the room? If the police find you here, you have no excuse. It is better to go outside and wait.'

I was just in time. The room was on the second floor. I started to walk down the stairs but I hadn't even got to the first floor when the police stopped me.

'You! Do you live here?'

'Me? No.'

'What are you doing here?'

'I'm looking for a friend. I thought he might be staying here. He's coming down from Canton. I don't know his room number.'

They looked me over very carefully but in the end they let me go. I was very well dressed. I didn't look like a robber. Also, although Canton and Hong Kong are so close to each other, you can easily tell a Canton man from a Hong Kong man just by looking at him. Kei was a Canton man. I was a Hong Kong man. Probably the police didn't think I would be part of a gang of Canton robbers.

So, in the end, only Kei was caught. He was sentenced to at least ten years in prison. And how did the police get to the lodging house so quickly? Naturally, they knew that there were four people in the gang so they knew Kei had some partners. As he refused to answer their questions, they searched his pockets. There they found a laundry bill. They went to the laundry and the staff there recognised Kei as being a regular customer who lived in the lodging house. That's how I was nearly caught.

Later, I met with the other gang members and told them I wasn't going to continue in the robbery line. Kei was a man I could trust. He had a cool head. He was a natural leader. He knew what to do when things became tough. Now that he was gone, I wasn't going to risk being involved any more. I persuaded the others that they too should go back to Canton. As they were obviously Canton people, the police would eventually stop and question them. They would inevitably be deported or sent to prison. They agreed. I never saw them again. But I did see Kei again. That's another story.

So that was the end of my career as a gangster. But I must tell you what my plan was. If this robbery had been successful, with that money I would have bought some equipment for my final robbery. We needed disguises, we needed guns and we needed a getaway car. I planned to do only one more robbery. I wanted to do such a big robbery that I would never have to do any more. What was my target? Not a bank. Even bigger than a bank. My next target would have been the Treasury of Hong Kong!

I must explain that the treasury in those days was right in the middle of Central district. It was an old building. From the street, you went up a few steps and into the main entrance. Inside was a big open office. There was a counter and behind the counter there were two very large safes. In those days there wasn't so much security. People were not so aware of the dangers of armed robbery. And why did I think the Treasury was a good target? Because I had been inside a few times. I knew one of the clerks there and had visited him occasionally. So, I knew what it was like. It was easier to attack than a bank because there weren't so many people around. Only about ten. One, maybe two, Europeans. The rest Chinese. I expected there would be about a million dollars. That would have been my next target. When I think back, I think maybe it would have been too ambitious. If we had gone ahead with this robbery, I planned to take part too. It would have been dangerous. I might have been caught and put in prison. I might have been shot and killed. With a robbery anything can happen. Maybe I was lucky the other robbery had gone wrong. Maybe God was protecting me.

What about Wong? His story had a happy ending. His second wife gave him a baby boy. With his first wife he only had one or two daughters. Naturally, his father was an old fashioned man. He wanted to have grandsons. As soon as he heard he had a grandson, he welcomed his son back into his household. His first wife had nothing to say about the matter. Later, I often used to drop in on his shop and borrow some money. Wong was always good to me.

'Earless' Lam

H IS REAL NAME WAS LAM KAI-WAH but everyone called him Mo Yee Jai, 'Earless'. He was the chief of the Wanchai triad at that time.

Wanchai was the same as it is now, a place of bars and nightclubs and girls. Nowadays there are topless bars but in those days all the nightclubs offered hostesses that you could dance with or sit and drink with. There weren't any girls on the street, they were all controlled in brothels. If you wanted a girl you just had to ask any of the old women on the street, or a rickshaw runner and they would take you there and collect a commission. That's how it worked. And Earless controlled everything.

Wanchai was busy. At one end were the bars and nightclubs that the Americans and British went to. At the other end were the Chinese nightclubs like the Tonnochy. The Tonnochy was where Earless operated from. Also, I knew all the triads and they knew me. I met most of them when I was working at the traffic office. That's where I met Earless. He had often come to ask for licences.

At that time I had nothing better to do. I had no work that would pay me anything like a decent wage. Perhaps I could have got a job sweating for twelve hours a day for very little money but why should I do that when I have friends I could drink with and borrow from for food for today and tomorrow? And Wanchai was the best place to go drinking.

Earless and I became friends. He respected me and I respected him. He was just a simple, rough, uneducated man. We often went drinking together. Why was he called Earless? The story was like this. Mo Yee Jai was just a simple country boy. He had only his strength and his courage to help him earn a living. He started off protecting an illegal mahjong parlour and then he built up a territory for himself. Of course he wasn't the only person trying this game so he often got into fights. He wasn't a clever fighter but he had one advantage over other people: he never backed down. Even if the other fighter was stronger than him he just kept fighting. Now this will scare other fighters. If I am a better fighter than you but I see that the only way to destroy you is to kill you then I will get scared myself and back off. One day he got into a fight with someone who was stronger than him and who he couldn't beat. He wasn't a big man and he didn't have good fighting technique. He was just strong and he was brave. But as he couldn't beat this other man and they were struggling together in the street he found himself staring at the other man's ear. He had an idea and bit hard. Naturally, the man was furious. Now, if we are so close that you can bite my ear then I must be close enough to bite your ear. So his opponent bit Lam's ear right off. Not all the ear. Just the lower half. But Lam still continued fighting and eventually the other one surrendered. This was a well-known story at that time. It was because of that fight and other fights like it that Lam established his reputation and then he started to attract associates and soon he had established himself in Wanchai.

One night, Earless and I nearly had a fight. One evening I went to the Tonnochy Nightclub. There was an illegal gambling room on the top floor. I went there because I was short of money. Sometimes I am lucky and sometimes I am very unlucky. This evening I lost. The more I lost, the more I tried to get my money back and I lost even more. I was down about $2,000 by the end. The problem was I didn't have any money. I had been betting on credit. They knew me so they let me continue gambling. But when I wanted to stop they asked me to settle up. I was a sucker that night. I lost to two people who didn't know me. I told them I would go and borrow some money and settle up my debt but they didn't trust me. They thought that once I had gone I would never return. In fact I could raise that amount of money without much trouble. But they refused to let me go and so they asked Earless to sort out the problem. Earless and I were on friendly terms but he didn't know me so well at that time.

'Mr Hui, you are not rich. We all know that. Once you start to lose you should stop.'

'You're right,' I agreed. 'Everybody knows that. But the fact is I lost the money in the heat of gambling. That's why I had bad luck. Now, what do you suggest I do?'

'Well, as you have no money, you must arrange for someone to bring the money here.'

'Good. Let me go and I will contact some friends and I will raise the money. Then I will come back and settle the debt. That is the best way.'

The fact is I would have to raise the money from a number of people. I didn't want to ask just one person for the whole amount. Earless wasn't happy with this suggestion.

'Ayah! You are giving me a lot of trouble. I am the boss here. I have my reputation to consider. If people win at my tables they must be paid or they won't come back. I am not the only boss. I have partners to consider.'

'Now, Mo Yee Jai,' I said, 'you and I are friends. I have no desire to cause you trouble but if you don't let me go then we are not friends. Ask all your partners and all your staff to come here and I will fight my way out. If I have to fight I will consider I don't have to repay the money.'

But he wouldn't let me go. We argued this way and that way back and forwards. But then I got angry. I pointed at his ear.

'You only have half an ear. I will fight with you and take the other half. If you don't want to let me go you must fight me.'

Now at this time Mo Yee Jai didn't know me so well. Maybe he knew I had a certain reputation. But I think he was impressed. I was on the top floor of his nightclub building but I showed I wasn't at all scared. I even challenged him to a fight – in his own headquarters! Naturally he had no desire to lose face.

'Well, Mr Hui. Just this once. But never again.'

'If you do me this favour I will do you a favour too. I will never come to this gambling room again to gamble.'

In fact he didn't know that I had so many rich friends. He thought I was just making an excuse so that I could escape. But in fact, because of this, I considered I didn't have to repay the debt. Mo Yee Jai must have paid it off. This shows you what kind of man he was because we remained friends.

I should explain something about what I know of the background.

How Mo Yee Jai came to control Wanchai I don't know. It didn't happen at one time. The triad situation at that time was very different from now. Now you just hear of triad gangs with names like 14K and Sun Yee On but in those days it was different. Each district was controlled by one gang. I told you how the Tiger group moved from the Hollywood Road area to Happy Valley at the beginning of the Japanese occupation. They stayed there. Even in the mid-sixties I was in contact with them. That was before I came to Cheung Chau. Once I came here I lost touch with everyone. Now, why did I contact them? Ah! It was the matter of my sixth daughter's birth certificate. I was trying to get her back to Hong Kong from China. I needed to prove that she was born in Hong Kong. But she had been born at home during the Japanese occupation. The only way I could prove it was to get a signed statement from the midwife who attended my wife. This woman was quite well-known. I asked Tiger to help me find her. It was no problem. He knew everybody.

There will always be small gangs that are nearly independent. But they must recognise the power of the chief triad group in that area. Each district had its own chief triad group. Earless Lam controlled Wanchai but before that there was another triad leader there called Ma Yue-bo. Ma was a very tricky man. He wasn't a fighter. But everyone was a little bit scared of him because he was mean. Maybe you would have a fight and beat him but after that you wouldn't know what he would do to your family to get revenge. So it was best to stay out of his way. But Ma was not so powerful as Earless. He knew he couldn't win in a fight. So he joined Earless's group and became a sort of lieutenant.

These groups respected each other and there were never any fights between them. But then the 14K came down from Canton. They didn't have any territory so they had to fight to take control. They got a reputation for ruthlessness. But at this time they were mainly centred in Kowloon. For many years the top gang was the 14K. But it is better to think of 14K not as one single gang but an association of different gangs. So, let's say you are moving into my territory and you are the 14K and I can see that I can't defeat you, then I will surrender and I will become 14K too. That way I can keep hold of my power. So that's what happened. People remained the same. Just the names changed. But the 14K were too brutal, too violent. I think this was their deliberate policy. They wanted to scare their opponents. But the danger of a reputation like this is that you make a lot of enemies and now they are not so strong. Now the Sun Yee On have taken over as the number one triad. They're new. I don't know anything about them.

Now, although I mixed with the triads and many of my friends were triads, I was never a triad member. Naturally, I was asked many times.

People said to me: 'Hui, with your intelligence and your abilities you could control half of Hong Kong.' But I never seriously considered it. When people said this I just laughed: 'Yes, it's true. If I had wanted to I could have been a powerful triad leader. On the other hand, I could have been killed five years ago. Who can say?'

Once, Tiger asked me to join the Hung Moon Group. I was still a police interpreter at that time and he often asked me for favours. One evening, he said to me: 'Mr Hui, you are a very capable man. I would like to invite you to join the Hung Moon Association. As you know, this is an old and venerable association.'

Now I did know something of the Hung Moon. My father told me stories about it when I was a boy. It started as a very benevolent association which had the aims of helping those who were in need of help. It had the same sort of reputation as Robin Hood. They stole from the rich and helped the poor. Now although their original reputation was good, it had become less respectable. Also, I was very proud of myself. I thought: 'They want to make use of me. What benefit can I get from joining them? Nothing. What benefit can they get from using me? A lot.' So I refused. Tiger was a clever man. He was not like the other triad leaders. He was a gentleman. He was always well-dressed and very courteous. He spoke well. We liked and respected each other. He understood that I thought they were just going to make use of me.

'You should think of it in this way, Mr Hui,' he said. 'You are an exceptional man. The Hung Moon Association still has a lot of influence. It will be easy for you to rise to a position of power in the organisation. Then you can do what you like. This would be a great advantage for you.'

What he said was true but I am like my father. I value my independence too much. My father was never a triad member either. But he knew all the triads. They respected him very much. I'll tell you a story. One day one of the staff of the Peninsula Hotel was walking with his uncle somewhere in Tsimshatsui and they were robbed. They each had to hand over their watches and fountain pens. It was just a common street robbery. Maybe they lost some money as well but the watches and fountain pens were worth something. They complained about this to my father. He told them to come to our house that evening for dinner and in the meantime he would see what he could do. That evening, when they arrived at our house, he led them into the dining room. On the table were two watches and two pens.

'Are these your watches and pens?'

The two men were amazed.

'Yes! Yes! How did you get them back?'

'I know the triad leader. He's a good friend of mine. He passed the word around that the watches and pens must be returned.'

Naturally the men wanted to pay my father something but he refused. He liked to help people. In that way also I am like my father.

So Tiger failed to persuade me to join the Hung Moon Association. I can tell you, when I was poor, I sometimes regretted my decision.

In fact another opportunity came up which I could have taken. The chairman of the Kowloon Godown Workers' Association died and the secretary came to see me.

'Mr Hui, many people have recommended you to me as an honourable and capable man and we would like to ask you to be our chairman.'

I nodded.

'We can't offer you very much salary but there is a way you can make some extra money which might be interesting to you. We all know you are a *kung fu* fighter. Some of our workers would like to accept lessons from you. We would suggest the sum of five dollars per worker a month for lessons. I have sounded out our members and I can say about three quarters would want to accept lessons. In this way you could make several thousand dollars a month. I hope you will consider this.'

I needed the money but I had to think very carefully about this. Now, it was always made very clear to me that a *kung fu* master was responsible for the actions of his students. The first thing my master, Lam Sai-wing, told me – and this lesson was passed down to him from his master, Wong Fei-hung, the most famous *kung fu* fighter in all of Chinese history – was that a *kung fu* fighter had to have a high level of morality. It's true now that most *kung fu* schools are very closely connected with triads – in fact, *kung fu* teachers nowadays are rubbish – but this wasn't true in my days. I can say that not one of my fellow students was a triad member. Thinking on this, the way I saw it, the porters at the godown were a rough crowd and the district they worked in, Yaumatei, was also a rough area. In those days, and even now, it is a place of low-class brothels and gambling dens and drug distribution. The association had over 1,000 members. If I taught them *kung fu*, how could I be sure that they would all use it for moral purposes? If I could be sure of one thing it was that there must be some members there who were not straight and honest men. They would abuse the skills I taught them. If there was a fight in the district I would have to intervene. If one of our members was at fault I would have to apologise and make some form of compensation. On the other hand, if our member was right then I would have to fight on his side and who knows who I would be fighting against. I might come against men who preferred to use guns. *Kung fu* is no use against a gun. I thought about this offer very seriously but in the end I refused it. It was too dangerous. If I used it for my own immoral purposes then maybe I could achieve something. I could become a senior triad leader with a large gang of fighters. But I had no such intention. I am not a greedy man. I have no desire to gain a fortune through protection, prostitution or drugs. I just want to fool around. If I was not serious enough to profit from the situation it was better not to take up the offer. So, very politely, I declined the invitation.

I am not made to be a criminal. I have done many foolish things. I have been corrupt. But I am not an evil man. I have helped more people than I have hurt. God will judge me mercifully.

Now, at this time, I was completely broke. I was miserable. And the more depressed I got the more I drank. I was always drinking and I was always getting into fights. I remember one evening I was drinking with Earless. We were in a basement bar drinking brandy. It was late. I was very drunk that night and Lam had to support me. We left the bar. Outside there were several policemen on patrol in the street. One saw me staggering and in a loud voice started to lecture me about drinking too much and causing a nuisance. Now, even though I was drunk my training is very good. I was annoyed with the man so I stepped up to him and with one quick movement I caught his arm and twisted it round to the back. At the same time I unbuttoned his holster and pulled his pistol out. I don't know why I did this. I think I did it to stop him taking the gun out. I had the thought that he might try to take his pistol out and shoot me. But I couldn't take the gun away because it was tied to the holster with a lanyard. So I pointed the pistol at the policeman's head. Of course this was a very stupid thing to do. There were several other policemen there and they were very alarmed at the situation. One, a sergeant, tried to creep up behind me but my senses were very alert. I didn't see him but I knew he was there. Maybe I heard something or saw his shadow, I can't say, but I sensed an attack so as he came at me I let go of the policeman and with a quick movement I twisted round and caught hold of his head which I held in a tight grip with my elbow. I have to laugh when I remember this. All the uniformed services require a minimum height of five foot six inches. I was a short man but I had defeated two policemen who were bigger than me. I had a gun pointing at one's head and I had the other head under my elbow. I had to laugh. But that was the end of the story. The other policemen saw how dangerous the situation was and they all dived on top of me. I was buried under them. I suppose they knew I couldn't shoot the gun as the safety catch was on. I had committed a serious offence but Mo Yee Jai was very influential. He apologised and explained I was drunk. As he was the triad boss of the district they accepted the situation and let me go.

A fight in a billiard hall

At that time there were a half-dozen billiard halls in Hong Kong. It was the American sailors who brought the game. It quickly became very popular and the halls were full all day.

One day, one of my friends came to see me.

'Mr Hui, I hope you can help me.' He sat down and told me the problem. He was the marker at one of the halls. Every day, a man came in with a few friends. He would select a table and then he would rub out the names of all the people who had signed up for that table. Then he would write his own name down in their place. No one ever dared to make trouble about this. Then he would go up to my friend and force him to take the table back from the people already playing on it. Most of the men in the hall were a rough crowd but no one dared complain because they all knew this man was the triad head in Western district. But he had to come down to Wanchai because there weren't any billiard halls in Western!

Now setting up a billiard hall is an expensive business. The tables are not cheap. The takings from each table were carefully accounted for. At the end of each week or each month he had to explain to the owners why one table was making less than the others – because, of course, this man never paid to play there.

'The boss says I have to solve the problem or lose my job.' This was a problem for him as he was a drug addict. It wouldn't be easy for him if he lost his job.

'My boss wants me to throw them out or call the police. But if I do that they'll kill me for sure. It's only a job. It's not worth dying for.'

'Why are you scared of them?'

I asked this because he was quite a big man.

'Mr Hui, they can attack me anytime they like. They know where I work. I'm there all day, every day. If they want to get revenge they know where to find me. They won't attack me one to one. And they might use knives. If they want to teach me a lesson they will want to hurt me badly. That's how it is. You must help me.'

'I can help you. That's true,' I said. 'But why should I? You are a drug addict. If I help you, you will just kill yourself anyway. Everything you earn goes to the drug dealer. I don't think it's worth it.'

'Mr Hui, if you can solve this problem I swear I will quit drugs.'

I laughed.

'Come on, how can I trust you? You will say anything now but afterwards how can I be sure you will keep your word?'

'Easy, Mr Hui. If I don't fulfil my side of the bargain you can ask these men to come back and plague me again.'

'All right. I'll help you.'

The next day I got a call.

'He's here.'

I went round to the hall and found my friend waiting for me.

'He's the one sitting near the counter.'

I saw the man was with a few friends. They were just sitting and talking and having a drink.

'Good. Now don't get involved.'

'He hasn't done anything yet but I guarantee he will come and ask me to clear a table soon.'

'Well, just do as he says. I'll wait until he starts playing.'

I got myself a cup of coffee and sat down about ten feet from him on a long bench.

Then, just as my friend had said he would, he got up and ordered my friend to clear a table. I let him play for a few minutes. I wanted to get a feel of the group. How many were there? Where did they stand? Then, just as he was about to play a shot I went up behind him, took hold of his cue with my right hand and twisted it out of his grip suddenly. He was very surprised.

'Hey! What did you do that for?'

'I am clearing you off this table just as you cleared the others before you,' I told him, 'if you don't go now I will hit you.'

He just stared at me. He took a quick look round to see how many friends I had with me.

'Maybe you think I am threatening you with this cue?' I smiled at him, 'here, you take it.' I handed it back to him. He still didn't move. I can say he was stunned. No one had ever challenged him like this before.

'If you ask your colleagues to help you then naturally I will fight in a different way. It's up to you. Either way is fine with me.'

He just glared at me. He was trying to judge who I was, what kind of person I was.

'There's no need to stare at me like that. There's nothing to think about. I am a man who is challenging you to a fight. I know you are a triad leader. I am just a common man who wants to fight you. Either you are scared or you are angry. That's your business.'

Now, no one will want to get into a fight with someone they don't know. He tried to reason with me.

'I don't know you. I didn't do anything wrong to you. What I do to other people is my business.'

'That's right. But what you do to my friends is my business. The marker here is my friend. Now I warn you very clearly, if you try to harm my friend or get revenge I will come and kill you. I know who you are. I warn you: I am a man who does what he says and I am not afraid of you. Even now, maybe you have guns or knives? Let's see them.'

I was getting more and more fierce as I spoke. He could see the anger in my face. I go very red when I am angry. His associates tried to intervene but I threw their hands off me and pushed them away.

'Now, fuck off. Go fuck your mother. Your time is up. What is your decision? Are you going to fight?'

He put the cue down.

'We are going. You will see what happens in the future.'

'Don't try to scare me,' I shouted after them, 'I will be here every afternoon this week. If you want to do anything I will be here waiting for you.'

Naturally, he asked around: 'Who is this small man who dares to challenge five men?'

'That must be Hui,' he would be told, 'don't ever mess with him or you will be killed!'

A chance to eat soft rice

WE HAVE A SAYING THAT a man is 'eating soft rice' when he is kept by a woman.

One day Earless and I were drinking.

'Mr Hui,' he said, 'please don't take what I am going to say in a bad way, but the fact is you are poor. Please, don't take this as an insult. I don't look down on you at all. You are a man with a lot of skills but the fact is you haven't got any money and I know you have a family and that you care about them.'

'So what of it?'

'I mention it only because I have an idea that you might be interested in. Actually, it is not my idea exactly.'

'What's this idea?'

'Well, the other night you were at the Tonnochy. One of the girls you sat with mentioned to me that she liked you.'

I couldn't remember any girl in particular. He described her but I couldn't remember her at all.

'She's one of the most popular girls there. I can say she probably earns the most. I know her well. We often have a midnight snack together. She needs a man to protect her. Your name came up. She asked me to invite you to have dinner with her.'

'What's all this about? What's behind this?' I was a bit surprised.

'Come on, Hui, that's obvious. She's rich. You're poor. She likes you. It should be easy to come to some form of financial arrangement.'

I understood. A girl makes a lot of money in that line but she must make sure she is safe from being squeezed by some punk. It is better to have a companion. A hostess can't marry a decent man unless she gives up her career. Maybe they hope for that. But if they are earning good money maybe they prefer to be independent. But a woman wants to have her own man. That was the proposition.

'Ask her what she wants. What are her terms?'

'You ask her yourself.'

'Earless, I have a problem. I can't remember what this girl looks like. I can't picture her.'

He laughed.

'That's easy. Come to the Tonnochy tonight or tomorrow night. Be my guest. I will introduce her to you and you can discuss this with her in person.'

So I agreed to go and meet the girl. What was her name? I should remember. She was a nice girl. Very attractive. She wasn't exactly Cantonese but she wasn't Shanghainese either. Maybe she was mixed. Very beautiful and entertaining. She was twenty-six or -seven years old I guessed. She was a girl with education and intelligence. She even knew some classical Chinese.

At the end of the evening we went to a restaurant for a late night snack and talked. I had already told Earless to tell the girl I would be happy to meet her and to talk but if she wanted anything she would have to bring the matter up herself. I wasn't going to state any terms.

We met several times in a friendly way and I can say we liked each other. Then, one evening, she said to me: 'Mo Yee Jai says you want to hear some terms from me.'

I nodded.

'Well, I think you understand the situation. Now the fact is I have some money but how much I have is my own business. Now I am prepared to offer you $200,000 cash. Later, if you have some ideas for a business, well, we can discuss that later. Maybe I will invest more money. That's what I can offer you.'

'I must think it over,' I said. 'Please understand I am not a greedy man. What you have offered me is very fair. I don't ask for more. But I must consider this matter very carefully.'

'Of course, please take your time.'

But I was curious to know why she wanted me. She laughed when I asked her.

She wanted me to marry her. She wanted the security and the title. Something like this I had to talk over with my wife. I mentioned it half-jokingly.

'If a rich girl wants to marry me. What would you say to that?'

She just shrugged her shoulders.

'Well, you can do what you want but you must support me and the children.'

But although she said she didn't mind, she didn't mean it. I thought about it and thought about it and in the end I realised I couldn't accept. If I married her she would control me absolutely. I have never trusted any woman. Never. But I understood this girl was very direct. It wasn't easy to offer such a large amount of your own property to someone you hardly knew. Either she was a fool or she was very clever. It's true, a clever person can see to the heart of things immediately. She was very experienced in the ways of the world. She could judge a man immediately. She honoured me by choosing me. She was beautiful and she had money. I appreciated that. But I have my own respect. To be controlled by a woman? I couldn't do it. People would laugh at me. They would consider me a pimp. Of course they would envy me too. I asked Earless to tell her my decision.

'You're a fool Hui. This is a good opportunity.'

'I know. But I have my reasons.'

'What?'

'My own private reasons.'

I send my family to China

FINALLY, I CAME TO REALISE that I couldn't afford to support my family in Hong Kong anymore. I had to send them to China. My wife was pregnant with our eighth child. There was no other alternative. I told her my decision and she accepted it.

It wasn't just money. I can say that I also loved Chairman Mao. I had read several of his books and what he said made sense. We Chinese should not live under foreign rule. The Westerners despised us in our own territory. Capitalism exploited the poor. It was best to share one's labour and share also the rewards of the labour. It is a simple idea and I came to believe in it. I was poor. But I couldn't earn a living in China so it was better for me to stay in Hong Kong. Also, my eldest son was ready to leave school and go to work. I decided to keep him in Hong Kong with me. Everyone else would go with my wife to live in Canton.

Once I made up my mind I moved quickly. The first thing I did was to sell our telephone. I had bought this when I was doing well in Canton. It cost a lot of money under the table to get a phone in those days. I had a friend who worked at the telephone company and he sold it for us for a small commission. My landlady heard I was leaving and demanded that she should have half of any key money I made from passing on the flat. I was so mad at her I passed it on for nothing to one of our sub-tenants. Then one day a truck came to take all our belongings down to the dock.

When we got to the dock, the truck driver unloaded everything on the pavement. There were my wife and seven children and myself and Fong-jeh, our clan sister, and another cousin were there to help us with the suitcases and bundles of clothing. As soon as we were unloaded from the truck we were surrounded by porters who immediately started picking up our baggage to take it on to the boat.

'What are you doing?' I shouted, 'Don't touch our baggage.'

'Don't worry. We'll get it on board for you.'

'Fuck off! Leave it alone.'

'I see you don't know the system. Only porters are allowed to carry heavy baggage on to the boats. Now let's see, this will cost you. . . .'

I was furious. People were pushing and shoving. My children were scared. They didn't know what was happening. All I knew was that I didn't intend to pay these porters one damn cent. I saw there was an Indian policeman standing a little way off. I ran over to him to complain about the porters.

'Ah well sir, it may be that they have a monopoly arrangement with the shipping company. I wouldn't know about that. Perhaps they have the right to receive porterage fees on any luggage passing through the pier.'

'Rubbish!' I shouted, 'I have been a government officer and I never heard of any law like that.'

But I understood he must have been paid off.

'Look, I am going to arrange things in my own way. If there is any trouble don't blame me.'

I ran back to the porters who were shouting at my wife and children.

'Get away,' I told them, 'Anyone of you insists that I must pay them even one cent, I will kill them. Now out of my way!'

The porters went into a huddle to discuss the situation but they had seen me talking to the police officer in English. They saw I must be someone. And I challenged ten strong men to a fight. Who would do that without any support? While they were still discussing the situation I organised everybody and we carried the baggage across a plank on to the ferry.

It is an overnight ferry ride to Canton. The next morning we were there. The porters there were cheap and I arranged for our baggage to be taken to a nearby lodging house. Then I set off on my own to look for somewhere for my family to live. My wife knew Canton much better than me and she told me which district I should go to. There were posters on walls everywhere advertising rooms and flats. The prices were so low I laughed. My troubles would soon be over. I really believed that. I went to look at a few flats and then I went with my wife and finally we agreed to take a flat at number 3, To Jung Hong – a little side street. Once we had moved in I had to go to the district security office to register my family. There were some benefits in being registered as an overseas Chinese. And when they were all settled in I returned to Hong Kong.

It was winter then. I remember that. I left my wife to organise the children. Canton was her home town. Although her father was dead she still had brothers and sisters. I didn't have anything to do with them but she must have kept in touch. Some were officials in the Communist Party. She would manage. I promised I would send them money from Hong Kong.

I did try to send them money. I did try. I know they suffered. But it wasn't easy for me either. There were times I didn't have even one cent in my pocket. My children blame me. I know that. They hate me. I have wanted to explain my side to them. But why should I justify myself if they don't talk to me about it? It's not for me to raise the subject. Where is my wife? I don't even know if she is alive. Is she still in China, or is she in Japan? I don't know why I think she might be in Japan. My second daughter used to love me so dearly but later she turned. She took my mother's side. Even my eldest son sometimes was very angry with me. He thought I was spending money on good food while my wife and children were starving. I remember once we were in a good restaurant with my girlfriend and him, just the three of us. We were having very good food. My son refused to eat. My lover left us for a moment.

'Why don't you eat?' I asked him.

'How can I when my mother is starving? Why don't we just eat noodles at a street stall and send the money we save to her?'

'I am not paying for this meal. It's not my money. You and I have been invited to dinner. We should take advantage of this to eat well.'

And in fact it was true.

This girlfriend was a very nice girl. In fact she did pay for the meal. Her friends liked me. They asked her: 'Hui is a good man. Why don't you marry him?'

And what did she say? I have to laugh. She was a very direct woman.

She said: 'I like him but when it comes to money he is useless. I need someone who can support me. I don't need someone who needs me to support him.'

She was a Macanese woman and she had already been married once and had a son. One day she said to me: 'I need to talk to you. I'm pregnant.'

'What do you want to do about it?' I asked.

'There's only one thing to do.'

We were lucky. She made a big commission about this time and used the money for an abortion. Then she went back to Macau.

Emperor Mao

I WENT UP TO CHINA WHEN I HAD THE CHANCE and my wife also came down to Hong Kong once or twice over the next few years. When I went up I would spend a week or two there at a time. It was very different now under the Communists. There was very little entertainment. There was not much business. Everybody was much poorer. But there were many good things too. I respected the discipline of the Communist officials. The streets were clean. People did their work and then went home. Everyone led a quiet life.

At that time I was very impressed by the basic ideas of Communism. Give what you can and take only what you need. We were all convinced that this was the way forward. But the truth of the matter is that people are selfish. They will work for themselves but not for others. Not everyone was willing to work hard. If I work harder than you but we get the same reward, naturally I will not be so happy. That is the fundamental problem that no amount of philosophy or propaganda can hide. It is a sad fact.

One of Mao's first orders was a very strange one. It was this. Households were only allowed to have one chopper for every five households. Every family wants to eat at more or less the same time. So we had to have a system for using the chopper and passing it on to our neighbour. Why did he order this? Maybe he was afraid the people might use the choppers to attack the Communists. Maybe it was a practical reason. Maybe he needed the iron. Or maybe it was a way to force families to co-operate with each other. That must have been the reason. It shows how damn smart he was. Five families have to share one chopper. They must rely on each other to be fair.

When I went up to Canton I would play with my children or I would sit in the tea shops and talk. There wasn't much else to do.

Suddenly, about a year after I moved the family to Canton, everything began to change. The first indication of this was that my wife and children couldn't get travel permits to come down to Hong Kong. I was furious. I went to the District Security office and asked them to approve travel permits. They refused. I was so angry I even banged the table. But they just smiled and asked me to calm down. They asked me to control myself.

'Look, I have a wife and eight children here in Canton. But I work in Hong Kong. I can't come here every weekend. It will affect my job. So sometimes my wife should come down to visit me in Hong Kong!'

I was furious but they were very calm about it all. That was their way. Always calm and smiling and firm as a rock. Immovable.

'Mr Hui, we understand. Everyone will want to spend time with his wife. This is natural. But we are living in tumultuous times. At such times as these everyone must suffer a little. We just have to accept it.'

But I wasn't happy at all.

'I want to speak to your senior officers about this. Please tell me where I can find them.'

'Mr Hui,' they said, 'you must believe us. Even our senior officers can do nothing. These orders came from Peking.'

'Who did they come from? Tell me. I will go to Peking myself and talk to them. This policy is breaking families apart. It's a bad policy.'

They just laughed.

'Mr Hui. These policies come from Chairman Mao himself.'

But I was so angry I said: 'I don't mind. Take me to see him. I will explain it to Mao himself. I am not afraid!'

But they just laughed louder and I realised there was nothing I could do.

In fact I had great respect for Mao at this time. I often read his quotations. It was there I saw a quotation that explained why the District Security Officers didn't get angry with me:

> The only way to settle questions of an ideological nature or controversial issues among the people is by the democratic method, the method of discussion, of criticism, of persuasion and education and not by the method of coercion or repression.

And there was another one:

A Communist must never be opinionated or domineering. He
must never lord it over others. Communists must listen attentive-
ly to the views of the people and let them have their say. If what
they say is right we ought to welcome it, and we should learn
from their strong points; if it is wrong we should let them finish
what they are saying and then patiently explain things to them.

This is what Mao wrote in his little red book. I can say it impressed
me a lot. The District Security people used this method very successfully.
Let's say you were found shouting something against Communism.
They would take you down to the District Security Office and argue
with you. After a while you might want to go home but they would
insist that you stayed until the argument was finished. And all the time
they would smile and be gentle and they would explain and discuss the
matter until you agreed with them. Until you said: 'You are right
comrades. I was wrong. Now I understand. Thank you for explaining it
so clearly to me.' Then you would understand that if you disagreed you
should keep your mouth shut. Even if in your heart you said 'No' you
would have to say 'Yes' on the outside. If you got into a fight with
someone they would take you to their offices and put you in a room and
say: 'Comrades, you want to fight. Go on please. Continue fighting.'
And they would make you fight until you were ready to drop dead. That
was their way of teaching you that fighting was not the right way to
settle disputes. If they caught you playing mahjong, they would force
you to play and keep on playing. You wouldn't be allowed to have a piss
or a bowl of rice. You would have to play until you were nearly dead. It
didn't matter if it took days or weeks or months. They had endless
patience. That was their discipline.

One time, I came up to Canton and found a large portrait of Mao
in our sitting room. Without thinking I just blurted out: 'Why do we
have to have that damn picture here?'

'Ssh!' My wife said. 'Not so loud. The neighbours will hear you.'

'What's all this about?'

'It's an order. Everybody has to have a picture of the Chairman in their
houses. Some people nearby did get into trouble already about this. If
we complain, even in our own home, our neighbours might hear and
report it.'

'I'm not afraid,' I told her, 'If they arrest me I will just talk to them reasonably. What could they do?'

Then she explained it.

'Even if you talk reasonably it will be no use. They won't torture you or anything like that but they will argue and argue with you until you agree. Even if it takes months. In the end even you will agree. You are a stubborn ox but they are much stronger.'

I understood that she was right and I never commented again about the portrait but it made me angry.

Another thing that concerned me was that schools stopped teaching anything except the words of Chairman Mao. I understood then that Mao wanted to be an emperor or even worse he wanted to be like God himself. But truly I did love his thoughts and revered him as a man. If anyone ever asked me: 'Why did you bring your family back to China?' I would say: 'Because I love Communism.'

One time, I was cycling along one of the main roads. I was stopped by an official for some reason. I had done something wrong. I could see from his face that I was in trouble. I apologised.

'I'm sorry comrade. I made a mistake.'

Well he was a typical official. If he can make life difficult for you he will.

'Well, you can't just apologise. You've broken the law. There must be some punishment.'

'I'm from Hong Kong. I brought my family to live here under Communism but I still live in Hong Kong. That's why I don't know all the rules,' I explained. I didn't want to pay a big fine.

'Hmm? You say you love Communism?' he said. 'What do you know about Mao's thoughts?'

In fact I had read quite a lot of Mao's thoughts and I liked to recite them to myself. I have a very good memory. If I read something several times then it is fixed in my mind. So I said I knew one or two things.

'Show me,' he said, 'recite some.'

'Capitalism is like a dying person who is sinking fast, like the sun setting beyond the western hills. Communism is full of youth and vitality sweeping the world with the momentum of an avalanche and the force of a thunderbolt.'

'That's very good. What else do you know?'

'Let me think. "A revolution is not a dinner party, or writing an essay, or painting a picture, or doing embroidery; it cannot be so refined, so leisurely, so gentle, so temperate, kind, courteous, restrained and magnanimous."'

'That's good. You recite very well. Give me another.'

'Another? What about: "We are advocates of the abolition of war. We do not want war; but war can only be abolished through war, and in order to get rid of the gun we must take up the gun."'

'That's true. Our enemies will not let us put down our guns. American aggression is everywhere. What else do you know?'

'I don't know so many. I never memorised them on purpose. But some have stayed in my memory. Let me see: "We must all learn the spirit of absolute selflessness. A man's ability may be great or small but if he has this spirit he is already noble-minded and pure, a man of moral integrity and above vulgar interests, a man who is of value to the people."'

'You really do have a good memory! I can say you are better than me. I try to remember them but they all get mixed up in my mind. Come on, recite me another one.'

'Let me think. I don't know so many,' I said. I was worried I would be there all night.

'Just two or three more and then you can go.'

'Okay. Here's one: "We must be modest. We Chinese people should never adopt an arrogant attitude of great power chauvinism. We should never become conceited because of the victory of our revolution or our achievements."'

'Do we have an arrogant attitude?'

'No. We are the victims of arrogance,' I told him, 'In Hong Kong it is the foreigners who are arrogant and domineering.'

'Is that so? What else do you remember?'

'"Be resolute, fear no sacrifice and surmount every difficulty to win victory."'

'Everyone can remember that one. Even me. One last one and you can go!'

'"It is not hard for one to do a bit of good. What is hard is to do good all one's life and never do anything bad. That is the hardest thing of all."'

By that time we were on friendly terms.

'You have a wonderful memory,' he told me, 'Wonderful!'

But I couldn't leave without reciting my favourite.

'Here is one more for you: "All men must die, but death can vary in its significance. The ancient Chinese writer Szuma Chien said: 'Though death befalls all men alike it may be weightier than Mount Tai or lighter than a feather.' To die for the people is weightier than Mount Tai, but to work for the fascists and die for the exploiters and oppressors is lighter than a feather. Thousands upon thousands of martyrs have heroically laid down their lives for the people; let us hold their banner high and march ahead along the path crimson with their blood."'

'You are right,' he said. 'That is very poetic and very profound.'

And so he let me go. What did he stop me for? It was dark. There were no street lights in those days and no one could afford batteries. It was very dangerous to cycle at night. So the law was that cyclists had to tie a bundle of lit incense sticks at both front and back. I had done that but I wasn't so good at tying on the sticks and the bundle at the back had fallen off. Naturally I didn't know that. It was behind me. I couldn't keep turning round. So, that's why he had stopped me.

Sunning House Champagne Room

WHEN I HAD NOTHING ELSE TO DO I sometimes went up to CL Li's office. There was always a group of hangers on chatting or playing cards. I was quite friendly with most of them. They knew my situation. It was one of them who suggested that I apply for the job of manager of the Champagne Room.

The first time the subject came up, I said I wasn't interested. Restaurant work is hard. The hours are long. You have to work twelve to thirteen hours a day.

'You have experience in this line,' he persisted.

'It's not so easy.' I really didn't want to get a job in a restaurant. But this man understood that I needed a job. I had been doing this and that for too long. And he knew the previous manager – the one who was leaving. He didn't have a replacement fixed up. He wanted to go back to China but it's not so good to leave a job if there is no one to replace you.

'The job would suit you. I know the manager. I know he would like to employ you.'

And in fact I had no good reason to turn down the job. As usual I was broke. And the job was a very good one. The Champagne Room in the Sunning House Hotel was one of the best restaurants in all Hong Kong. So, in the end, I phoned the hotel manager. When he heard I had worked for the Hongkong Hotel and that I had experience of managing restaurants he hired me right away. Maybe he knew I was a relative of Ho Tim. This would be another good reason to give me the job.

When I started at the job I took a strong line. A restaurant manager has to be in control. I had no problems that way. It was the hotel's policy to steal staff from the Hongkong Hotel. They knew then that their staff would be well trained. So the staff all knew me already. Naturally they respected me. So every day when they started work, I inspected the fingernails of all the waiters and bar attendants. There is nothing more disgusting than dirty fingernails near food. I also checked their shoes were properly shined and that their hair was clean. These are the elementary things. I learnt this at the Hongkong Hotel.

Now, I must say this. I was a first-class restaurant manager. Why do I say this? For one very simple reason. I have been a rich man. I have eaten as a guest at all the best restaurants in town. I knew how I liked to be served and what made me angry. I knew the psychology of people who are used to being served. Let me give you an example. The question of lighting cigarettes. I warned all my staff that a guest must never be allowed to light his own cigarette. Except in one circumstance. If a waiter sees a woman take a cigarette he must immediately look to see if the man with her is about to light it. If I were a man and I was about to light my partner's cigarette and a waiter beat me to it I would be damn angry. So the waiter must first check. If the man was not going to do anything then the waiter should offer a light. I taught the staff many small things like this that I understood because I had once been a rich man myself.

The Champagne Room was the top restaurant in Hong Kong. All the rich businessmen, all the high government officials, film stars, even the governor. They all came and ate at our restaurant. You would think that such a famous restaurant must be big, but in fact it was very small. There were only thirteen tables. Each table had four chairs. It looked bigger than that because the walls were mirrored. I remember once a visitor to Hong Kong entered the restaurant and was very surprised: 'Mr Hui? Is this really the Champagne Room that I have heard so much about?' He was surprised it was so small. I was surprised myself.

'How do you know my name?'

'Oh, Mr Hui,' he said, 'you are famous. All my friends who come to Hong Kong told me: "You must go to the Champagne Room. You must meet the manager, Mr Hui. He is a real character!" So here I am!'

William Holden and Ava Gardner both came to the restaurant several times. We talked a few times and got on in a very friendly way. I remember once he said to me: 'Mr Hui, you are the most handsome Chinese man I have ever seen!'

I laughed. It was true. William Holden was a very handsome man too so I told him that. He made a face and waved away the compliment.

'Well,' he said, 'I am a famous film star. Naturally, many people say that to me.'

'Well,' I responded, 'Many people have told me I am handsome too! But whether I am handsome or not, I don't care. As long as I can enjoy myself!'

Holden raised his glass.

'I'll drink to that!'

Customers are always right, of course, but sometimes. . . I remember one customer. He was very proud, like some of my rich friends. He was British. He had ordered smoked salmon. When the waiter served him he just made an unpleasant face. After a few minutes the waiter noticed that he hadn't touched it.

'Is everything all right sir?' he asked.

'I ordered smoked salmon!' the man said.

'This is smoked salmon sir.'

'This is not smoked salmon. Take it away and bring me smoked salmon!'

The waiter was very confused. He took the dish away but he didn't know what to do. I had been observing everything from a distance. The waiter came over to me and explained the problem.

'He says this is not smoked salmon but it is. What should I do?'

I took the plate and went over to the customer.

'May I help you sir,' I said very politely. He didn't appear to be angry. He was very relaxed.

'I ordered smoked salmon.'

'This is smoked salmon sir, I assure you!'

'What are those?' he asked, pointing at the sliced tomato placed along the side of the dish. I was a bit surprised.

'That's tomato sir. That's how we serve smoked salmon here.'

'Smoked salmon should never be served with tomato.'

'Would you like me to serve you smoked salmon without any tomato?' I asked.

'Yes, please. That would be most kind of you.'

So I took the plate to the kitchen and put the smoked salmon on to a different plate without any tomato and took it back to him.

'Thank you,' he said and started to eat it.

If I didn't understand the very rich perhaps I would have been angry.

But customers weren't always so easy. I remember there was a young man. I knew that he was the aide-de-camp to the governor. He was drinking with a girl and another man. They were just having a drink so the bill was not so large, $40 or so. But he was too proud of himself. He asked for the bill, in those days we didn't call it a bill, we called it a 'chit'. The waiter gave it to him and he said: 'It's all right. I'll just sign it.'

Some people liked to arrange to sign their chits, like in a club. Our policy was that they could only do this if they had made the arrangement in advance. The captain explained the rule to the customer.

'Oh don't worry about that. I'm the ADC to the governor. You know me. I've been here many times. Now, I'll just sign the bill and we can settle it up later.'

The captain came to ask me to handle it. Everyone in the restaurant was aware of the situation. I went over to the table and explained our policy on signing chits. The problem was clear to everyone. He wanted to impress his friends but he hadn't brought enough cash. I was very polite: 'I am sorry but we have to refuse you. Even if I knew you were a millionaire, I would still refuse you. Our policy is fixed. We can't change it for anyone. I do apologise.'

He was silly to let the situation get to this point but now he had to lose face. So he got very angry.

'Oh come sir! The amount is very small. It's trifling. I'm not going to run away from Hong Kong without paying it. If you don't let me sign this chit I will refuse to pay!'

I stood very straight and looked at him very sternly.

'You have that choice sir!' I was aware the restaurant had gone quiet as all the other guests watched with interest to see what would happen.

'Now, there are only two ways in which we can settle this problem. One way is for you and me to go outside and settle this man-to-man. I am a slight man and you are much bigger than me. But don't be surprised if I knock you down. In fact, I can guarantee that I will knock you down. But I have no wish to fight you. I am only trying to do my job as politely as I can. The second way is for you to pay this bill right now.'

Naturally, he had no desire to have a fight and he was a bit surprised that I should challenge him. He looked very embarrassed.

'I'm sorry,' he said. 'It's just that I assumed I could sign and so I didn't bring much money with me. I think your regulations are unreasonable.'

The girl who was with him leaned forward.

'Please, manager, it's all right. I will settle the bill.'

She paid and they left immediately. They must have felt very embarrassed because I noticed they hadn't even finished their drinks.

I never did have to fight any of my customers but the nearest I came was with a man called Carter. He was the colonel of the Volunteer Regiment. He was well known in every restaurant and café in Hong Kong. Naturally, I heard all about him before I met him. Other restaurant managers told me: 'Kei gaw, if you ever come across this man you can beat him like hell. Do it for me! Every time he comes to our restaurant he causes trouble!' He came to the Champagne Room two or three times while I was there. The first two times he didn't cause any problems. He just sat by himself and had a drink. The other staff who knew him pointed him out to me. I kept a close eye on him. Some people are like that. When they get drunk they get mean. It depends how drunk they are. Carter was like that. If he got drunk he had to cause some trouble. The third time he came he sat at a table drinking whisky. Then he got up and went over to the pianist, a Filipino called Lupo, and made a request. Lupo nodded but explained that he already had a number of requests and Carter would have to wait his turn. If someone made a request it was always put on a piece of paper. Lupo showed Carter that he had a few requests waiting.

'I don't care!' Carter shouted, 'I want you to play my song now!'

Lupo knew I was watching everything. He knew I would give him hell if he played Carter's request out of turn. He apologised again. Carter was standing in the middle of the restaurant with his glass of whisky. He tipped his glass and poured his drink all over the keys of the piano. At that I rushed over and started shouting at him.

'What did you do that for? Do you know how much this piano cost? At least $20,000! Are you going to pay for a new piano?'

Carter just glared at me drunkenly.

'Don't you stare at me! I'm in charge here. Now tell me, why did you do that?'

'I just asked the pianist to play a song and he refused me,' Carter mumbled, 'No trouble. That's all!' and he turned his back on me and walked back to his table grumbling.

'You're not the only customer here!' I shouted at his back, 'You have to wait your turn.' But he just ignored me. Then he called for his chit. I waved the waiters away.

'I'll deal with him myself,' I told them. I gave him the bill and he tried to focus on it. It was obvious he was very drunk. He just looked at the bill for a very long time.

'Please pay now,' I said.

'I want to sign.'

I didn't know if he had any arrangement but I was not going to let him sign.

'You are not allowed to sign. You must pay cash!'

He glared at me.

'Do you know who I am?' he asked. I had to laugh.

'I know who you are. I know very well. Everyone knows you. Your name is Carter. I don't wish to insult you but I can say you are well known as a very rough man. Everyone knows that you are a drunkard.'

Maybe he was surprised. But in fact he didn't do anything. He just sat at his table with his drink in his hand. Maybe he was so drunk he was confused. But by now he was annoying everyone in the restaurant so I spoke to him again.

'Either you pay or we can call the police.' I was angry. But he still didn't move so I continued talking. 'If you like there is a third way: you and I can go outside and fight. You are a military man so you must know something about fighting. Also you are a big European man. I am a slight Chinese man. I would like to fight you. If you can beat me, you don't need to pay a cent. But if I beat you I can tell you that not only will you have to pay but you will also be badly hurt.' He looked at me with some surprise. Then he nodded slowly to himself and pulled himself to his feet.

'To the door!' he said.

This time I was surprised. I can say I was happily surprised. 'Ah Kei. This is your chance to beat him to hell!' I told myself. But actually he was just embarrassed and a bit ashamed. As we approached the door he stopped and pulled his wallet out. The bill was for $30 but he gave me $40. Then he shuffled off out the door. He never came back.

A restaurant is like that. There are always some awkward customers. But those were the worst. I never did have to hit a customer.

There was another customer at the Champagne Room that I remember. She was a very famous Chinese singer: Lee Heung-lan. She used to sing propaganda songs for the Japanese, praising their intervention in

China, praising them for fighting gloriously against the Western allies. I think she was Manchurian. Certainly she wasn't Cantonese. She was not a beautiful woman. She was short and very flat-chested but she had a nice face. I think her nickname was 'Oriental Butterfly' or something like that. She gave talks on the radio in English about the glorious Japanese. When she came into the restaurant I recognised her face immediately. She was with a group of four or five European Immigration Department officials. They didn't have a reservation. I thought to myself: 'You bitch! You think you're a high-class girl. You are so famous. But you mix with low-class government officials.' Now why did I react in this way? I can't say. Not because I thought she was a traitor. No one blamed her for collaborating with the Japanese. After the war she disappeared for a while and then after a few years she re-emerged.

'Do you have a table for us?' she asked.

'I am afraid we're full,' I told her.

'There's no reservation sign on that table.'

'I have it marked down in my book. I'm very sorry. You'd better come back another night.'

So she left. But she did come back several times. Each time she was with a European government official. Each time I told her all the tables were reserved. Each time she smiled and accepted my excuse with a polite nod. On the fifth time she came back she had learnt my name.

'Mr Hui, good evening. How is my luck tonight? Do you think you can find me a table tonight?'

I looked at her and thought that she really was a lady. I had refused her many times and yet she was still polite to me.

'How many?'

'Just two of us.'

Her companion was another European government officer. He just nodded at me. I thought I had been too petty. I led them to a table.

'Tonight you are lucky. This table is not reserved.'

'Thank you,' she said, 'you are very kind.'

After that I didn't hate her.

My wife came down from Canton once or twice that year. When that happened I had to find a room in a lodging house because I was staying at the staff quarters. There was no privacy there for a wife. No privacy for a girlfriend either! But that didn't stop her! She was a Shanghainese girl. Once or twice she came to the staff quarters at two or three o'clock in the morning. She was a cabaret girl at the Camay ballroom in Causeway Bay. I would sometimes go there after work with KF. I shouldn't have gone. Two out of three times I paid. It wasn't good. My wife needed the money. But that's how it was. Sometimes I even borrowed money to pay the bills. I did send money back to China as soon as I was paid. The Champagne Room closed at one in the morning and the ballroom closed at two. We got to know each other there. It became a regular habit. Afterwards we would have a snack together and if we felt hot we would rent a room. Really she loved me so much it scared me. Soon she would tell the mamasans to stop bothering her.

'Can't you see I'm talking to Mr Hui?' she would say in a loud voice. She had no shame at all. One day she invited me to have dinner at her home. She had told me she was married but it didn't seem real to me. It was just part of her private life. But when I went to her flat and met her husband I felt bad. Not that I was cheating him. I wasn't. He knew what she was doing. He encouraged it. He just wanted her to earn the money for him to live. This made a very bad impression on me. I think Confucius said something like this: If you fool around with someone else's wife of course it is pleasurable but how will you feel if someone fools around with your wife? This is a good point. This is good philosophy. After this, I stopped going to the Camay. But she started to chase me. She would bang on the door early in the morning. Of course everyone would wake up. She would use the shared toilet without shame. It was all very embarrassing. I remember one morning one of the staff commented to me: 'Your girlfriend is very attractive.'

'She's a cabaret girl.'

'Ah yes! We thought so,' he said.

I was afraid I would lose my job because she was disturbing everyone. Also it wasn't good for respect. One day I got angry and shouted at her.

'If you do this again I will call the police.' I was furious. But to be fair, she didn't understand the situation. I hadn't told her I was married and had children. There had never been any good reason to tell her.

'Why do you stay in this staff quarters? You're single. Let's get a flat together. I will pay the rent. We can live together. What's wrong with that?' she asked.

'I can't do that,' I explained, 'If things were perfect then I would marry you. But now I think it's better not to get more involved. Please leave me alone. I might lose my job.'

I was frightened how strong her feelings were. It was too much. It was excessive. Why did women fall in love with me?

Now, the Sunning House Hotel was owned by the Lee family, that Lee family that my first lover Leung Chui-yee married into. I had been working at the restaurant only a week or so when Lee Shuen-ho entered with one of her sisters.

'Mr Hui!' she said with surprise, 'I haven't seen you for so long! Which table are you sitting at?'

I was a bit embarrassed.

'I am not a customer. I am working here. I am the new manager.'

She just nodded.

'Yes, I heard things were not going so well with you.'

What could I say? I nodded. There was a short silence. In my mind I said: 'Now you have something to say to Leung Chui-yee about the man she might have married if you hadn't interfered.'

But she was friendly to me: 'Well, I hope this job suits you.'

'Thank you. Now let me take you to your table and show you that I can do a good job serving you.'

I made it easy for them. An employer cannot be friends with his employees. The rich cannot be good friends with those who have no money. We could not continue our old relationship.

In fact all the Lee brothers and sisters often came to eat at the Champagne Room. The eldest brother, Dick Lee, and the second brother, Harold Lee were both regulars. Once or twice the fifth brother – Leung Chui-yee's husband – also came. He knew who I was and naturally I knew him too. But he was always very polite and proper towards me. But Chui-yee herself never came. I was on good terms with all of them except Harold Lee. The problem was that Harold Lee was the one in charge of the hotel operations. He was my direct boss. When he came to eat in the restaurant I took the view that he was part of the hotel staff and so I should not pay so much attention to him as I did to other customers. He had a different attitude. The way he saw it, he was my boss and so I should pay extra special attention to him. Perhaps my way of thinking was more modern and his way was more traditional.

One evening Harold Lee was drunk. He came to the Champagne Room and continued to drink. I could see he was in a bad mood so I didn't bother him. As he was leaving I saw him stagger. I put out my hand to steady him.

'Are you alright Mr Lee?' I asked, 'Can I help you to your car?'

But he knocked my hand away and glared at me. Then he walked on. I knew that if it had been anyone else he would have hit him but he knew my reputation. The next day he told the manager of the hotel that I had ignored him. The manager called me in to have a word with me. I was not prepared to defend myself. I walked out. But this time I had a job waiting for me.

I had been approached by another restaurant and they were offering me a better salary. So I left the Champagne Room and took over as manager at the Kings Restaurant and the Blue Heaven Nightclub.

Who would have thought that I would spend so many years working in restaurants?

KF

I REMEMBER ONE NIGHT KF SAID: 'Come on Hui, let's go to the Camay ballroom.'

'I haven't got any money,' I told him.

But KF was crazy. He didn't care about anything.

'Ah, don't be silly, Hui,' he said. 'You don't have to pay anything.'

Naturally I assumed he had some money. So we went to the Camay and fooled around with some girls. One of them was a regular companion of KF's. Towards two o'clock, closing time, naturally we had to settle the bill.

'Okay, pay up!' I said.

'We have a problem. I had hoped to bump into some friends I could borrow from but I couldn't see anybody.'

He turned to his companion.

'How about lending us the money.'

'You're crazy!' she said and left us.

'KF,' I said, 'this is a lesson for you. You think people are friends but when you need them they leave you.'

'Well, the only thing we can do is fight our way out,' KF said.

Now I was in a good mood and I had no intention of fighting. Why should I fight? We were in the wrong.

'Look KF,' I said, 'I don't mind fighting but the trouble will just come back to you tomorrow and it will be much worse for you. Everybody here knows you.'

But KF never understood the consequences. He would do anything he wanted on the spur of the moment. That's the way it is for sons of rich men.

'We have no choice. We must ask them to call the police,' I said. So the police came and took us to the station. It was all very friendly. At about three o'clock I phoned Cyril Kotewall to come down and bail us out. He owed me some big favours so naturally he came.

Afterwards, as we were leaving the station he turned to me. 'Hui, I have done this for you this time. Promise me now that you will never ask me again.'

I promised him. But actually it wasn't such a big thing to ask. He was my friend and KF's friend. For a true friend there is no end to friendship. But I never did ask Cyril for a big favour again. Later, we had an argument. I wanted to hit him. He knew it. I bumped into him outside the Bank of China in Central. He was scared. We stopped and faced each other.

'I expected you would hit me,' he said.

'I wanted to,' I told him, 'I thought to myself, the next time I see Cyril I am going to hit him. But I can't. You are my friend. How can I hit you?' I walked away from him. And I never spoke to him again. I can still feel everything I felt that day. It could have been yesterday. But it was something he did. He betrayed his friendship to KF and myself. Some things cannot be forgiven. How did he betray the friendship? Some things should not be said, not even hinted at. I walked from him and we never spoke again.

But KF was crazy. Cat thought it was my fault. She thought I was leading him astray. The fact is, if I was drinking with him I tried to slow him down. One morning I met Cat at the Jockey Club.

'Where's my husband?' she asked me. I could see she was angry.

'I don't know,' I told her, 'I left him about ten o'clock last night.'

She didn't believe me.

'It's your fault he gets drunk all the time. You taught him your bad habits!'

But the truth is he was always a bad drinker. He couldn't control himself. Cat was getting tired of his drunkenness. A year or two later she left him. I don't blame her. A drunk is disgusting. He has no dignity. He will do anything he wants for no reason at all except that he wants to do it now. I think this time one of his drinking friends found Cat and told her he was sleeping on the floor of a ballroom where they had left him.

So my relations with Cat suffered at this time. I was her husband's best friend and she was tired of being humiliated by him. Poor Cat. We were the closest friends but KF was even closer. I could never desert him even when all his other friends had, when he was drunk and penniless.

One day, at the Jockey Club bar, he saw me and took me aside.

'Peter, I'm in a jam. I can't settle my bar bill for this month. Lend me three hundred will you? If I don't pay them today they'll post me. It will be very embarrassing.' I didn't have so much money myself but I could manage $300. He had just retired from being a jockey. The fact is he was drunk so often no one would hire him. It was sad. He was one of the top jockeys. Only Kenny Kwok was better. But who wants a drunk riding your horse? Now, I'll tell you something. The races in those days were often fixed. There was a syndicate. But a lot of owners didn't know this. Now if you are the owner of a horse, naturally, before the race, you will ask the jockey: 'Are we going to win today?' and the jockey might say: 'We've got a good chance but I can't promise anything.' Now the owner will say: 'You're riding the favourite. Do everything you can to win.' What can the jockey do? He has already been told by the syndicate to hold up the horse. If he doesn't they'll break his legs or do something else to punish him. But naturally he can't tell the owner this. So the owner bets a lot of money and loses it. I know some horse owners who have been ruined by their jockeys.

Anyway KF was so drunk that soon everybody started to avoid him. He couldn't get a ride. So he spent every day sitting in the bar of the club running up bills. And now he didn't have any income coming in. The following month he came to me and took me aside and said: 'Peter, you've got to help me out. I owe the bar $600. They'll post me if I don't settle the bill today.' So I lent him the money and told him to sort things out. The third month came along and he took me aside and said: 'Peter, I'm going to be ruined. My bill is over a thousand. I can't pay. The secretary is threatening to post me. I will lose face. Please help me.'

But I was furious with him.

'You think I'm a sucker. Every month I pay your bills. My family are starving in China and I am paying your bar bills! Enough is enough. This time I can't help you with money.'

KF was almost crying.

'What can I do? What can I do?'

'Stay here. I will talk to the secretary.'

The secretary was very understanding. He agreed to tear up the bills and not post KF on condition that KF stopped using the club. Cat had some money and they set up a small shop in Wanchai Road. That kept them going for a few years. Cat's father was still alive. He rented them a small shop space. KF's drinking was under better control now that he had to work. But it's some people's fate that they have to fall right to the bottom. KF's behaviour degenerated. In the end, Cat had no choice but to leave him. But I am his oldest friend. There is no end to the burdens of friendship. I could not desert him. When I came to Cheung Chau he followed me. His behaviour didn't improve. One day, Mr Fung, one of the village elders, said to me: 'I understand Mr Chu is an old school friend of yours.'

'Yes, I have known him all my life.'

'I regret to tell you he is causing a lot of trouble. He abuses shop-keepers. He shouts at women. He is always drunk. I have been asked to have him thrown off the island.' He could arrange this very easily. I grasped his hand.

'Please give me some face. He is my oldest friend. Please don't throw him off the island. He has nowhere else to go.'

'Mr Hui, you are an educated man. Everyone on Cheung Chau respects you. You are always polite. But Mr Chu has upset many people.'

'Please. For my sake. I will do what I can to control him.'

'Very well,' Mr Fung said. But the truth is there was no hope for KF. He had passed beyond the bounds of decency. If he needed a drink at three o'clock in the morning he would hammer on the shop grille and shout and curse the whole world until someone came down to give him what he wanted.

Near the end, before he died, I said to him: 'I have been a good friend to you.'

'Yes, Peter,' he said. 'You have been a very good friend. The best friend a man could hope to have.'

'And do you know why I have stood by you all these years?'

He shook his head.

'Because I remember, before the war, when I had no money, you carried me along. You paid for everything. You did it without thinking. I have always valued that. Do you remember, one time, you gave me a blank cheque. I could have filled it in for millions. You trusted me that much. You trusted me absolutely. That is why I have stood by you all these years. For the sake of our long friendship.'

'But I have given you back more than you ever gave me. I have given it back many times over. I have given you millions. If it was all counted up. Not including the meals I paid for. Millions.'

'Yes, Peter, you have been very good to me.'

'The burdens of friendship are without end.'

'Thank you Peter. You have been very good to me.'

The woodwork shop

IT WAS MY FRIEND CHONG WHO HELPED ME out one time when I didn't even have a roof over my head. His father had a woodwork shop in Wanchai and he said I could sleep there at nights. There were six or seven staff there and at night, when the shop was closed, they would pull out their beds. This was fine for me but not for my son. Chong arranged for him to stay overnight at his office in Central and during the day he paid him to be a clerk. In this way he learnt something about office life. Later I got him a job in a Kowloon incense stick factory. Then, maybe a year later, Ho Tim got him a job as a waiter in the Weissman Café in Central. I could have asked Ho Tim for a job too but we have a saying: A good horse never goes back to old pastures.

The staff at the wood shop knew I was a trained *kung fu* man. One evening they bought a bottle of brandy and offered me a drink, and then another and another. Then when I had had quite a few drinks and was a little drunk they raised the subject of my *kung fu*. Naturally, I boasted about my successes. They asked me to demonstrate my skills. So they got some pieces of wood and I broke them in pieces with my hand.

'Wah!' they said. 'You really are something. Try another!'

So I broke three or four pieces of wood. Then one of them said: 'Here's one you can't break.'

'Don't be silly! I can break any wood.'

So they brought out a piece of wood and I used all my force to hit it, and my hand just bounced away without damaging it.

'What! I really must be drunk!' I said.

They all laughed.

'Drunk or not you will never be able to break this one. It's rattan. If you hit it your hand will just bounce off.'

Then I realised they had set this up. It was a good joke. I had to laugh too.

But my luck hadn't stopped going downhill. It was not long after I put my family in China that I was arrested. It happened like this. Wu

Hor-kuen was a friend of mine from before the war. I remember that he had asked a mutual friend to introduce him to me because he had heard great stories about me. Although he was a few years older than me we became friendly and at this time when I was poor I often made a point of going to visit him. You must understand that I am an educated person and Wu Hor-kuen was an educated person too. But the other people I mixed with at this time were not. I enjoyed Wu's conversation from time to time so I made a point of going to see him.

Now, Wu's elder brother was a high official in the Kuomintang and in fact he was the head of one of the leading factions. I remember it was called the CC Group. I have no idea what CC means. The Kuomintang had established itself in Taiwan but they were very corrupt and there was a lot of political in-fighting between the different factions. Wu wasn't involved in this. He had set up a school in Mongkok and in fact it was doing quite well.

One day he told me he had sold his school. I was surprised. A school isn't like an import-export company. It should be for a lifetime.

'My brother wants me to help him in Taiwan,' he explained.

Naturally, if an elder brother needs our help we must do what we can to give whatever help is needed. I knew he planned to go soon so I went to visit him.

When I got there I found his flat door open and there were people inside searching it. I could see they were police. I should have gone immediately but I just stood there.

'What do you want?'

'I've come to see my friend Mr Wu Hor-kuen.'

'Do you know where he is?'

I thought this was a stupid question.

'Of course not. I've come here to pay him a visit.'

'I see. Please sit down,' he said.

I sat down and they continued to search the flat. I thought: why am I sitting here?

'Why should I stay here?' I asked.

'You have to wait for us. We want to question you.'

So I waited. It took a long time.

'What's the matter?' I asked one of the policemen.

'I can't tell you. You'll find out later.'

I waited for over an hour and soon, naturally, I started to get angry.

'Excuse me, I am just a visitor. Even if Wu Hor-kuen has killed someone it doesn't concern me. If you want to ask me anything, then ask me and I will answer it. But this is Hong Kong. We have laws here. We have rights. You can't just detain me for no reason. So please can you either let me go or question me immediately as I am getting tired of waiting.'

The European inspector was not impolite.

'Well,' he said, 'you may be a visitor or maybe you aren't just a visitor. Let us just say I have my doubts. And, as for the law, we have the right to detain you as long as we like. But, in fact, we won't keep you much longer.'

After about fifteen minutes more we left. They took me to the Mongkok Police Station and started to question me. Who are you? What's your name? What's your job? What's your connection with Mr Wu? One thing was bad for me. I didn't have a steady job at this time. Naturally, that must look suspicious. Nevertheless, I protested my innocence.

'Inspector,' I said to him, 'I am an honest man and I am a brave man. If I am involved in something wrong I have the guts to admit it. But I am involved in nothing at all. You haven't told me anything about why you were searching Mr Wu's flat. Has he committed a crime? If so, I don't know anything about it. If it is a political matter I know that Mr Wu is involved with the Kuomintang. He is a gentleman. He is an educated man. But it is possible he is involved with politics. If so, I know nothing about it. That's the truth. Now please let me go!'

The inspector just looked at me.

'I have to think about what you've told me carefully. Would you like a drink?'

Now, I had gone to Wu's flat at about midday and it was now early evening. I was a little annoyed. When he asked me if I wanted to have a drink I decided to show my character.

'Yes please,' I said. 'I would like to have a brandy!'

He smiled.

'I'm sorry, Mr Hui. We don't have brandy. I can offer you a coffee.'

'Okay. Give me a coffee!'

They let me go at eight o'clock.

Two days later, early in the morning, there was a knock on the door. It was the police. They had come to take me away for more questioning. They had more information now, they said. They knew that Wu had been involved in a lot of political activities. I was his friend or close associate. They had to assume that I was also involved in the same political activities. I denied it strongly but it was no use. They sent me to Victoria Prison, just next to Central Police Station. That's where they kept all the political prisoners. The Hong Kong authorities have always been very sensitive about political matters. Hong Kong is caught between the Communists in mainland China and the Kuomintang in Taiwan. Anything that might annoy the Communists or disturb the stability of Hong Kong was stamped on quickly. No one was allowed to organise any political party or group in Hong Kong. Every kind of politics was illegal.

In fact Victoria Prison is a nice place. Very comfortable. The life of a political prisoner is completely different from that of a criminal. I was given a room but it wasn't locked. There was some reading material. You could read what you wanted and you could send down to the kitchen to have anything you wanted to eat. I ordered brandy to see what would happen. They gave me some. I got two pecks a day. Just two small measures. For a drinker like me this was nothing. For the first few days I just stayed in my room but when I realised I could wander about I went downstairs to the kitchen. I was thinking about food when suddenly I saw a familiar face.

'Kei!'

'Mr Hui! What are you doing here?'

'What about you?' I asked. I hadn't seen or heard of him since his arrest after the robbery went wrong.

'I'm the chief cook here. It's a good arrangement. I'm comfortable.'

This was obvious. He had put on quite a lot of weight. I told him something about the Wu Hor-kuen affair. He said he had heard something about it. It was in the newspapers.

I was kept in prison for ten days. Every day I was taken to Police Headquarters and questioned. There were four different officers. They took it in turn to question me. I gave them all the same answers. This was easy as I was telling them the truth. I was innocent. Why should I lie?

I had a very good friend, a senior officer in the CID. He was the one who had recommended that I apply for the job of police interpreter. I wondered if it would help me if I get in touch with him. But then I said to myself: 'Better not! He must know I am in prison. If he can help me he is already doing something. If I mention his name to these officers maybe it will be bad for his career.' So I said nothing. But I am certain he was doing what he could in the background. Later he retired a very rich man. He had a very beautiful wife. In those days being a policeman could be very profitable.

Every day, after the questioning, I spent many hours talking to Kei. He told me I could eat as much as I liked. Six meals a day if I wanted, even at midnight. He gave me the very best food.

On the last day of questioning, the inspector who was interrogating me mentioned the word 'deportation'. This was a very serious matter. I lost my temper. I pointed my finger at him.

'You don't have the right to deport me. I was born in Hong Kong. I am a Hong Kong citizen. If you deport me I will take the case all the way to London. You have no evidence that I am involved in anything. I warn you that I understand the law. I was once chairman of the Hong Kong Solicitors' Clerks Association. I know something about the law. You can't deport anyone who was born in Hong Kong.'

They asked me to calm down and that was the end of it. I was taken back to prison but early the next morning I was freed.

Some time later, Kei was freed and he came to visit me before going home to Canton. I offered him some money but he could see my situation wasn't good.

'Don't worry, all the time I was in jail I was earning money as a cook,' he said.

Over the years I often met Wong, the man who had introduced me to Kei. He was a rich man now. I suppose his father had died. Wong now went around in a chauffeur-driven car. I can tell you he was always generous to me. Maybe we met once a week or at least once every two weeks. He always handed me some money. He turned out to be a good friend. Even much later, I introduced my second wife to him, and my children. This was a precaution. I wanted him to know them just in case anything happened to me. They could go to him for help if necessary. Once I asked Wong if he had heard anything of Kei. He told me that

Kei had gone back to his home town and then, a few years later, he had suddenly collapsed and died. It had been very sudden. He would have been in his late thirties. Why do some people die young and others die of old age? How can we know what is in God's mind.

Now, Wu Hor-kuen? What happened to him? I have no idea.

Tinker tailor soldier sailor

WHEN I WAS RELEASED FROM PRISON I went back to Mr Chong's wood shop in Wanchai. I was so depressed. I had reached bottom. It was a very bad time for me.

To make money I had a little trick. I sometimes went to the billiard rooms and sat on the tables. I didn't do this too often. Maybe once a month. I would say: 'Right! If you want me to go you'll have to pay me $40.' I never asked more than that. I just smiled and sat on the table. 'Come on, give me $40 and you can play.' In fact everyone knew me well and they always gave me what I asked without any problem. On the one hand they knew I had a family in China to support, on the other hand they knew I was a bloody *kung fu* fighter and it wouldn't be so easy to defeat me. They might get hurt.

In fact $40 was quite a lot of money in those days. A careful man could live for a week on that. Not me but somebody else. But for them it was not too much. I didn't sit on just anybody's table. I waited until I saw one of the Shanghainese gangs playing against one of the Cantonese gangs. Then I knew they were playing for money: about $300 usually, maybe $500. So $40 was nothing to them.

People understood I did this only because I was broke.

One day, someone I knew suggested that I should become a tailor.

'Tailor?'

'Of course! There's the war in Korea. You've seen all the soldiers and sailors in the bars. They're crazy about Hong Kong. They spend hundreds, thousands of dollars on clothes.'

'So?'

'All you have to do is get their business. You speak English.'

'And when I get the business?'

'You pay a cutter to make it up.'

Of course! It was so easy! So I became a tailor.

Once I had the idea, I saw how I could make a lot of money. I knew a European girl. We had met in one of the bars. I asked her if she knew any girls who wanted to earn good commissions. They didn't need to be very good looking, I told her, but they should be reasonable. She introduced me to some girls. One was very black. Two others were Eurasians. They were my sales girls. They got ten per cent commission on anything they sold. Their job was to serve soft drinks or beer to any sailor who came into the shop and talk and entertain them in any way they wanted. They could go out with them and show them the town if that's what they wanted. They were free agents.

They were nice girls and they had a lot of fun and they made very good money. They were happy and had a good time. They received a lot of attention from the sailors. I warned them: Have a good time but don't ever get serious. Don't ever marry one of these sailors. They may get hot and passionate after a few drinks. Maybe they will look at the moon and get very romantic. But always remember this: they're sailors. There's a war on. Who can say what might happen? If they survive, will they be able to get a good job later? Will they be able to support you? And all the time you will be here. You will have to live apart. Don't misunderstand me. Don't think I'm saying this just to keep you. I'm saying this from my heart for your own good. They listened to me. These girls were very faithful to me. They stayed with me to the end.

Now, the shop itself wasn't mine. Naturally, I couldn't afford to rent a space or buy stocks of material. I would have an arrangement with a shop so that when I wanted I would pretend it was mine. I had two or three shops where I had this arrangement. Naturally the tailor who owned the shop was very happy to do this because I would pay him rent and buy my cloth from him. He told me his prices and I added my mark up.

But we didn't just wait for business. That's a quick way to starve. I couldn't wait for sailors to pass my shop. I had to go out and get them and I had to get them before any of my competitors could get them. In fact all the others like me co-operated. When there was business there was plenty for everyone. And when there was no business we hung around the waterfront and waited. We would sit in a coffee shop on the waterfront. One of my overheads was buying the girls drinks while we waited. We could spend days or even weeks waiting.

But then, even before the ships had entered the harbour, we knew they were coming and we rushed to the *wallah wallah* boats and raced out to meet them. How did we know they were coming? One of the larger tailor shops had a connection with the radio officer at the us Navy Reception Centre. The ships always radioed ahead to inform the centre they were coming. There was a signal. Maybe something to do with flags. Maybe a telephone call. And once we saw the signal we had to race to the boats.

Often we got to the ships before they even anchored and we followed them until they dropped anchor, and then we climbed on board any way we could. Of course the captain and the other officers would try to throw us off. It was no use going up the gangway. You were certain to be pushed back. Many times I climbed up the anchor chain itself. Although I was forty years old I was strong and agile. Aircraft carriers were easiest as they were big and they had more decks, and there were things sticking out you could put your feet on. That made it easier. Often the sailors would push us back but I always talked in a very gentle, smooth way. The important thing was to get inside the boat as quickly as possible. When I saw one of the crew I would ask the way to the Recreation Officer's cabin. Sometimes they would even take me there personally.

From time to time one of the tailors would be unlucky and be pushed over the side of the ship into the harbour. This happened occasionally. They wouldn't be hurt of course but he would get soaked and of course that was the end of the day for him. Naturally no one will do business with a tailor in a wet suit. Afterwards you can laugh but at the time. . .!

It wasn't just the tailors who went to greet the warships coming into the harbour. There were always junks and sampans. These fishing people had a little trick. They would shout to the sailors to throw down small coins and then the young boys would dive for them. The water in the harbour wasn't so dirty then. For the sailors it was a game but for the fishing people it was real money.

For us, once we got on the ship, we had to run as fast as we could to find the Recreation Officer. He was the man who was in charge of all welfare activities like this. The Recreation Officers were usually okay. Once you got to his cabin you were safe. That was the usual rule. I know some of my competitors complained that they had been thrown out. But that never happened to me. I suppose my manner was different from the others. I always acted like a gentleman. I was always treated with respect. I would tell them that I was ready to take measurements if anyone wanted to order suits straight away. Or I would hand out my cards. The officer would pass the word to the crew and very quickly I would be showing my book of cloth samples and taking measurements. Some crew couldn't go ashore. They were on duty. But they still wanted to buy suits and jackets and trousers.

I might be two or three hours taking measurements and then I would take some others to the shop itself so that they could look at the material and have a drink and so on. I would tell them I would introduce them to some nice girls. They were all young boys and they just wanted to have a good time. We never asked for a deposit but we asked them to sign the ordering book. That was the standard practice. There was never any problem.

It wasn't an easy business. The ships always came together. For a week or two there would be nothing and then the whole fleet would arrive for five days. For those five days you had to work twenty-four hours a day. The cutters never got more than a few hours sleep a night. We all made a lot of money. It was a good business. But nothing lasts forever. I got into the business late. I was a tailor for about one year.

Then the Korean War ended and soon I was broke again. Money doesn't stick to me.

I nearly drowned again

I NEARLY DROWNED AGAIN. This was after the war, in the fifties or sixties. I was with KF at Shek O beach at the south-eastern end of Hong Kong Island. We often went off to the beach if we had nothing else to do. On this day there were very few swimmers, probably because the red flag was up. This means it's very dangerous to swim. The beach faces south to the open sea so it is quite common for a dangerous swell to come in. Now the red flag never worried me because I am a strong swimmer. We were on a raft moored about a hundred yards out from the shore.

There were three British servicemen, KF and myself. The raft was rolling and heaving quite strongly and we could see that the waves were getting stronger. The three servicemen decided to leave. As soon as they had gone we realised that it was getting quite dangerous.

'We'd better get back now, while we can,' KF said.

'Yes, that would be wise,' I agreed. So we set off ourselves a few minutes after the servicemen. Now, by this time, the waves were maybe eight feet high. I quickly lost sight of KF. The waves threw us up and then down. When I was up, KF was down. Frankly, I was a bit worried. KF wasn't as good a swimmer as me. I just hoped he was safe and kept swimming towards the shore. Then I heard a cry for help. Actually, I heard two people crying for help. One voice was a woman's and the other was a man's. I decided I should try to rescue the woman and started to swim in that direction but the man was closer. In fact it was one of the servicemen we had been on the raft with. So, since he was nearest me, I felt I should try to help him because I couldn't see the woman at all. I swam towards him. I wanted to hold him by the back of his head so that he could breathe but he was at that point of life and death and was panicking. He grabbed me close to him and he was a very strong man. I don't mind admitting I was scared. He held me with the death clasp of a dying man. My fear gave me an extra power and I used my *kung fu* to push his arms off and kick his body away. With one powerful movement I stretched my arms and legs together. Once I had got rid of him I swam straight for shore. I asked God to forgive me but I had to save myself first. When I got to the shore I found the life-guards were putting out a boat. In fact they picked up the woman, the serviceman and a young boy. When they brought the serviceman to shore he looked awful. His whole body was dull grey in colour. It looked bruised all over. I think we all thought we was dead but the next day the newspaper carried the story that three people had been rescued alive. But where was KF? I was very worried for him but after about ten or fifteen minutes he managed to struggle to the shore.

So, I nearly drowned again but I am still here alive at the age of seventy-nine according to the Chinese calendar. I don't go swimming so much now. When I first came here I would swim right across the bay and back but since my heart problems started I only swim round the floats of the swimming area on the beach in front of my house. An old man shouldn't pretend to be like a young man.

Snow White

I ONLY HAD ABOUT $50 on me when I bumped into my two friends, Mr Luk and Mr Wan. We were all good drinking friends.

'Mr Hui!' they greeted me. 'Where have you been? Come on. Let's go and have dinner.' So we went and had dinner and some brandy. It is good to drink with old friends.

'Come on, Hui, tonight let's celebrate. Let's have a happy time. Let's go to a ballroom.'

I thought about my money situation.

'No, you go. It's better I don't.'

'Why? You're a damn playboy. We know you like to fool around. You don't have any job to go to so what's the problem?'

'Money. I can't pay my share.'

'Mr Hui,' they said, 'we're friends. Don't worry about money. Tonight we're paying.'

So I was happy to go with them but I made a suggestion.

'If we go to a ballroom, there will be girls and that will be expensive. Actually, it seems to me that we want to drink and have fun so why don't we go to a nightclub instead.'

Actually there would be no problem of getting a drink in a ballroom. They would serve it in a teapot. Legally, at the ballrooms you got girls and no drinks and at the nightclubs you got drinks but no hostesses. That was the law but no one stuck to it. If they did they would go out of business very quickly. So the ballrooms served brandy in teapots and nightclubs employed 'waitresses' who sat with customers if they wanted.

'Good idea,' they said, and so we went to the Tonnochy Nightclub in Wanchai.

That night the lead singer was a young woman whose speciality was Japanese love songs. Her professional name was 'Snow White'.

'You know, she has a very good voice!' I said to my friends. They winked and laughed. They thought I meant something else. When I wasn't looking they wrote a note to her to ask her to join us. They were regular customers so naturally she had to give them face. When she had finished her set she came over and joined us and we all introduced ourselves. Now, when it comes to women I enjoy talking. I have said this before. I am very straightforward and women like that. They don't like tricky men. They like to feel safe. That's the main thing. Now Miss Tong saw that my friends were giving me a lot of respect and she saw that I was a friendly, well-behaved man. As for her, people said she was beautiful but I never thought so. She was attractive perhaps. What she had was a beautiful singing voice and I will say she had a very good figure. Naturally, she knew how to laugh and talk to men and to flatter them. Later she told me that she had been introduced to the business by her sister, who was also a singer, during the Japanese occupation. She was just eleven or twelve when she started singing in nightclubs. It seemed she enjoyed our company because that evening she spent all the time with us when she wasn't singing. Towards the end of the evening she turned to me: 'Mr Hui, I have enjoyed talking with you. I would like to invite you to have dinner with me one evening at my home. Would you like that?' I was a little embarrassed. A man in his forties should have the money to entertain a beautiful singer in her twenties. I had nothing.

'It is difficult for me to say but if I am free I certainly would enjoy having dinner with you one evening.'

I was lying. I had plenty of time. But even if she invited me to dinner it would involve money. She went off to get her things and I turned to my friends.

'It's clear she likes you very much,' Mr Wan said.

'What's your secret?' asked Mr Luk.

'Don't be silly,' I protested, 'this is just normal for a girl in her profession. She wants to trap a man. This is their way.'

'Then why doesn't she invite me to dinner?' Wan said.

'But what should I do?'

'Mr Hui, you must be a gentleman. She has asked you to have dinner with her so you must have dinner with her.'

'Don't be a fool! She won't kill you! You're experienced enough to protect yourself. Just go and have a drink with her.' So I did. I took her for a snack and then I took her to her home and we talked and I found that she was a nice girl. It was clear that she enjoyed my company. In fact, it was soon clear that she liked me very much.

After that night, I went to visit her quite often. Not at the nightclub but at her house. Usually in the afternoon. Since she was a singer she would start work at about two in the morning. I rarely went to the nightclub. I couldn't even afford to pay the taxi fare. Also she didn't want people to know she had a boyfriend. It would be bad for business. If people thought she was free they would spend money on her. It's funny. She didn't care about money. She didn't care I was poor. She loved me. She was, she still is, a stubborn woman. I can say that even now she still loves me. But let me go back to those early days. I enjoyed her company and she showed very clearly that she loved me, so naturally I warmed towards her. But this question of money concerned me. And she was much younger than me. So I kept a certain reserve. I wanted to test her love for me. I tell you honestly I didn't touch her for six months. And then it was she who insisted we make love.

I tried to be careful but the fact is I don't like precautions and it's all or nothing for me. If I'm uncomfortable or something gets in the way then it's no use. So she became pregnant. She didn't tell me at first and it didn't show. When she did tell me we agreed she should have an abortion. I didn't continue working. It was a bad situation. I rang my friend Inspector Tin at Wanchai Police Station and he gave me the name of the best back-street abortionist. We went to see him. He was a good man. Very straight. He gave her a check and then he spoke to us.

'Mr Hui, Miss Tong, the situation is this. The pregnancy is three months along. You have come to me a bit late. I can do it but it will be very dangerous and frankly I don't want to do it. There will be a lot of bleeding and this could threaten your life. Why don't you get married and have the baby and be happy?'

We went away and thought about it and decided that was the best thing to do. So, she became my second wife.

This child in her belly. What pain he brought me.

Now, one day, in Causeway Bay, my wife was very obviously pregnant, maybe six or seven months, and naturally a woman doesn't look her best at this time. We were shopping. Suddenly we came face to face with my old lover Margaret. I hadn't seen her for about ten years. She was still very beautiful and tall and elegant.

'Hello Peter,' she greeted me. Naturally I had to introduce them.

'Margaret, this is my second wife.'

Margaret looked at me very strangely and then at my wife. My wife too knew who this was. I had told her everything. They examined each other and I stood there feeling very embarrassed. I knew what Margaret was thinking. 'How was it he refused to marry me but now he has a second wife?'

It was a very short awkward meeting. It was the last time we met.

There are some things that should be forgotten forever

THERE ARE SOME THINGS that should be forgotten forever. The short, sad life of my fourth son is one of them. His birth brings back memories of pain. His death too. How can I think of his death? It was the most miserable thing to happen to me in my whole life. Once I broke down and cried. I was with KF. We were standing in a bus queue outside the hospital and I could not stop the tears. Everyone in the queue was scared. Not just tears. Not just crying. The death of a child. How can you ever deal with such a thing? God can be very cruel.

When he was born, as usual, I was broke. I was so damn poor it hurt. To have the responsibility of a child and to have no money. This is a terrible burden. I had seven dollars in my pocket. I remember this very clearly. I went up to the hospital to see my wife and my new son. For me it was not such a novel event. I had eight children already. But the nurse asked me if I had brought tissues and pads and powder and so many other things. This had never happened to me before. I thought I understood everything. But this hospital was a cheap hospital though it had a good reputation. They expected you to buy everything. But all these things would cost me about twenty dollars. So I walked back down the hill into the city to borrow some money from some friends to buy the things my wife needed. It is a humiliation to have to borrow money for the pads your wife needs after she has given birth to your son. I felt the need to get drunk. But I had only borrowed enough money to buy the things I needed. I only had about two dollars on me when I left the hospital. But I felt a kind of rage inside me to get drunk. Where could I go? Who should I get drunk with? I decided to go and see Lam Chu. Lam Chu was the nephew of my old *kung fu* master Lam Sai-wing. We were friends from those days when I first took up *kung fu*. Now he had his own *kung fu* school. Actually he took over Lam's studio. We were old friends but I hadn't seen him for some time.

Lam Chu and his wife greeted me warmly. Probably they could see things weren't so good with me.

'I need a drink,' I said.

They pointed at the cabinet. It was full of wines of different types. Chinese wines.

'Help yourself,' Lam said. 'Drink what you like. We are old friends. Don't stand on formality.'

I opened the cabinet and saw a large bottle of Ko Leung. This is one of the three most famous Chinese wines: Ko Leung, Ng Ka Pei and Mui Kwai Lo. These are the three classic Chinese wines. Nowadays everyone knows Maotai but it wasn't so famous in those days. It only became famous after President Nixon went to Beijing. I drank the first bottle in about twenty minutes.

'Go on,' Lam Chu waved his hand, 'My students are always giving me bottles of wine. Drink what you like. I don't drink so much myself.'

So I took out another bottle of Ko Leung and drank that too. Dinner time came and they brought food to the table. But I had no appetite. I just felt this hurt in my pride. I had a son but I had no money to support him. I didn't tell them that I had a new son. I just told them I hadn't got a job. So they ate their dinner and I drank all their Ko Leung. I had maybe three or four bottles. Then I found they had no more large bottles left. Only small ones. So I took out a bottle of Mui Kwai Lo. That means something like 'Rosy Dew Wine' in English. It seems as if I had only had a few mouthfuls when that bottle was finished too. Now I can tell you I was still absolutely sober. Lam and his wife knew how fierce I could be when I was drunk. If I had shown I was drunk they would have made excuses to get rid of me. But they just continued to invite me to drink. This time, when I looked in the cabinet, I caught sight of a bottle of Ng Ka Pei. It suddenly appealed to my sense of humour to have that too. To drink a bottle of each of the three most famous Chinese wines in one evening. That would be something worth doing.

By the time I had finished that I was beginning to feel the effects. I decided it was time to leave them and go home. As it happened there was a bus from where they lived in Canal Road to where we lived in Happy Valley. In those days there was a conductor who had a machine with several rolls of tickets and a punch to put a hole in it before giving it to you. When they walked up and down they would click their punch.

I sat down at the front of the bus and leant forward. I could feel all the wine going up to my head. I was beginning to feel very sick and very drunk. Naturally, the conductor knew I was drunk. He could see it from my expression and the way I sat. Maybe it is not an easy job. He was irritated with me. I could tell by the way he clicked his punch. Click. Click. Click. All I could hear was the clicking of the punch.

'Stop that!' I yelled at him.

'Stop what?'

'That clicking. You're driving me crazy.'

'So what? I'll do what I like.'

'I warn you. Stop it or I'll hit you.'

He just saw this small, middle-aged drunk. What could I do to him? But I got up and pushed him hard back. Naturally he fell back on the floor of the aisle. The driver saw that something was happening so he braked and the bus came to a stop. The doors opened and all the passengers got out. The driver got out too. Only the conductor and I were left on the bus. I was standing over him.

'Come on. Get up. I want to hit you again.'

But the conductor had no desire to fight. He got to his feet and got off the bus himself. So I was the only person left on the bus. I can tell you I was feeling very drunk so I sat down and put my head on my arms. When I think about it now I have to laugh. I remember everything so clearly. The bus driver was shouting at the conductor to go up and throw me off the bus but the conductor knew how strong I was. The driver himself then started to come into the bus. I got to my feet and stood at the top of the stairs. The driver looked at me and had second thoughts. Even if I were not so strong I could easily kick him as he came towards me. So the driver went back to his cabin and started the engine. The conductor and the passengers stayed where they were. The driver then drove off with me in the back. I had no idea where he was going. In fact he drove all the way to Central Police Station. I was so damn drunk that I fell asleep. I didn't know anything else but when I came to my senses again I was locked in the cell in the charge room at the station. How they got me off the bus I have no idea.

'Hey! Let me out of here. Let me go. I want to go home!'

But the constables just cursed me and told me to shut up.

I banged on the bars and kept on shouting. I was shouting so loud that the inspector on duty came in and asked what was going on. The cops explained everything and the driver was still there making a statement. The inspector asked to see me and told the constables to open the cell door.

I was furious and started to tell him my side of the story but the officers shouted at me to shut up. Now, I don't like people shouting at me. I felt insulted. So I started to hit the officer nearest me. Then I hit out at everyone in the room. The British inspector was a big man. Over six foot tall. I pushed him with my arms crossed back hard against the wall. I had my arms against his throat. I could see he was surprised. He was so big and I was so small. But he couldn't do anything. You can't hit very hard from the side. There's no room to swing your arms. As soon as I did this all the officers in the room drew out their truncheons and started to beat me. When I was a young *kung fu* student I used to ask the other students to hit me hard on the body. I had some training in this and the drink gave me strength. They hit me round the back and head and shoulders. They were furious and all their blows had no effect at all. I didn't feel a thing until the last strike on my head knocked me unconscious. They were a bit scared. They could see I was bleeding so they took me straight away to Queen Mary Hospital. I woke up there in the casualty ward. They could see I was more or less all right. They put some stitches in my head. Then I was taken back to the station. By this time there had been a change of shift and my friend Inspector Lau had come on duty.

'Mr Hui!' he greeted me. 'How are you feeling?'

We were good friends. He knew me very well. He told the others who I was. Lau was a good man. He laughed when I told him the story. He gave me a coffee and we sat up talking for a few hours.

'If this didn't involve the bus company I would let you go,' he said. 'But they will demand action so there's nothing I can do. I have to take you before the magistrate tomorrow morning. I'm sorry.'

I understood I could not get off so easily so I didn't blame him. He didn't ask me to go back into the cell. He could see I was completely calm now. I lay down on a bench and tried to sleep but I could only think of the birth of my son. I still hadn't told anyone. How could I explain it? No one knew what I was thinking. No one knew what was happening to me. Not even me.

Later the next morning the shift changed again and it was the same shift that had been on duty the night before. I saw another of my old friends, Inspector Wan. He had an ugly mark on his face. A large bruise. It looked like the impression of a hand.

'What happened to you?' I asked.

'You don't remember hitting me?' he asked.

He had had the bad luck to come into the room just as the fight was starting. He was the first one I had hit. I just saw a police uniform in front of me and lashed out. By this time all the officers knew who I was and were feeling more friendly. One of them said: 'You know Mr Hui, you are wonderful. When I hit you, you felt nothing. And I hit you with my full force. I thought you must be a ghost. How can a human being be hit so hard with a truncheon and not feel anything at all?'

I was taken before the magistrate. I saw it was someone I had once helped during the Japanese occupation. This magistrate was very good. Naturally we didn't show that we knew each other. And Lau made sure the evidence was presented in a way that was favourable for me so I was fined a few hundred dollars.

But let me tell you about my son. He was a bright boy. Mischievous. Clever. He was my favourite. Of all my sons he was the only one who looked like me. I loved him with all my heart. When he was three he fell ill. There was a measles epidemic. Measles is not such a serious thing. I told my wife she shouldn't worry too much. She wanted to take him to hospital but I told her measles was just a common thing. We didn't bother with doctors. Just keep the skin powdered. Make sure he doesn't scratch himself and keep his temperature down. That's what I told her. But she was inexperienced in these things. I don't blame her. She didn't realise it until it was too late. When we finally took him to the hospital, the doctor told us he had to stay there in a special room. It wasn't measles. It was meningitis. We had come too late. He died three days later. There are some things we shouldn't remember.

An evening of cheating

ONE AFTERNOON I BUMPED INTO MY FRIEND Lee Bo in Central district. He was the eldest son of a very rich merchant, Lee Yu-kee.

'Hui,' he greeted me, 'I'm glad I bumped into you. Let's go to a cabaret and fool around. Later we have been invited to do some gambling.'

I didn't have much money on me at that time.

'I don't want to go with you,' I told him, 'the fact is, I have a little money but I don't want to spend it in this way.'

'Don't worry, I will take care of that. You will be my guest.'

So, this arranged, we went to a cabaret and then we took some girls out and went to a restaurant in Shek Tong Tsui, the red-light district in Western district.

'Why have we come here?' I asked.

'This is where the game is.'

'Well, we don't need the girls if we are gambling.'

So we arranged with the girls that they could go back to the cabaret and then later we would meet them there or they could come back to meet us at this restaurant for a light meal. Cabaret girls always like to have a light snack after finishing work at about two in the morning. With that arranged we went in and found the gambling party.

The game was going on in a private room. There were about ten people in the room playing *pai kau*, the domino game. As soon as we entered I recognised two or three men who I knew to be cheats. When I saw that these cheats were there I understood that there were one or two other associates among the players and that the rest were being suckered. I thought to myself: Poor Lee Bo. His luck will be bad tonight. I turned to him: 'Well, Lee, how long will you be playing here?'

'You can join in if you like,' he replied.

'I won't gamble myself but I will take a quarter share of yours.' I said this in a loud voice and made sure the cheats heard. They knew I knew they were cheats. I was warning them to be careful. 'But I don't want to gamble any large sums.'

The cheats saw that they weren't going to get very much from Lee that evening. I caught the eye of one of them and said to Lee: 'Well, Lee, I'm going to the toilet. I'll be about fifteen minutes. You carry on.'

So I left the room and this cheat followed me out. In the toilet we made sure we were alone before speaking.

'Mr Hui. Please. I think we understand each other. We hope you won't interfere. We don't want any trouble. We just want to make some money.'

'Well, that's fine by me. Now, I don't know how many of you there are but I think that my share should be twenty per cent. I think that's reasonable.'

As soon as I said this he smiled.

'That's easy, Mr Hui!'

So we went back to the room. I stayed for a while and then left. While I was there Lee lost just a hundred or so, so my losses were not so great. Two days later one of the cheats came to my home and paid me quite a large sum. I was very happy to take it.

'Why don't you join us? You can make a lot of money this way.'

I told him I would think about it. But I never did do this kind of work.

Some time later I bumped into Lee.

'How did you do?' I asked.

'I lost a few hundred.'

'Are you going back there?'

'I don't think so. *Pai kau* is not my game. I prefer poker.'

'You should be careful. There are a lot of cheats around. You are a well-known rich man's son. People know you're a gambler. You are a natural target.'

'I know,' he said, 'but what can I do? I enjoy gambling. If I don't know the other people I don't bet so much.'

'You are wise!' I told him.

I hurt my back

MR YIP WAS A RICH MAN about fifteen years older than me. At that time he was financing a business idea I had. Actually he didn't need to risk his money but I think he enjoyed my company. So with his backing I bought a lot of fishing boat equipment very cheap and had it stored in a godown.

One evening Mr Yip and I were having dinner. Naturally he was paying so we had the best of everything. I had drunk quite a lot of brandy and I can confess to you that I was a little drunk. Now I have a very good head for drinking but sometimes I do get a bit drunk. If I get very drunk I just black out for ten minutes. I just black out and then, when I wake up, I am sober again. Anyway I had been drinking and I was happy. We were talking about our business and I suddenly had the urge to go to the godown to inspect our goods. Stealing from godowns was very common.

'We'd better go and check our goods. Make sure they're okay!' I said.

Mr Yip tried to stop me.

'No need. Another time. You're tired. It's late. You've been drinking. Leave it for now. It's my money. I'm not worried about the goods.'

But I insisted.

'No. This is my business. Although it's your money, this is my idea. I have to take care of my ideas.'

So Mr Yip and I went to the godown to check our goods.

All the goods were packed away on a cockloft. The only way to get to them was to climb up a ladder. The ladder there was not a round bamboo ladder but one made of hard wood. It was a heavy ladder. I leant the ladder up against the cockloft and started to climb up. As I got near to the top I could feel the ladder slipping away. I must have been very drunk. Everything happened very quickly. It slipped away very quickly. I could feel it go and I knew there was nothing I could do to stop it. I had a sudden thought that I should kick the ladder away. I think my thoughts were confused but I had the idea that it would fall on top of me if I didn't kick it away so I kicked as hard as I could but naturally there was nothing to kick away from. If I hadn't tried to kick it I would probably have been all right. But when I tried to kick the ladder away I lost my balance completely. The ladder fell to the ground and I fell on top of it. Now it is better to fall on the flat ground than on to a ladder. My body came down hard on the hard square struts of the ladder. This meant that my buttocks and my neck took the whole weight of the fall. My back itself wasn't hurt at all. I felt a terrible pain. I managed to get to my feet. Mr Yip was very concerned and wanted to take me to hospital but I insisted I was all right so he accompanied me home.

When I got home I took my shoes and jacket off and fell into bed. That was normal for me if I came home drunk. I never bothered to get undressed. Early the next morning, say about five thirty, I felt I needed a pee. I tried to get up but I couldn't. 'You damn silly drunkard!' I said to myself, 'What's the matter with you? Why can't you get up?' I tried to push myself but I couldn't do anything. Now I was worried. I tried to turn my head to speak to my wife but I couldn't even do that. I can tell you, I was scared. I knew I was seriously injured.

'Ah Shuet!' I called out. 'Ah Shuet!' I had to call out several times.

'What's the matter?' She was rather cross. Because of her job she went to bed late and got up about mid-day.

'I can't move.'

'Why can't you move? You bloody fool!'

'Please help me. I need to have a pee.'

She started to grumble and curse me. She thought I was just drunk and had a hangover.

'No listen,' I pleaded with her, 'Listen, this is serious. I had a fall. I think this time I am seriously wounded.' I don't think she believed me. She got out of bed and came round to my side. Then she tried to lift me up but my head just fell back on the pillow. This scared her.

'What's the matter? What did you do?'

'I don't know. I don't understand why my neck won't support my head.' At that time we were very hard up and we were sharing the flat with another small family. My wife shouted to the other family to help. They quickly came and I could see they were scared too. I was scared. I was in some pain but that didn't worry me so much. It was the fact that

I couldn't move. I was worried I was paralysed. Naturally, the first thing to do was to get me to a doctor.

Now, with anything to do with bones we Chinese naturally think first of going to see a bone-setter. These people are very skilled in fixing any kind of problem affecting the bones. There is a natural connection with *kung fu*. If you know about *kung fu* naturally you will have a good knowledge of bones. Thinking in this way I told my wife to take me to see my friend Lam Chu. Now I should explain that I had helped Lam Chu in many things. Once, during the Japanese occupation, I gave his wife a large sum of money. They had wanted to go to Macau to live. Lam had four or five children. His wife came to me and said she planned to go to Macau to sell her mother's house. She asked for $10,000 but I told her that wouldn't be enough and I gave her $20,000. The fact is, although she promised to pay me back as soon as she had sold the house I never heard anything more about the money. Not even after the war. She never mentioned it again. I am not the kind of man to demand repayment. As far as I am concerned if I borrow money from a friend I never say thank you and I never mention it again. But when I can afford to repay the debt then I do so. I expect other people to do the same.

Now, since Lam was an old friend and he knew about bones I decided to go to him first of all. He would know what the problem was. So with some help we managed to get me downstairs and into a taxi. I had to hold my own head in my hands while four people carried me – two to the legs and two to the side.

We got to Lam's studio and Lam checked me carefully. He told me I had displaced the vertebrae in my neck and at the bottom of my spine. He knew what to do. He did some manipulation and massaged me with some special herbal oil. He did a good job. He told me to go back the next day.

My wife managed to contact my eldest son and the next day he accompanied us to Lam Chu's. While Lam was doing his manipulation his wife asked my son to go to the next room. 'Your father is an old friend of ours,' she said, 'and he will need a long period of help. We don't want to charge you each time. It's better if you just pay one lump sum to cover the whole period. Let's say $1,500. Lam Chu will do everything he can to help your father get better. If you don't have the full amount now maybe you can pay a deposit. I don't want to worry your father about money now as I know he is having a hard time these days.' My son was annoyed about this. He knew it wasn't the right way to do things. But he didn't want to make a fuss. Certainly he didn't want to annoy me as I was in such pain. So he paid something on account. He didn't tell me about it. However, he told my wife what had happened and she told me.

'Deposit!' I shouted, 'That bloody woman!' Actually I thought of ruder words than that. 'Right! I will never go to Lam Chu's again. I know someone else who is just as good. We will go there.'

So we took the taxi to Canal Road, to the house of Kun Tak-hoi, another *kung fu* fighter who was famous for his monkey-style *kung fu*.

'Mr Hui!' he said when we arrived, 'What's the problem? What have you done?'

I explained everything and asked him to help me.

'Of course! Of course!' he said. He looked me over carefully.

'You are very seriously injured. But you won't be paralysed. However, it will take at least three months for you to recover. This was the same as Lam Chu had said. He knew Lam Chu well and knew that he and I were good friends. He was puzzled that I had come to him.

'Mr Hui, I hope you don't mind my asking but why is it you didn't go to see Lam Chu?'

I explained the whole situation to him. 'Yeah!' he agreed, 'His wife's such a bloody woman. That's not something you should do to a friend.'

So every day I went to Kun and he massaged me. I already knew I was going to recover. I could move all my limbs again. My neck could support my head. By the ninth day I was already about eighty per cent recovered. I could walk downstairs slowly by myself. On the next day I told Kun I was feeling much better and that I was pleased with my progress. Then, on the eleventh day, we couldn't get a rickshaw or a taxi to go home. After waiting for a while I told my wife that I was sure I could manage it.

'What do you mean manage it?'

'I mean walk home myself.'

It wasn't so far. Maybe half a mile. So we set off walking very slowly. As it happened Kun was looking out of the window and caught sight of us.

'That's a bloody miracle!' he said to himself, 'Only eleven days and he's walking.'

'Mr Hui,' he said the next time I saw him. 'This is remarkable. I would never have imagined that you could recover so quickly. I can only explain it like this. With all your *kung fu* training you developed so much external power that it went down deeply into your tissues and you developed internal power too. Even though you never tried to achieve internal power you have achieved it through your development of external power.'

I understood clearly what he was saying to me. *Kung fu* consists of two disciplines. The first discipline is to obtain external power. Once that has been achieved you can go on to develop internal power. If you have not fully achieved external power it is very dangerous to try to attain internal power. It can hurt your organs. Some people go mad. Some people even die. Nowadays there is a fashion for *qigong*. This is a system for the development of internal power. It is very dangerous. There are stories of people getting a big rush of energy to the brain. They are not trained to control this power. It can drive some people mad.

Soon I was completely well. As for Lam Chu, I never went to visit him again. I am sure he knows why. Maybe he didn't know his wife asked for the money at that time but he would have found out. He would have wondered why I didn't go back for more treatment. I tell you, Chinese women are greedy. My father once told me: 'Never give a woman enough to eat until she's fifty.' My mother overheard him and shouted at him like hell. 'What nonsense are you teaching my son!' But it's true. I have something of my father's character. A man must never allow himself to be controlled by his wife.

Bodyguard

I KNEW MR LAI from the time we had taken a photography course together when I was seventeen. He was the younger brother of a well-known actress. There was some connection because the photography teacher was hired to take still photographs of the actress for promotional material. From time to time I bumped into Mr Lai because he was chasing a girl who lived near us in Happy Valley. Normally we just waved to each other but one day he crossed over. He had something he wanted to talk to me about.

He explained that he was working for an overseas Chinese shipowner by the name of Alexander Kwong. I'm not sure where he came from originally: Malaysia, Singapore, perhaps Indonesia. This man was having some financial difficulties, he had borrowed a million dollars from someone, and he hadn't paid it back. Now he had heard there was a contract out with one of the triads. If something happened to Mr Kwong then the company would collapse and he would lose his job. For this reason he had recommended to Mr Kwong that I be hired as a bodyguard. I was doubtful. I thought that my temper wasn't suitable. Also I could see that it might be dangerous. I might be killed. I was concerned about my responsibilities to my wife and our seven children.

I went to see Mr Kwong at his office in Central. He was a slight man too, about two inches taller than me and about five years older. My first impression of him was good. He treated me in a very friendly way and he showed me respect.

'I would very much appreciate it if you would be my bodyguard for a few months.'

'Maybe I can help. I have some connections. Tell me who is chasing you.'

'I thank you for your offer, Mr Hui, but you must trust me. I cannot tell you who is chasing me.'

'How much do you want to pay?' I asked.

'I would like to suggest $800 a month,' he said. 'Naturally, I will pay all your expenses while you are working for me.' This was quite good money at that time. The rent of my flat which had two large bedrooms, two bathrooms, a large sitting room and servants' quarters was only $140. I remember that a tael of gold in those days was $200. Now it is about $4,000. That gives some idea of the value.

'That's fine.'

'If that is not enough, maybe I can offer more,' he said. I am not a greedy man. I said: 'I have already accepted $800. If I need any extra money I will ask for it.'

He nodded. I could see that we understood each other.

My job was to stay with Mr Kwong twenty-four hours a day. During the daytime I sat outside his office. When he went to the bathroom I went with him and when we went back to his flat in MacDonnell Road, I went there too. He had a mistress. She was a nice girl, always very polite. In fact, Mr Kwong always treated me as a friend who was doing him a favour rather than an employee. He was a natural gentleman. I was very comfortable in his guestroom.

The threat was a real one, I discovered one day. There were about twelve staff in the office but they didn't have much to do. Business was bad. That's why Kwong owed the money. I was sitting at a desk just outside Mr Kwong's office. Anyone going into the office first had to get past me. Suddenly a young man entered the office and headed straight towards Mr Kwong's office. He was in his mid to late twenties and he had a cold, hard expression on his face. It was clear he had been there before. He knew where Kwong's office was. The other staff were obviously afraid of him and didn't do anything to stop him. I guessed immediately from his attitude that this man was the collector. As he approached, I got to my feet and stood in front of him.

'What can I do for you sir?' I was very polite.

'None of your business!' he said and tried to push past me. I immediately put my hand up to warn him.

'You must excuse me sir, but if you want to see anyone you must let me know first. I'm afraid I must insist you let me know your business.'

He was surprised. He was used to people being scared of him. But he could see that I wasn't, even though I was shorter than him. He hesitated. Maybe I was just a new employee who didn't understand the situation. He stared at me hard, looking me up and down.

'You don't have to try to judge who I am. I can tell you. If you wish to see someone you must ask me first. Otherwise the only way for you to go through that door is to knock me down.'

He immediately took two steps back. He looked like a killer. I waited. I assumed he was giving himself some room to attack me.

'Who are you?' he asked.

'I am Mr Kwong's bodyguard. If Mr Kwong has done something bad to you or to your boss then I am sorry. I regret that. But I am here and you have to talk to me first or fight. That's the choice.'

He looked hard at me. I guessed he was a Shanghainese, and that he was connected with the Green gang in North Point. Later I found that I had guessed right. I thought he should know who I was. I told him my name.

'Don't worry,' I told him, 'I am not a killer. I have never killed anyone. I have knocked many people down but, at the last moment, I have always stopped myself from killing them.'

He was at least seven years younger than me and five or six inches taller. He would expect to be able to defeat me. I knew that he wasn't carrying a gun. A top fighter like this doesn't need a gun. For a *kung fu* fighter, every part of his body is a potential weapon. Also, we have a saying that a hero always respects another hero. Perhaps he thought in that way. He nodded to me and turned and went away. He never came back.

I asked around and found out that this was a very famous Shanghainese fighter by the name of To Tung-sang. Any fighter, no matter how good, will always delay a fight until he knows how good his opponent is. There is a saying: 'Know yourself. Know your enemy. A hundred fights. A hundred victories.' Once he heard who I was from Small Tong and my other Shanghainese triad friends he backed off. Maybe he still thought he could beat me. But it wasn't certain. A fighter like that must be certain he can win. Otherwise, if he loses a fight, he will also lose his reputation. I heard that he suggested to his boss that he should settle the matter amicably with Kwong. That's what happened. After about four months Kwong told me I wasn't needed any more.

We kept in touch. He visited my home a few times and distributed lucky money to my children. I helped him to sell his race horses for a good price. Then he left Hong Kong. The last I heard he was in Singapore.

Some girls are just lucky

THIS IS A STORY ABOUT A MAN NAMED NELSON and a girl named Sally. The world is a funny place. Sometimes there is a kind of madness in us. Sometimes fate gives us a chance that we could never hope for.

This was before the Vietnam war, but a lot of US servicemen still came to Hong Kong and I was back in the tailoring business. I had got myself a job with a high-class tailor shop in Kowloon called Henry's Tailor Shop.

At Henry's we did very good business. Why? Because the boss was the brother-in-law of the driver of the bus that brought the sailors into town from the airport. He always stopped the bus outside the shop. The sailors who came to Tsimshatsui were officers and higher-ranking seamen. And it was an easy job because the sailors came straight to our shop in Cameron Road. I didn't have to go out looking for business. The bus brought maybe two or three dozen officers. Naturally, not all of them would buy something but even two or three was good enough. I was happy. I had a basic salary and a commission and sometimes people would trust me to buy them presents. They didn't have a long leave. They didn't want to spend the whole time shopping so they would say they wanted to buy this and that, and I would offer to get everything for them. I remember one black sailor passed me a long list of the things he wanted: watches, clothes, jewellery, fountain pens and so on. The total cost came to about $20,000. I would make maybe ten per cent. There was a small jewellery counter in the shop. Actually it was a separate business. The owner couldn't speak much English so I was happy to introduce his goods to the customers and from this I learnt something about jewellery. He showed me how diamonds were cut and so on. I did this just as a favour but at the end of the month he gave me a commission on what I had sold for him. I never expected it but he insisted. It was good business for him to do this. We had quite a few black sailors as customers. They liked to have nice clothes. I liked them. They were very straight. If they thought something was very expensive they just said so. 'Hey man! Why's this cloth more expensive than that one?' I would explain that it was special silk or high quality wool. They liked me.

Now, gradually word went round that I was somebody they could trust. I was friendly and I would show them round and introduce them to nice girls and so on and I never charged for this. It was my pleasure to do this for customers of the shop or for people who trusted me to buy their presents for them or just friends of friends. Most of the sailors were from the Philippines, or Vietnam or from Guam. All my customers would go back and tell their friends to look out for me. So, soon I was doing very well again. Also I had many connections in the hotels in Tsimshatsui. I still had some connections at the Peninsula Hotel from the old days and also in the other hotels. Everyone knew me. Everyone respected me. I was doing well again and I didn't have to work long hours. This was much better than working in a restaurant.

One morning I got a call from someone I had introduced to the Miramar Hotel. It was early. Maybe seven o'clock.

'There's a crazy Yankee sailor here who's throwing money around. He's giving everyone ten-dollar tips just to get him a drink. He's been here twenty-four hours and he hasn't been out of the room. He's just drinking like crazy. Then he said: "I just want two things. Get me a tailor and get me a girl." So you better come over here fast or someone else will get the business.'

I hurried over to the hotel and got there at about eight o'clock. I knocked on the door and he called me to go in. My friend had already told the man something about me.

'So you're Peter Hui. Glad to meet you,' he waved his hand to a seat, 'have a drink. My name's Nelson and I've been in Okinawa for ten years. I never got out of Okinawa. Now here I am.'

Ten years in Okinawa! Later we talked and talked. He needed a friend. He needed someone to show him round. He was mad to have a girl. Not having a girl for so long can make you crazy. Nelson was crazy.

'Okay Peter,' he said. 'First let's go and have breakfast. Then I'll come to your shop to make up some clothes and then I want you help me find a suitable female companion.'

'I will help you get anything you want.'

So after breakfast we went to the shop. Now this Nelson was a strong drinker. We had already finished more than a bottle of whiskey between us. He ordered six suits at $300-400 each and some shirts and other clothes. It was a good order.

'Now, I will introduce you to a nice girl.'

I had in mind a girl named Juliana. She was a nice-looking girl and also a nice person. I wanted to choose a very nice girl for my new friend Nelson and Juliana was the best I could think of. So we went to her flat and knocked on the door.

'Who is it?' the door opened a crack.

'Is Juliana there?'

'No. She is out.'

She saw it was me and opened the door. It was Sally, who shared the flat with Juliana. Well, Sally wasn't such a nice girl as Juliana but she wasn't so bad and she was there. I introduced her to Nelson. I could see he was almost crazy with excitement. We went and had lunch together and then I left them. I told him Sally would show him round and that he knew where to find me if he wanted anything. I saw him again that night and almost every day we had lunch together or a drink.

About the third day, Nelson dropped by the shop with Sally on his arm. She was wearing an expensive fur. I could see she was milking him for everything she could. I didn't blame her. When you're lucky you must make the most of it. I could see he had no thoughts about anything but having a good time. He was just throwing money away.

'Be careful,' I warned him, 'spend your money on things that are worthwhile. Enjoy yourself. Don't spend it in the wrong way.'

'Ah Peter, you are an experienced man!' he said.

But he was crazy about Sally and he was crazy with his money.

About a week later he told me something that nearly knocked me off my chair. He had bought Sally a flat. Crazy. How much would it cost? A 700 square foot flat in Tsimshatsui? At least HK$100,000! Maybe even $200,000.

Then two weeks later Nelson left Hong Kong and I never saw him again. What happened to Nelson? I would like to know what happened to him.

Now that wasn't the end of the story. Although I introduced many sailors to girls I never once took a cent from the girls. I'm not a pimp. I was happy to do this as a favour. But this case was different. I didn't even think of any commission. I had made maybe $6,000 from Nelson myself. But Sally's girlfriends and the mamasans in the bars heard about the story. They knew she hadn't given me anything in return. I had done

her such a big favour. Even the pimps blamed her. They knew I hadn't
asked for a commission, but still, they thought, I should get something.
That's our way of thinking. If you do me a big favour I should give you
a small thank-you present. So one day she invited me to lunch. At the
end she suddenly looked serious.

'Peter, you did me a very big favour.'

I laughed.

'It was just Juliana's bad luck and your good luck. Who can say when
fate will bring us good fortune.'

'You did me a very big favour. I know you don't want any commission
but still I would like to give you a present.'

'Don't be silly. There's no need.'

But she insisted.

'I don't know what kind of present I should buy you so I will just give
you this *lai see*.' And she gave a little red 'lucky money' packet with some
notes inside.

'Come on, Sally, I can't accept this. I know you girls have to work
hard. You wouldn't be in this line of business if life wasn't so hard. That's
why I don't like to receive a cent from you girls.'

But she insisted and in the end I put it in my pocket. When I opened
it I found it contained $3,000.

I got a letter from Nelson. In it he told me that he had wanted to
marry Sally. But the naval authorities had rules. They checked Sally out
and refused Nelson permission to marry her. That's what he said. I think
he spent his entire life savings in two weeks. Sally was a Shanghainese.
Those Shanghainese girls know how to entertain a man. They are much
better than Cantonese girls.

Maybe everyone is crazy in their own way. Nelson was crazy about
girls. I am crazy also, but in a different way. I had a good job. I was
making good money. My second wife was giving me children. We had
four altogether. Two girls and another boy. Then one day I said to myself:
'You are earning good money, Peter, but you will never be rich.' I thought
about this a lot. It seemed to be a very mean existence always to be serving
other people and never having the chance to be rich. So I quit the
tailoring business and set myself up in business. But I'm no good at
business. It didn't work out. I was not meant to be rich.

Trouble over pond mud

IN 1952, I TOOK MY FAMILY UP TO CHINA. In 1954 the Chinese government imposed travel restrictions. It became very difficult for my first wife to come to Hong Kong. It was impossible to emigrate back to Hong Kong. Then the situation grew worse. There was no education for the children. Not real education. The only thing students learnt was the *Little Red Book* of Mao's quotations. They just memorised his thoughts. Mao wanted to brainwash the entire population of China. He wanted to be treated like a kind of god. He wanted to be worshipped in every house. Mao's portrait stared down on us in our own sitting room. The situation was becoming intolerable. In fact, the situation for my own children was not as bad as for the children of other families. We were registered as overseas Chinese. That gave us some privileges. My children didn't have to work for years at a time in remote country districts. We were lucky. But still, life was dull. It would only get worse. Meanwhile, I had work now so I could afford more. My eldest son too helped. I am proud to say that my eldest son is a very capable and hard-working man. He is a good son.

We had to be careful what we said but we finally agreed that we should bring all the family out as fast as we could. We had to think how to do this. Now, a two-way travel permit that would allow you out and back again could be obtained if you could persuade a neighbour to guarantee your return. So we decided to try with two children first. My second daughter insisted on staying with her mother so the first two to come out were my third son and fourth daughter. Our plan was to see what the consequences would be if they didn't return. We got on well with our neighbours so it was no problem to get a guarantee. We got the permit and they came down to Hong Kong. Then we waited. If there was any problem my wife was to say that I had detained them in Hong Kong. If the consequences for our neighbours were serious then they would have to go back. We just waited to see what would happen. In fact nothing happened. The neighbourhood security office accepted my wife's explanations and nothing happened to my neighbours.

A year or two later we did the same again. My fifth daughter also refused to leave her mother. Such a bright, attractive and mischievous girl. But she was very loyal to her mother. So the second time it was my sixth daughter and seventh son. Again we waited and again nothing happened. Then, some time later, we did it again for my eighth daughter. It was more difficult for her because she was born in China but in the end we managed it. The security office questioned the neighbours: 'Why did you guarantee these children?'

The neighbours replied: 'It's quite natural that they should want to stay with their father. He is overseas Chinese. The mother is still here with the other children. What's the harm?' So nothing happened. We were very lucky. A few years later the situation in China became much worse.

It was then, in the early sixties that I first came to Cheung Chau. It was my eldest son who solved the problem of accommodation. For a while they were living in the premises of a shop that had gone bankrupt. Then my son made contact with an old schoolmate whose father was Mr Fung, who was chairman of the Cheung Chau Chamber of Commerce. With his help we found a flat on the island.

When my son first told me about it I cursed him like crazy.

'Cheung Chau? Why so far away? Couldn't you find something more convenient?'

In those days Cheung Chau seemed very remote. It was only eight miles south of Hong Kong Island and it only took an hour by ferry to get there, but no one would ever think of going there if they didn't have to. My life has been mostly spent in a few square miles of Hong Kong. Now my family was living far away on this remote island. It was like going back to China. I didn't go with them when they first moved there but after a few months I went to see how they were doing. I got on the ferry and I grumbled the whole way. Until I got there. It was just a small island with two hills and a low strip of land in between where the town was. There was a wide bay filled with fishing boats. There was a long waterfront. It was a world away from the city. My life wasn't easy at this time. I was trying to earn a living and I was arguing with my wife a lot. And suddenly I came to Cheung Chau and I saw that life could be easy.

I was getting old. I didn't need to run around all the time. If you wanted to sit and drink you just put a table up in one of the alleys and you sat there and watched the world go by. What could be better? I said to myself: 'This is wonderful!' I decided immediately to move in with my children.

I describe it so simply but it didn't just happen like that. All these years I went up to China from time to time and all these years I had a young family and my second wife was insisting that she go back to work. I wasn't earning enough to keep her and the family. I hated the idea of her being a nightclub singer. It was something we argued about all the time. But she is a stubborn woman. I couldn't stop her. It was the only life she knew. She didn't know anything about being a mother. I won't say she was a bad mother but how can you bring up young children if you don't get to bed until four o'clock in the morning? Her argument was that she could earn more as a singer than I could in any kind of business. She was right. But I hated it. All those men in nightclubs looking at her, I knew what they were thinking. I knew they said to themselves: 'For $1,000 I could sleep with her.' The entertainment world is like that. If you have money it's not so difficult to persuade a singer to spend the night with you. It's almost expected. I may say many things about my wife but she is a virtuous woman and I never had any fears about that. But other people wouldn't know that. They would say to themselves: 'Peter Hui thinks he's so clever. He's so proud of himself but he's married to an entertainer!' or else they would say: 'Peter Hui can't earn a living for himself. He likes to eat soft rice.'

With my first wife I fooled around with other girls and it never worried me and I never hid it from my wife. She always said to me: 'You do what you like but just make sure you can take care of us. That's all I ask.' I did this because we had a traditional marriage. But my second wife was different. I had chosen her myself. So I never once fooled around with other girls while I was married to her. Not once. I was very faithful. Her girlfriends all teased her. She had told them what a romantic man I was but they laughed at her: 'You say he's so romantic but he has never once tried to make a suggestion to any of us. Are you sure he really is romantic?' But I know one thing well. My wife loved me very much. She loved me more than I loved her. That is always the way. One side loves more than the other. That is a fact. Even though we are divorced she still loves me. I know this.

My first wife knew about my second wife. I didn't tell her but of course the children did. She accepted the situation. It was my traditional right. At that time it was possible to register two wives. This didn't apply to me as neither of my marriages were officially registered. As far as I was concerned I was married. In the case of my first wife the marriage was recognised but the second time we didn't even have a dinner. Once my first wife came down to Hong Kong herself. I asked my second wife to go and pay her respects but she refused. She was too embarrassed by the situation. But she let the children go. When she came down, I stayed with her in a lodging house near Western Market but this didn't happen often. She only managed to come down to Hong Kong a few times. Almost every month I went up to China. I took with me provisions of all sorts: rice, cloth, sugar, everything. It was difficult to get enough of all the basic necessities in China. Everything was rationed. Every time I went through customs going in and out they inspected my bags very carefully. What did they expect to find? I can't say. They were obsessed with the idea that people from Hong Kong and Macau were coming to China to spy for the Americans. Everyone was warned that they should be careful of spies. Spies? What was there to find out? I asked my family but they just told me to be careful what I said in case people suspected me of being a spy. I laughed. I listened for news that someone had been arrested for spying, some Hong Kong or Macau compatriot. But I can't remember that I heard of anyone being caught. But everyone was concerned about spies. The customs officers would look at my lighter.

'What's in here?' they asked.

'Some gasoline, some cotton, some flint.'

But they were very suspicious.

'What else?'

'Nothing else. It's just a lighter.'

'Where did you buy it?'

'What? I don't know. I've had it for years.'

'How much did it cost?'

They just kept on asking more and more questions. Finally I got so mad at them.

'Here take it,' I said, 'I don't want it. Please keep it. I'll use matches.' Then they let me go.

When I went up to China I liked to get fishpond mud. This is a very rich kind of soil and it's very good for plants. I have always liked plants and I used to take some dried bricks of this fishpond mud back to Hong Kong. It's very fertile. Now the older Customs officers were educated men and they knew all about fishpond mud but the young Customs officers were just uneducated peasants who knew nothing about anything.

'What's that?' one young officer asked looking at the dried brick of mud I was taking back to Hong Kong. I explained what it was.

'What's inside?'

'Nothing!'

'How do I know nothing is inside?'

'Do you want to see?' I asked. He nodded. So I put the brick flat on the table and hit it hard with my fist so that it broke up into small pieces. He just looked at me in amazement.

'There!' I said. 'You can see. There's nothing inside.'

'How about that piece?' he asked pointing at another brick. I had half a dozen bricks.

'There's nothing in there. I told you!' I was getting very angry.

'How do I know?'

Time was passing and I was afraid I might miss the train. If I missed it I would have to wait another day and go through this procedure again.

'Look! I'm not going to hit them all. I don't want to hurt my hand. Haven't you got an X-ray machine?'

They didn't.

'Look,' I said to the officer, 'You are so stupid. I have a family here. My wife and seven children live here. Do you think I would be so stupid to smuggle anything? Do you think I'm a spy? You're crazy. If I did anything bad like that you could arrest my whole family. Would I be so stupid? Now, you are suspicious of these bricks. Take them. Look at them. Cut them up. Do anything you want. If you find anything wrong then arrest my family. If everything is all right then you can give it back to me the next time I come through. How about that?'

Very reluctantly they decided to let me take the bricks out. Later, they started to sell flat tiles of this mud at the exit. It was me and one or two other overseas Chinese who knew about fishpond mud who taught them.

I went up to China nearly every month. I can say it was a hard time for me. If I went up I would have to stay at least a week. How could I earn a living? How could I support my wife and family back in Hong Kong? This was a very bad time. I did many jobs. Nothing for very long. My wife made more money than I did with her singing. But I felt insulted and humiliated by the situation. But I also had to think of the children. I didn't want to harm them. I knew if I let my anger out it could only have one result. This is the only time in my life I have been able to control my temper for so long.

But finally I couldn't restrain myself any longer. My second wife and I were in a restaurant and we started discussing this question. I asked her to give up singing and she refused. I lost my temper and she lost her temper and we started to shout at each other. Finally, I said: 'If you won't give up then I must separate from you.'

She just glared at me: 'Good idea.'

'We'll go and see a solicitor this afternoon.'

'Let's do that!'

I understood she was talking hard but her heart was soft. She didn't want it. I too was talking harder than I felt. But neither of us would back down. So after lunch we went to see a solicitor. Now, we both knew several solicitors but which one should we use?

'I don't want you to think I am trying to get an unfair advantage over you,' I said to her, 'So you choose which solicitor we use.'

She chose Hsien Ping-hei, a well-known society lawyer. He was an old friend of hers, an old admirer. I had never met him myself but I had no objections. We went to his office. Naturally he was a bit surprised to see us, especially as we both looked so angry.

'We need a divorce,' I told him. He looked at my wife and she nodded.

'I don't need anything,' I said, 'but I want to keep the children.'

She didn't argue but she looked at me very sadly.

'Why do you want them?'

'They're my children.'

'They're mine too.'

'You're a singer. You don't have the time or energy to look after them. You work at night. You spend most of the day in bed.' At that time I was doing some private tutoring on Cheung Chau and I had my other children around.

'I can take care of them better than you.'

Mr Hsien listened to everything and at the end he spoke to my wife: 'Miss Tong, you and I are old friends but I am afraid I must agree with Mr Hui. He is better suited to look after the children. Your life and work are upside down. It would not be suitable for bringing up your children. I am just trying to be fair and equitable. I suggest therefore that he be given care of the children. In addition, I must add that if you want to see the children you must first have Mr Hui's permission.' At this my wife started to cry. I thought this was a very hard condition but I didn't say anything. When everything was completed I said to her: 'You can come and see them anytime. You don't need to ask my permission.'

A separation contract was important. Even though we weren't properly married we both needed to know that if the future was brighter we wouldn't be sued later. Maybe I would become a millionaire or she would marry one. Nothing was impossible. It was best to sort this thing out officially. I took the children to live with us in Cheung Chau. My youngest son was three years old at that time. His sisters were four and five. My other children helped me to look after them. They liked my second wife.

'Why did you have to divorce her?' they asked me. 'Auntie is all right.'

'I have my reasons. We couldn't agree on her singing career. It was intolerable to live together like that. Now we are free to live as we like.'

And then I became a spy.

ONE DAY, IN THE LATE AUTUMN of 1965, a well-known sports reporter by the name of Ma Siu-wah came to see me. We knew each other well.

'I've got something for you,' he said. 'I think you might be interested.'

'What is it?'

'An American agent approached me to do a job. I told him I wasn't qualified but that I knew someone who might be suitable. I was thinking of you. Would you be interested?'

'I need money,' I admitted, 'How well does it pay?'

'It shouldn't be bad. Frankly, I don't know. You can discuss that with them directly. If you want I can arrange a meeting. He's a Japanese but he speaks English.'

I agreed and a meeting was arranged for the next day. Ma introduced me to the Japanese agent.

'If I take this job what kind of work do I have to do?' I asked.

'Well, it's simple, you're new to this kind of work and you're new to us so we'll start slowly and see how we get on. We'll start with something very simple.'

'What do you mean simple?'

'Well, you go up to Canton quite often to visit your family?'

'Yes.'

'Just keep your eyes open. Tell us what you notice. We don't want to specify anything. Just study people and everyday life. Just tell us anything that strikes you.'

'That's an easy job. What do you pay?'

'Well, you can choose. Either you get paid for each trip or you get paid monthly. Up to you.'

I didn't have to think.

'I am not a greedy man. I have a family so I would like to be paid monthly and then each job will be different so the risk will vary so I will charge a separate amount for each trip. If it's harder or more risky I will charge more.'

I think we agreed that they would pay me $450 a month plus expenses and a fee per trip. I could live on it but I wasn't going to get rich. But it was such an easy job. Naturally I didn't tell anyone what I was doing.

Now, at this time China was closed to the outside world. Foreigners couldn't enter the country without special reasons. The only people who went in and out were people like me with family in China. Naturally, the Chinese officials suspected everyone of being an American spy. I don't know how many people the Americans recruited. So I went up to China more and more often. Before this I had gone up once a month, later I was going up three or four times a month. The Americans just wanted to know what was happening on the streets of China. From this they could guess what was going on in Beijing. They knew there was a power struggle. Any information they could get would be useful.

Once they asked me to find out information about harvests. Not just in Guangdong but in other provinces. Actually, there was no difficulty finding out this kind of information. It was common knowledge. Everyone had relatives in other parts of China. If they were short of anything they would ask relatives elsewhere to send it to them. It was easy to find out and not difficult or dangerous to ask. It was the sort of information that everyone liked to know.

In 1965 the Red Guards began. Then in 1966 China went crazy and they became powerful. Red Guard sympathisers started a bombing campaign in Hong Kong. Every night you could hear two or three bombs exploding. Many people were killed. For a year there were bombs everywhere. Then suddenly they stopped. Everyone in Hong Kong was disgusted with the bombers. A young girl was killed at a tram stop. Overnight they stopped. But in Canton it was different. There were no bombs there but there was a lot of fighting.

The background was this. Mao Tse-tung was losing power. So he launched a youth movement to attack the government. But the Red Guards were not centrally controlled. They belonged to factions. There were provincial factions and ideological factions. Red Guards travelled all over the country free of charge. It was a time of wildness and freedom. They felt they could do everything they wanted. They felt they could change the whole world. But the Red Guard factions would disagree with each other and when they disagreed they would attack each other physically.

All round the city each faction of Red Guards would put up small character posters explaining their political views. Some of these were about petty ideological matters that I didn't understand, and maybe no one really understood. There were hundreds of these posters on different subjects. One of my jobs was to memorise as many of these posters as I could. Now, as you know, I have been gifted with a good memory. But it is not photographic. I didn't dare make any written notes. That would prove I was a spy. What did it matter who read these posters? But those times were not times of reason. If they suspected you of being a spy they would kill you straight away. If you disagreed with them they would beat you up or kill you without even thinking. Let's say a poster would argue that farmers should keep half of what they produced and give the rest to the government. Now, if a Red Guard saw you reading this poster he might come up to you and say: 'Well, comrade, what do you think of that?' Naturally, you might reply: 'It makes sense.' But, if this Red Guard belonged to a different faction you would be in big trouble. Maybe he would think the farmers should only keep thirty per cent of the harvest and give seventy per cent to the government. Every policy matter like this would be argued using obscure political language. So, you can see, reading the posters was a dangerous thing to do. My family warned me not to read them too obviously. But it was my job so I had to read them. The way I solved this problem was like this. I would read one poster for say five minutes and then walk away for a while and then come back after twenty minutes and read another poster and then walk away again. All the walls would be covered with posters so it wasn't an easy job to remember all of them. The Red Guards were really frightening. Not just the boys, the girls as well. They carried all sorts of weapons: knives, choppers, iron rods, wooden staves, *kung fu* weapons – these were very popular – lengths of rope, chain, tools, everything they could lay their hands on, every kind of weapon you could imagine. Faction attacked faction without mercy. I saw this happen once. I must explain that the factions used to drive round the city in open trucks. They weren't big trucks but they could carry forty or fifty people. They thought nothing of killing people. Really, it was a common sight to see corpses lying in the streets and side lanes. They might even hang bodies up on street lamps. I saw that many times.

One day, I was just walking along the street near the East Asia Hotel when I saw two trucks coming towards me. At the side of the hotel there was a colonnaded walkway. Suddenly the two trucks stopped and I saw another two or three trucks coming from the left. They also stopped and without a word they all jumped off their trucks and started to attack each other. I hid behind a column. I didn't dare look round. It was common for bystanders to be killed just for watching. The fight lasted maybe fifteen minutes and then one side fled leaving maybe a dozen of their friends dead or dying. They just left them. No one cared about the injured at all. They were just left on the street. You can't imagine what it was like if you weren't there. It was horrible.

My reports were so good that they began to suspect that I was a double agent. How could I memorise everything so clearly? As soon as I smelled this I just laughed at them: 'You know why I enjoy doing this? Because I hate that bloody Mao. He keeps my family in Canton. I'm doing it for their sakes. I'm doing it for my sake too.' But I made it clear that if a job was too dangerous I would reject it.

The biggest job they gave me was to find a military air base near the town of Foshan. They knew there was a base somewhere near there but they didn't know exactly where. I think they had some pictures from their spy planes but they weren't too clear. So one day I took the train past Foshan and got off at a small station. I didn't know this area at all and I had intended to ask someone for information but when I got off the train the other passengers who got off hurried away and I found myself completely alone. The station was a small country station so there was no town there – just flat rice fields and fields of vegetables. In the distance there were some hills. I had no idea which way to walk: north, south, east or west. Now, my reason for choosing this station was simply that it was one stop from Foshan. I wanted to get back to Foshan before nightfall so that I could return that night to my family in Canton. I had told the local neighbourhood police office that I was going for a trip to Foshan and that I expected to be back that evening. If I was delayed – if something went wrong and I didn't get back until the next day then I would have to go and explain to them. They might punish me if they thought I was telling lies. I started to get worried but in the end I decided that if I was late, too bad, I would just talk my way out. So I stood on the edge of the paddy fields and looked round. It was obvious there wasn't an airfield in the immediate area. Since there were some hills in the distance I decided to walk up to the top of one of them and see if I could see anything from there. So I set off. As I walked I became aware of the sound of planes. After a while I got to the hill and looking down from the top I could see some planes descending to land in a place hidden by another hill. I set off to climb this higher hill and when I got to the top I looked down and I could see the whole airfield spread out below me – but something was wrong, I couldn't see any planes. Then I realised that they were all camouflaged and hidden. I think they expected to be attacked by Taiwan.

I had no trouble walking back to the railway line and getting a train back to Canton. No one bothered me. At that time people minded their own business. When I gave my report back to the Americans they were very impressed. Actually they were suspicious. How could I measure the distances so accurately? I explained that I walked between three and four miles an hour. I had timed everything. Later they said they had a message from Washington praising my efforts.

'If they think I'm doing a good job why don't they give me a medal?' I asked.

'In our line we hide everything,' the spy explained. 'In this line we never get medals.'

Actually I didn't need a medal. You can't eat medals. But I was interested to know what support I might be able to get.

'If I ever need any help in the future from the American government, can I tell them I worked for you?'

'No, we will never admit it.'

One day the Japanese spy said to me: 'Be careful. I work for America too and I've been in this business longer than you. If they ask you to do anything dangerous you must look out for yourself. Ask for what you want and if necessary refuse to do anything that's too dangerous. Don't try to impress them. If you do a good job don't think they will trust you. They will always suspect you. Don't think you are building up merit with them. That's not how they think. They will use you and then throw you away.'

I was very grateful to him for saying that. Maybe it was because he was an Asian like me.

One day they asked me to take something into China. I forget now what it was, a handkerchief or a salted fish. Now, obviously this fish or handkerchief had to contain a secret message. I decided this was very dangerous. If I was caught then the evidence would be too clear. How could I talk my way out of it. I would be shot out of hand. For myself I wasn't worried but what about my family. I thought about it and then I told them that I would do it but only if they paid me $40,000. They said they couldn't do it. I was asking for too much money. So, that was our last meeting.

But I had very good reasons for being afraid. Actually, I think the Chinese side were suspicious of me. Before I was a spy I used to go up only once every month or six weeks but later I started to go up three to four times a month. Maybe they asked themselves why is he coming up so often? Anyway, one day in Canton I realised I was being watched. I was waiting to cross a road when I saw two men coming towards me. One was hiding something with a book. I saw they were trying to approach me in a particular way. I guessed immediately what the situation was. They wanted to take my photograph. Actually they weren't very clever or well-trained and the camera they were using was very bulky. When the shutter was clicked you could hear it. As soon as I saw him move to press the shutter I looked straight at them and pulled a funny face. That shocked them. Of course it was a stupid thing to do but I have always been confident in myself. Too confident sometimes. I don't know what I had intended to do that day but I immediately changed my mind. Instead I just walked and walked. All day I walked. Canton is a large city and I walked around a lot of it that day. If they were following me let them suffer. When I got back home my wife was worried. People had been asking the neighbours about me. So I went back to Hong Kong and didn't go back up for a while. Everyone said I should stay away.

So that's how my career as a spy started and ended.

I was a good father

I WAS A GOOD FATHER. I taught my son to swim. We went swimming every day. But of course bringing up children alone isn't easy. The girls? After a time, they went to live with their mother. It's not easy for a man to look after girls. My older children helped but then they too got work. They moved off the island. They went to Hong Kong, they went to America, Australia. I never took any money from them. But my youngest son, Hing Jai, stayed with me.

I needed a job. Someone suggested that I teach *kung fu* because I was so good. I did think about it but in fact I never taught *kung fu*. I'll tell you why. If you want to study *kung fu* you have to practise hard for at least five hours a day. But before a true master will agree to teach a student he must be sure of the student's character. A *kung fu* fighter should have a good heart. *Kung fu* should be used for good purposes not for bad. In the old days, when I was young, that's how it was. There were no triads in the *kung fu* schools in those days. Now the situation is the other way round.

I will never teach anyone *kung fu* unless I am a hundred per cent sure that I could trust them. I never taught any of my sons. When I myself trained my own master made this very clear. If you teach someone how to kill others then you must bear responsibility for any deaths that result. Nowadays it's different. Nine out of ten *kung fu* teachers are connected to triads.

But Hing Jai wanted to learn *kung fu*. He had heard all my stories and wanted to learn for himself. Since I refused he went to see Ng Fat, who runs a local *kung fu* school and trains the lion dance troupe. When Hing Jai first asked him Ng Fat was surprised.

'Why do you ask me? Your father is much better.'

'But he won't teach me.'

'Then if I teach you your father will blame me. We are friends. I don't want him to be angry with me.'

Actually Hing Jai is a weak person and it was not a good idea for him to learn *kung fu*. I think he learned a little. But unless you have a fighting heart it is better that you don't learn. If you know something you may try to use your knowledge when it would be wiser to just back away from a dangerous situation. That's just how it is. We each of us have our own different gifts.

In fact Hing Jai did get involved with the local triads. I am sad to say this because I have never joined a triad myself. He started to skip school. I didn't know this at the time as I was working from early morning to late in the evening. I was working as a teacher in Hong Kong. I taught Chinese and English. For ten years I was a teacher. I taught at ten different schools. Each year I was invited to go to a new school for a bit more money and if it involved less travelling time I agreed. I didn't want to do it but there was no work for me on Cheung Chau and I had to support myself somehow. Maybe I could have asked my children to support me. That is the traditional way. But I never did take money from them. Even now that some of them are doing well and I am broke. But I was telling you about Hing Jai. For three months he didn't attend school. At this time his sisters were with their mother so there was just him and me. From the age of eight or ten he was a member of the Sun Yee On. They used him to carry heroin to the addicts around the island. One day he was nearly caught. The police surrounded the area he was in and started searching everyone, even the children. He had six packets in his pocket. What could he do? Luckily, a *kung fu* master who understood the situation saw him and took him round the corner. When no one could see them he told Hing Jai to take the packets out of his pocket and put them under a stone. In those days there were old grind stones in all the alleys. So Hing Jai did as he was told and then walked through the cordon. This friend told me. That's how I discovered he hadn't been attending school. I had been paying the school fees and the school hadn't told me he was not attending. I complained and his teacher lost his job.

All my life I have believed in God. Not this god or that god – just God. But a few years after coming to Cheung Chau the pastor of the local church became my friend and kept chasing me to become a Christian. I laughed. I told him: 'I am not a good man. I smoke. I drink. I chase after girls. I fool around. How can I qualify to be a Christian?'

But he persisted. He told me it didn't matter what I did. As long as I believed in God and went to church, slowly my habits would improve. So I agreed to become baptised. I was taken down to the sea and the pastor pushed my head and my whole body under the water.

Did it change me? Maybe you can say so. I am more moderate perhaps. I don't fool around so much. But maybe that is just getting old. Every Sunday I go to church and I listen to the wise words of the Bible. It must have some effect. But although I am a Christian I don't have much respect for my fellow church-goers or the pastors. The pastor who baptised me was a good man but he died young. The pastors who came afterwards are rubbish. They won't help anyone. They are not true Christians. One time I needed a signature on a job application. Just a signature but when I asked the pastor he refused to sign the paper. Another time I was short of money. It was really urgent. He pretended he didn't understand I was asking to borrow money. So I go to church and I pray to God but I have nothing to say to my fellow church members. As far as I am concerned they are just hypocrites.

Approaching the end

IT'S THE FIFTH DAY OF CHINESE NEW YEAR. The weather is sharply cold as it generally is at this time of year. As I make my way to Peter's rooms I leave the bustle of the village streets to the flushed, boisterous, still brightly dressed children. It is now dark and the beach area is deserted. It has been two years now since we started these Tuesday evening sessions. I have recorded maybe seventy sessions. I come down about six and we set up the small cassette recorder and we talk. But it has been clear now for the last few weeks that we are running out of subject matter. It is time to bring our project to an end. I am in any case half frightened that we will uncover a new rich seam of memory. We already have too much material. But now we are reduced to talking about Peter's expertise as a drinker. Last week he gave me detailed instructions on how to win a drinking competition – but I am no great drinker. I doubt I will be able to make use of his secrets. The trick is to mix as much air into the opponent's drink without him knowing. He told me of Olympian drinking sessions that still live in his mind. He is proud of his exploits.

'All our great heroes liked to drink. Drinking and being a hero. These are things that go together. Look at me. I am a hero and I love drinking.'

He went on to tell me how he had fooled some young men who wanted to get him drunk. He laughed as he told me how he had played along with them.

'One night I was in a local bar. There were some lads I know. They were drinking something they called "killer". It was tequila. Actually I had never tried tequila before. They saw I had had a few drinks and they thought they would play a game on me.

'Hey, Peter! How about some killer? Have a drink.'

They explained how to drink it with salt. They bought me a glass and I drank it. Now as soon as I had finished it I saw them smiling at each other. I thought to myself: I know what you're doing! You're trying to make a fool of Peter Hui. We'll see. So I decided to play along. So when they asked me how I felt I said maybe just a little dizzy. Actually it had no affect on me at all. So they bought me another one.

'It's okay,' I said. They laughed some more to themselves. They thought Peter Hui will soon be making a fool of himself. Maybe they thought I would pass out or be sick. I don't know. They joked about the name.

'Maybe you should be careful. This is a killer,' they said and laughed. 'Don't worry about me!'

So they bought me a third and I drank that too. They stayed and I stayed and nothing happened at all. They were very disappointed. They were waiting for me to fall over. They would have to give me the whole bottle and then some more. It's expensive playing those games on me.'

Are we going to have another evening of drinking stories? I wonder. I know Peter enjoys these evenings. He can relive his past with an ardent listener. That is something, to find someone who will listen. And who knows, perhaps he will become famous when the book is written. Perhaps he will become immortal. And then, afterwards, there is the dinner and the quarter-bottle of French cognac that we share. That, too, is something to look forward to.

But we are coming to the end. Perhaps it's as well that it is Chinese New Year. Maybe this will be the last evening. I climb the stairs and rap on the metal grille. Inside, two frisky dogs scrabble at the door and then Peter shoos them away.

'Come in,' he welcomes me while hustling the dogs out of the way. He is smartly dressed in a tie-less white shirt that doesn't seem warm enough and a dark jacket. I compliment him and he flashes me a mischievous smile of gold fillings. He enjoys being smart. We settle down in our usual places. The room is brightly decorated with the trappings of New Year. I ask Peter to tell me about the New Year. I want his take on things. Peter is happy to oblige. I switch on the recorder and he starts to talk.

'This is the fifth day of the New Year. The year of the Monkey. I wasn't born in the year of the Monkey but somehow my mother used to think he was my patron. Maybe she thought I was a monkey too! I am seventy-eight years old. In the Chinese calendar I am seventy-nine. Next year I will be eighty. Eighty! But this is the first day of the New Year. My family should be with me. I have eleven children. But it can't be helped. I don't blame them. I was born to be alone.

'I have decorated my room with flowers. In a large vase on my desk I have six big yellow chrysanthemums and four pink gladioli. They will last a few days only but the chrysanthemums will last a few weeks before the flowers die. In another vase I have a flower that we call *gum jee yuk*. That means golden twigs and jade leaves. They cost $35 each. I got four of them. I like the little yellow blossoms. They should last a month. Then the silver willow branches. They will last three or four months. They look very beautiful together. And by the window I have a narcissus bulb. This one is very good. It has eight stems. Another one in my bedroom has only six stems. That cost me $6 a stem so it was $84 just for the narcissus. All the flowers together cost me $250. Naturally I took the flowers I wanted and at the end I asked for a discount so it came to $250 altogether. These flowers make me feel very good. They are just breaking through.

'Mostly, people like to have peach blossom at this time of year, but it's too expensive. Cheap ones are not so good. You must pay a lot for a good one. My father's favourite flower at this time of year was what we call "hanging bells". He didn't mind paying a good sum for the right plant. Each clump breaks up into eight white blossoms that look like hanging bells. The idea with most of these lucky plants like peach blossom and narcissus is for the plant to blossom in the first week of the New Year. Of course if it blossoms on the first day that is wonderful but any time in the first week is all right. It takes a lot of skill to bring the plants to this point at the right time. A plant that is just on the point of blossoming is just right and of course it will cost more. But it is very lucky so people don't mind to pay more. Sometimes it's too warm and the trees all blossom too early. Of course no one wants them then, certainly they won't pay good money for them. Maybe they will buy it just for decoration. If that happens it is a disaster for the plant growers. They just have one chance in the year to sell their flowers for a good price.

'Also clothes. If possible we like to have a complete set of new clothes. I can't afford that. I just bought myself some shirts.

'Now Chinese New Year is like this. On the last night we like to have a big dinner with lots of meat: roast pork, duck, chicken and of course other good and auspicious foods. One thing we always have on the last day, on the first day, as often as possible is *fat choy*. This is a long hair-like vegetable. Why *fat choy?* Because it sounds like 'prosperity'. If you eat a lot you will get rich. It's a joke but also we like to do things like this that have a symbolic meaning. Then at midnight . . . when I was young, even if I was asleep, my mother would wake me up and I would pray at the family altar. This involves bowing with incense sticks and pouring a little wine in front of the altar from three small cups. Chinese are just like Christians: we also believe in one god in charge of Heaven. There are some differences but on this we agree. After worshipping the gods we would kneel in front of our parents and offer them a cup of tea and some New Year candies. We did this to show our respect. Also when my children were young they did this to me too. Nowadays these customs are not followed. I like these old traditions. They allow children to show their respect for their parents.

'Now, in the cup of tea that I offered to my parents there would be a red date. Red is a lucky colour. Everything we celebrate involves the colour red. Brides wear red wedding dresses and so on, even the groom wears a red ribbon. Now when children give their parents the tea, the parents must give their children a little red packet containing some lucky money. One thing I must mention about this lucky money is that it must always be an even number, never an odd one. It would not be good to give someone five dollars because it is unbalanced. Even numbers are balanced. And, of course, everyone wishes everyone else *Kung Hei Fat Choy:* "Have a prosperous new year". Then there are the New Year candies. These are sweets like candied lotus root, lotus seeds, melon seeds and other things. Each of these has a meaning. Melon seeds are red so they stand for money. Lotus seeds stand for sons. In the old days a couple might be wished *Teem Ding Fat Choy,* meaning have more sons in the coming year. But this is out of fashion nowadays. Young people don't want to have so many children. One or two is enough. Now you hardly hear this at all.

'Now on the first day we need to eat one meal that is just vegetarian food. Actually, we just make one dish called *Lohan jai.* The Lohan are the disciples of the Buddha and there are eighteen of them so this dish has eighteen ingredients. Each family makes its own style. It will have many different kinds of vegetable and beancurd and nuts and mushrooms and fungus and even dried oysters – we believe oysters are vegetables. After that we have another rich feast in the evening.

'This first day is reserved for visiting our close family members. That means the family of the husband. On the second day we will visit the wife's relatives or friends. On the third day we are free. This is the day for arguments. Psychologically this makes sense. Who can celebrate, eating and drinking for three nights in a row without needing a rest? Naturally it is easy for people to fight on this day. So everyone is allowed to do what they want. The seventh day is everybody's birthday. The fifteenth day is the last day of the New Year.

'Now, of course, only my youngest son lives in Hong Kong. All the others? Two in Australia. Some in America. Most of them I don't know. They don't keep in touch. My youngest son should come to visit me but we haven't arranged anything yet. I talked to my grandson on the phone. My son's wife is a good girl. She doesn't know much about traditional politeness and she's not courageous enough. She should force her husband to come and see me. She should tell him: "Come on! He's your father!" That's the only thing I will say against her. Otherwise she is a good wife for him and a good mother. Today they are probably resting because my son is a hairdresser. Everyone wants to have their hair cut before the New Year. He was probably working until midnight. Business is good and they charge double. But of course he will have no work for a few weeks now. Now I have to be honest and say my youngest son is not as good to me as he should be. He's so unsteady. Sometimes he's working here, sometimes there. Sometimes in Kowloon, sometimes in Hong Kong, sometimes in the New Territories. He never sticks to one place. He has tried to run his own shop but he just lost money. He is lucky his wife can earn a good living. He's not such a good son. I have to say that. But I love my grandson very much so I go to see them as often as I can.

'All the others live elsewhere. My eldest son is the best. I think that's because we stuck together when the rest of the family went back to Canton. He stayed with me. Maybe he doesn't think I was a perfect father but he is a loyal son. He is always concerned about my health and he always asks the others to make sure I have everything I need. But he is in Australia. He's been there for over twenty years. Now he's an Australian citizen. He did well for himself. He's a hard worker. My eighth daughter is also down there. She went just two years ago. Her husband was a senior civil servant. He took early retirement and they emigrated to Australia.

'My fourth daughter lives in America. Her husband is a third-generation American Chinese but his family thought that American-born Chinese girls weren't suitable – too Westernised. So he came back to Hong Kong. A friend introduced him to my daughter. They decided they were suitable for each other and got married. That was about sixteen years ago. They have one son. He's ten years old.

'Also my ninth daughter. She had the chance to go there seven years ago. She was working in a travel agency. They set up an office in San Francisco. I don't know if it was completely legal but she has been there for seven years so she qualifies for citizenship. Actually she is back in Hong Kong now. She's been back for two months. I've talked to her on the phone. She's with her boyfriend. I think they're planning to get married. My youngest son says that they have had some business problems and they're looking for work in Hong Kong. I don't think this is a happy time for her. I don't know if I'll see her. She hasn't come out to visit me yet.

'Her sister, my tenth daughter, is married and has a son. She travels a lot with her husband round Southeast Asia. He's a nice man. But I can say that there's one bad thing about him – he likes to gamble too much. Everywhere they go, they go into the casino. He makes a lot of money but he's also lost a lot of money. And she's a spendthrift like me. She spends a lot of money. She also gambles. She's a silly gambler. She plays mahjong. She's not so good at the game. There are many good players. It's not so easy to win at mahjong.

'So who else? My seventh son? He's very funny. I haven't seen him for over ten years. He doesn't care about anything. He's not a bad boy but he's reckless. He's very unsteady. He never paid any attention to me. He never cared about me. I think he's forgotten about me. He goes from country to country. I sometimes ask the others if they have seen him. They say he just turns up out of nowhere and then disappears again. As a kid he was very smart. Actually I love him. He doesn't hate me. Maybe one could say he is a bad son but in fact he's fine. He just doesn't know how to behave. I think he just cares nothing for anybody.

'My third son is different. He does hate me a little bit. It's easy to understand why. I don't blame them. But he doesn't know the whole story. He and my second daughter suffered most. They were the eldest of the children who went to China with my wife. When I couldn't send money naturally they suffered because they also needed food. They can't forgive me for the hard times. But it is hard to support such a large family. That's something maybe they don't think about. I did everything I could for my family. Those were difficult times and we were separated for a long time. I have never tried to explain my story to them. I had some opportunities but I never did.

'My second daughter never married. She stuck to her mother. She is a good girl. She is a woman in her fifties now but I haven't seen her for a long time. I don't even know where she is. You know something? I don't even know if my first wife is still alive. My children have never mentioned anything to me about her. I never say anything about her to them either. We don't talk about it. My second daughter is a good person but I know that she hates me and she is bitter. Naturally, when she was very young she loved me completely but her experiences after they all went up to China left a bad impression. She never wanted to marry, she said, because it was so hard to get a good husband. If she married it might cause her more suffering than if she stayed single. Maybe she had a bad impression of men because of me. Maybe she didn't want a husband who was always fooling around. I am a little sad when I think of these things.

'My fifth daughter also stuck with her mother. She was cute and clever and gentle. A very capable, healthy, good-looking Chinese girl. She wasn't beautiful but she had nice features. Also she had a very strong sense of right and wrong. I don't know if she ever married. Someone told me once that they all three of them went to Japan. This was one of my wife's relatives. I didn't ask about it. But I wondered about it. How was it possible? All I could think was that maybe my son had introduced her to a Japanese man and they got married and she took my mother and second sister to live with her. This is possible. I never asked my son. He would know.

'My sixth daughter? Best not to talk of her. I blame her for stirring things up. I may not see everything but I am smart. When I look at something I can see it clearly. She stirred up a lot of bad feelings and hatred towards me. Where is she now? I don't know. When we all got together and lived on Cheung Chau, we could have been like a family again.

'I don't know so many things. For fifteen years I have not asked anyone about my family. Why didn't I ask? Because I know that once I start to ask I will want to ask so many things. I will want to know all the details about all their lives. I will want to know everything. I know that once I start to ask them questions they will want to ask me questions and there will be a need for so many explanations. Explanations will lead on to arguments. But now that I am approaching eighty I don't care so much. Even if there are some arguments, I won't care about it. I want to know. It's a big gap. Maybe I was wrong not to ask. I should know something. All my children have only heard one side of things. They have only heard my wife. I am sure she complained. How can I be so sure? Because it is inevitable. Every Chinese wife complains about her husband. This is a fact. Chinese wives store up bad feelings so that they have some weapons they can use when the time comes. I know this. I have seen it many times. Perhaps it's understandable. It's a way of defending themselves. I can tell you, even a perfect husband could not escape criticism. I don't want to say I have been a perfect husband but actually I was a good husband to both my wives.

'Now I am an old man I want to see something of my family again. Of course, I don't expect all my children to suddenly forget the past. Some things are not possible. I don't care so much whether my children love me or not. That is for them to decide. But I do care about my grandchildren. I love my grandchildren very much. I don't even know how many I have. It must be about twenty including all my sons and daughters. You know, I don't have pictures of many of them. I have never seen them. This saddens me. I mind so much about my grandchildren and think about them so much that I find myself loving all babies and young kids that I see. I love them all. You know why? Because their virtue is so pure and open. They aren't stained or dirtied by life. Adults are tricky. You can never believe what an adult says. But children are straight. If they like something they say so. If they don't like something they say so. You can say there is something of the child in me but I am stained too. No one can go through life with a pure and innocent spirit. But children have this spirit and while they have it we should enjoy them and love them. I will try to write to my eldest son soon. I will ask him some questions about my first wife and my children and my grand-children. I think I should know something before I die.

'I am not afraid of death but I don't think I will die soon. Maybe I will live to a hundred and ten. Why should I not? Only my heart is a little weak. But the rest of me is strong. In any case, what does it matter if I die? I have lived a long life and a full life. I have been at the top and at the bottom. I don't think anyone else in the whole world has had so much contact with so many different levels of society. I have been up and down. Not just once but several times. I have no regrets. If God wants me to go to him tomorrow I can say that I am ready. No one will have to put a silver coin in my mouth to make my eyes and mouth close up. I have had my fill of life and I want to go on living life fully. Believe me. When my time comes to die I will die with my eyes closed.'

And this, I felt, was a good place to end. I unclipped the microphone from his shirt and put away the recorder and we went round the corner to our usual restaurant and celebrated – this time I felt the occasion merited a half-bottle of cognac.

Eleven months later, shortly before the New Year, at approximately six o'clock on February 6th 1993, Peter had a stroke. The Cheung Chau Police Station received an anonymous call saying he had collapsed in the RSPCA office. When officers arrived they found him bruised and in a confused state of mind. He was taken to hospital in Hong Kong. The stroke left him paralysed, unable to speak, and humiliatingly dependent on nurses for the slightest release from his discomforts. His powerful will to live gradually succumbed to the horror he felt at his situation. And then, after six weeks, God was merciful. Peter died on Monday, 21st March. He was almost exactly eighty years old as the Chinese calculate age – seventy-nine years old according to Western practice.

He had had a good life. His death could have been worse.